Critique of Everyday Life

VOLUME III

Critique of Everyday Life

VOLUME III

From Modernity to Modernism
(Towards a Metaphilosophy of Daily Life)

◆

HENRI LEFEBVRE

Translated by Gregory Elliott

With a Preface by Michel Trebitsch

VERSO

London • New York

Liberté · Égalité · Fraternité
RÉPUBLIQUE FRANÇAISE

This book is supported by the French Ministry for Foreign Affairs as part
of the Burgess Programme, headed by the French Embassy in London
by the Institut Français du Royaume Uni

First published by Verso 2005
This edition published by Verso 2008
Copyright © Verso 2008
Translation © Gregory Elliott 2005
Preface © Michel Trebitsch 2005
Preface translation © Gregory Elliott 2005
First published as *Critique de la vie quotidienne III: De la modernité au modernisme
(pour une metaphilosophie du quotidien)*
Copyright © L'Arche Editeur Paris 1981

1 3 5 7 9 10 8 6 4 2

Verso
UK: 6 Meard Street, London W1F 0EG
USA: 180 Varick Street, New York, NY 10014-4606
www.versobooks.com

Verso is the imprint of New Left Books

ISBN-13: 978-1-84467-193-9

British Library Cataloguing in Publication Data
A catalogue record for this book is available from the British Library

Library of Congress Cataloging-in-Publication Data
A catalog record for this book is available from the Library of Congress

Printed in the USA by Maple Vail

Contents

Preface

Presentation: Twenty Years After

Michel Trebitsch

This book represents a leave-taking – in the first instance, for Henri Lefebvre himself – since it closes a long cycle, wholly unpremeditated at its inception, extending from volume one of *Critique of Everyday Life*, published in 1947, to the third volume, which dates from 1981. The philosopher, who had retired in 1973, died ten years later, at the age of 90. There is no better way of indicating that these three volumes span almost half a century of intellectual history – especially when we recall that Lefebvre's questions were inspired by theoretical lines of inquiry going back to the pre-war period and that to the trilogy we need to add one of the signature books of 1968, *Everyday Life in the Modern World* (not to mention a number of articles).[1]

The decades separating these works were full of historical upheavals: that is why this preface, in contrast to those to the previous volumes, will not merely offer a presentation or, rather, contextualization. Nothing could be less straightforward than jumping from the years around 1968, which postdate the second volume, to (in the French case) the arrival of the Left in power, which coincided with this work, not to mention the collapse of the Eastern bloc foreshadowed by events in Poland. But we must go further (and perhaps we should have done in the earlier prefaces) by considering not only the context – the reconstruction of the conditions of production of each of these texts in its own right – but also the effects they produced – that is to say, the conditions of their reception. Thus, as is well known, it was the first volume of *Critique of Everyday Life* that had the main impact on

COBRA and then on the Situationists; while the second volume (however densely theoretical, even abstract), which was contemporaneous with close relations with the Situationists, was construed by them as ratifying the summons to total revolution they thought they had deciphered in volume one and in those of Lefebvre's texts that they regarded as veritable manifestos, especially the article on 'revolutionary romanticism'. That is why it is worth returning to what was in fact at the heart of the reception of Lefebvre's conception of the everyday: the close relation between this conceptual endeavour and a component of *la pensée 68* – precisely what eludes the utterly one-sided analysis of Luc Ferry and Alain Renaut, obsessed as they are with anti-humanism.[2] Above all, we shall have to extend this examination by seeking to understand Lefebvre's evolution from the 'radical critique' of the 1960s to the more complex stance, albeit one still stamped by the need for critical radicalism, characteristic of the 1980s.

But this final preface also affords the requisite occasion for a more general appraisal. Not so much of the French variety of Marxism and its crisis in the second half of the twentieth century – a subject that has spawned a whole host of commentaries (not always of the highest quality) – as of the place of Lefebvre's own thought in the philosophical and ideological reconfiguration of the period, the position of his thinking in a landscape ranging from the French brand of phenomenology, and then existentialism, to the structuralism and deconstructionist theories of the years after 1968. The rather perfunctory observations I shall make will certainly not compensate for the surprising absence of Lefebvre in the (rather rare) histories of contemporary philosophy (one thinks, for example, of the works of Vincent Descombes or Christian Delacampagne).[3] Was Lefebvre too much of a sociologist and not enough of an officially recognized philosopher? Too much of a Marxist, but unaffiliated to respectable post-Althusserian orthodoxy? Without venturing an overly generic explanation, we shall try to read the partial oblivion that the work of Henri Lefebvre has fallen into as one of the symptoms of the end of an era of thinking that became apparent at the turn of the 1980s.

*

We must, however, do a little history. 1961–1981: twenty years separate this volume from the preceding one – years marked by profound historical changes. During them, Lefebvre reached the peak of his celebrity, first of all as one of the brains behind the radical critique of the 1960s, but also – in a complex relationship with institutions and institutional realities – as one of the pioneers in thinking about space and cities, especially during the 1970s, before various retreats and turns at the end of the decade tended to exclude and marginalize him. Thus, we could track his progress in an excursion through events which, on the one hand, continued to be borne along by the prosperity and growth of the *trente glorieuses*, while on the other they remained dominated by the idea of revolution, despite successive, cumulative setbacks.

Let us play with some symbols. Nineteen sixty-one, publication date of the second volume of *Critique of Everyday Life*, was the year of the Eichmann trial, the first man in space (Gagarin), and the Berlin Wall. From colour television to the RER (*réseau express regional*), from Concord to the Apollo mission to the Moon, there was an acceleration in technological breakthroughs, diffusing throughout the developed countries what came to be called the consumer society – the very thing Lefebvre analyzed and denounced while seeking, unsuccessfully, to define it in more complex fashion as a 'bureaucratic society of managed consumption'. Faced with this growth and its political, social and cultural effects, the great protest movement that dominated the decade had as its rallying cry the rejection of the Soviet model, whose crisis, official since 1956, crystallized with the fall of Khrushchev and the Brezhnev years. The search for alternative models, which tended to be rather martial in cast at the beginning of the 1960s (Vietnam, the Chinese Cultural Revolution, Che Guevara), and then became more democratic (Czech 'socialism with a human face', the brief Allende experiment in Chile, Eurocommunism and, in France, the Common Programme), in each instance ended in failure. This phase – still dominated by the idea that a revolutionary perspective was possible – was obviously symbolized by the shock of the events of May '68.

The phase of Lefebvre's greatest productivity and intellectual influence, and his attempt to conceive a model of radical critique that he would gradually distance himself from only at the end of the 1970s, was situated around 1968. Here we must go back over some points about this period that were dealt with rather hastily, particularly as regards the Situationists, in my preface to the second volume of *Critique of Everyday Life*. This provides an opportunity to fill in some gaps and correct some errors.[4] We should remember that after launching a 'research group on everyday life' at the CNRS in 1960, Lefebvre was made a professor at Strasbourg in 1961, where he remained until his appointment to the recently created faculty at Nanterre in 1965. At Strasbourg as at Nanterre, he inaugurated an academic practice that was unconventional for the time, encouraging students to work in self-directed groups, signing contracts with public institutions, and embarking on market studies, in particular in order to finance a number of young intellectuals. According to Eleonore Kofman and Elizabeth Lebas, having established contact through the New Left milieu in 1958 with the young Georges Perec, who at the time was doing his military service, Lefebvre employed him on various studies in Normandy and the Oise.[5] A friendship was born out of this and Perec subsequently stayed on several occasions at Navarrenx, Lefebvre's house in the Pyrenees, which is where he probably became fully committed to becoming a writer. Hence this was a significant encounter for both men, as Perec's biographer David Bellos has emphasized,[6] involving mutual influence, as demonstrated by recent work in the context of the seminar of the George Perec association at the University of Paris VII.[7] Thus, in his *Introduction to Modernity* (1962), Lefebvre draws a parallel between *Ligne générale*, a small avant-garde group Perec belonged to, and the Situationist group as one of the spearheads of a 'new romanticism' that was revolutionary in character. Above all, he refers to Perec's oeuvre, especially *Les Choses* (1965), several times in *Everyday Life in the Modern World*. As for Perec, the influence of *Critique of Everyday Life* and, more generally, of Lefebvre's thinking on alienation, on the cult of objects and commodities, on the banal, and on the 'infra-ordinary', finds numerous echoes not only in *Les Choses*, but also in *Un homme qui dort* (1967), and even *Espèces d'espaces* (1974) and *La Vie: mode d'emploi* (1978).

The proximity Lefebvre detected between Georges Perec and Guy Debord prompts us also to return to his relations with the Situationists. At the time of the publication of volume two of *Critique of Everyday Life*, relations were good, even if (as indicated in my previous preface) they were never straightforward, given that the Situationists were forever criticizing Lefebvre for his relations with the 'New Left' and the *Arguments* group and for lacking a revolutionary political project. To the bibliography I used at the time, in addition to the issues of *Internationale situationniste* and Lefebvre's autobiographical work *Le Temps de méprises* (1975), there have now been added not only a pile of studies of varying value, but Guy Debord's correspondence in particular, three volumes of which (covering 1957–60, 1960–64 and 1965–68) have been published to date.[8] This correspondence confirms and clarifies the very close links that briefly existed between them, while tending to relativize the consistency in their positions so adamantly asserted by the Situationists. As is well known, it was Lefebvre's article 'Vers un romantisme révolutionnaire', published in *NRF* in 1957, that attracted their attention in the first number of *Internationale situationniste* (June 1958). But it was apparently through Asger Jorn that Debord became aware of the theory of 'moments' as Lefebvre had just defined it in *La Somme et le reste* (letter from Debord to Jorn of 2 July 1959). The year 1960 would appear to mark the peak of their friendship, as indicated by the exchange of a considerable number of letters between Lefebvre and Debord from January to May. The major trips to Navarrenx, and the evenings of drunken debates in the tiny place where Debord lived with Michèle Bernstein, date from this time. In addition, it was Lefebvre, to whom Raoul Vaneigem had sent his manuscript *Fragments pour une poétique* (letter from Vaneigem to Lefebvre of 18 July 1960), who got Debord to read it, put the young Belgian in touch, and helped integrate him into the Situationist group. This ideological and political accord, marked by their joint signature of the 'Manifesto of the 121' and Debord's talk to the research group on everyday life in May 1961, would not survive beyond 1962. The Situationists reacted heatedly to the conclusions of *Introduction to Modernity* where the thinker they nicknamed 'Amédée', resuming and modifying his analysis of 'revolutionary romanticism', placed their activity in the category of youth revolt. Above all, there was the famous episode (I myself have already referred to it) when they accused Lefebvre of plagiarism over the pages on revolution as festival published in *Arguments* and foreshadowing his 1965 book, *Proclamation de la Commune*. The break was violent, sanctioned by the tract 'Aux poubelles de l'histoire' (21 February 1963); and the attacks on the '*Versaillais* of culture' would recur in the last three issues of *Internationale situationniste* (in 1966, 1967 and 1969). The additional

information on this affair furnished by the publication of the correspondence is that Debord was initially prepared to restore relations,
on condition of a public explanation at any rate (letter to Michèle
Bernstein at the end of February 1963); but also that the political
break was coupled with some rather ugly personal quarrels.[9] The
conflict proved permanent, Debord treating Lefebvre as an 'old
sponger' leading a filthy existence, whereas the latter would reply in
kind in 1965 with his abusive letter to Asger Jorn, characterized as
a 'dirty swine' for having referred to the Situationists' accusation of
plagiarism.[10]

If there are good reasons for going back over the relations between
Lefebvre and the Situationists – the recent publications I referred to –
there are also bad ones: the massive wave of 'Debordmania' relayed,
in particular, by prominent figures from the ex-avant-garde, which
serves to conceal 'the era of the void' already diagnosed a good few
years ago. In this respect, the form of Debord's published correspondence, especially coming from a major publisher such as Fayard, is (to
say the least) surprising, because it flouts the basic rules in such
matters: slim volumes with excessive margins, no means of knowing
whether we are dealing with a complete or a selected correspondence,
and no critical apparatus, except for a few ill-humoured 'notes'. Such
publications in connection with Debord in particular, and now
Vaneigem, are certainly not without interest. But they form part of a
kind of deification, or at least heroization, utterly contrary to
Situationist intentions. Whatever the heavily influential role played by
the model of André Breton (infinitely more pontifical than his descen-
dent, it is true), up until his suicide in 1994 Guy Debord lived through
the troubled period from the 1960s to the 1990s without ever making
the slightest concession to what allowed many other intellectuals
among his contemporaries to set up shop and hawk their junk. This is
why it is so shocking to see him instrumentalized in current commercial and editorial conditions. And hence it seems all the more
important to recall, rather acrimoniously if needs be, this intellectual
and even moral rectitude, on the one hand because of the problems
of reception it poses – especially the diversions created by particular
Anglo-American readings of 'French theory' – and on the other hand
because it was in these terms, of joy and rigour, that the intellectual
and personal relations between Debord and Lefebvre in the 1960s

were played out. And it is also in these terms that we can decipher not only the influence of the latter on the former at this point in time, but also the more long-term impact of certain Situationist themes on Lefebvre.

*

This reminder of the relations between Lefebvre and the Situationists also has the function of reopening the debate on May '68 and the philosopher's actual place in it. Here we face a paradoxical situation: often presented at the time of the 'events' as a kind of *deus ex machina* of the student turbulence, particularly by his most conservative colleagues such as Didier Anzieu (Épistémon),[11] silence has since descended as to Lefebvre's role, so that the further removed we are from the years immediately following the 'events', the fewer references to Lefebvre we find, at any rate in the 'major' histories of May 1968.[12] As for his book written in the heat of the moment, like several other contemporary essays it long ago disappeared from the bibliographies and even more so from the histories, until its recent republication under a stupidly abridged title.[13] In truth, apart from the strange and brilliant essay by Greil Marcus on the 1960s, *Lipstick Traces*, where Lefebvre cuts a novelistic figure, it was not until Bernard Brillant's recent thesis that his role was recalled in a balanced fashion and his own ideas on 1968 analyzed in any detail.[14]

By the time of Lefebvre's move from Strasbourg to Nanterre in 1965, the break with the Situationists had been consummated. But that does not mean that this unusual sociologist, whose courses generally attracted the students most disposed to protest, and who enjoyed a nefarious reputation with the Strasbourg bourgeoisie, was not going to distil a certain line of questioning in the student milieu. Even so, it was after his departure that the Situationist scandals erupted at Strasbourg, making it a capital of the student revolt prior to 1968. These scandals initially involved the sociology department – in particular, in 1965–66, the cyberneticist Abraham Moles, whom Lefebvre had hired as his assistant and whom the Situationists treated as a 'conformist robot' devoting himself to 'programming young cadres'. After various uproars, they prevented him from delivering the inaugural lecture for his chair in psycho-sociology in October 1966. The second 'Strasbourg scandal', mentioned in *Internationale*

xiii

situationniste and the local press, coincided with the Situationists' seizure of power in the local branch of the students' union UNEF. Accusing it of reformism, they decided to dissolve it and sell off its assets. The affair was taken to court and the assets sequestrated, provoking a reaction among teachers in the sociology department at Nanterre.[15] Meanwhile, the Situationists had despatched Mustapha Khayati to Strasbourg, where on behalf of the students he wrote a manifesto – read at the beginning of the new academic year – that was destined to have a certain resonance and which was rapidly diffused in a number of universities, *De la misère en milieu étudiant, considérée sous son aspect économique, politique, psychologique, sexuel, et notamment intellectuel, et de quelques moyens pour y remédier*, published in 1967.[16] Let us recall that the two principal Situationist texts – Guy Debord's *The Society of the Spectacle* and Raoul Vaneigem's *Traité de savoir vivre à l'usage des jeunes générations* – also date from 1967.

There is a paradox about Lefebvre in 1968, especially when compared with the current silence. While his contemporaries – or at least those of his colleagues most opposed to the student agitation – thought they had discovered in him the *deus ex machina* of the troubles at Nanterre, Lefebvre was rather invisible during the events, particular after the month of May, when the main action shifted to Paris. Yet even before 1968 his influence was undeniable. Appointed to Nanterre in 1965, he initially had the aura of an unusual professor. Head of the sociology department for a year, he was succeeded by Alain Touraine in 1967. Lefebvre surrounded himself with unconventional teachers (some of whom did not hold the *aggrégation*) – François Bourricaud, Michel Crozier, and then Henry Reymond, René Lourau, and Jean Baudrillard – whom he invited every Friday to eat together in his office with students. Without himself engaging in institutional pedagogy – the preserve of Georges Lapassade and René Lourau – he taught in a non-controlling, spontaneous sort of way, inviting Jean-Jacques Lebel, for example, for a lecture-demonstration on the 'happening' on 10 February 1967. Or, to take another example, without it being possible to speak of some discovery on his part, he gave a course on 'Sexuality and Society' in 1966–67, which coincided with the initial confrontations at the university halls of residence over the right of male students to enter the females' building. Thus, Lefebvre was the figurehead in what was unquestionably a troubled sociology department. There is no doubt that the sociologists, teachers and students alike, played a significant role in the 'events'. It has often been observed that the sociology students were particularly dynamic at Nanterre, including in the battered students' union. Moreover, it was a young, active Christian sociologist – Philippe Meyer – who launched the movement against selection; and there is no need to recall the role played by Dany Cohn-Bendit, who on several occasions was to acknowledge, alongside the influence of *Socialism or Barbarism* and various anarchist and Situationist texts, his debt to Lefebvre. This was a purely intellectual debt, for Lefebvre, free of any political affiliation, had no ex officio relationship with the Trotskyist, Maoist, anarchist and Situationist *groupuscules* that divided the campus between them in these years.

The unrest began at Nanterre in March 1967 with the occupation of the female hall of residence. But it was with the new academic year, in November, that the movement launched over the issue of the equivalence between the old and new second-year degrees adopted the struggle against selection as its key theme. The sociology teachers were soon calling for a strike and the celebrated disturbances began at the end of November with the occupation of buildings – including administrative buildings – by students, who thus broke with the traditional methods of student union struggle and more or less imposed their own negotiating structures (the Dean, Grappin, agreed to a dialogue). Accused by his colleagues of fomenting the revolt, Lefebvre was to play a role during the extraordinary faculty meeting convened on the 25th in the presence of a student delegation, which was to lead to the setting up of committees with equal staff/student representation.[17] In the meeting that was henceforth in permanent session at Nanterre, where *enragés* advancing provocative slogans ruled, Lefebvre was a significant presence, participating in staff-student meetings and the cultural turbulence in an ambiance of the happening and the festival that prefigured May – notably, for example, during the visit of the Living Theatre in December or, in March 1968, during the lecture by Mme Revault d'Allonnes on Reich's *Sexual Revolution*.[18] In January, Cohn-Bendit was threatened with suspension after the famous swimming pool episode (8 January) when he challenged the minister François Missoffe, whose official report on youth ignored the subject of sexuality. On 26 January, a demonstration of support, which denounced alleged 'blacklists' of students, turned into a riot and involved aggression against Dean Grappin. During the University Council and General Assembly of the Faculty convened on the 27th, Lefebvre, while condemning the violence, defended Cohn-Bendit and in turn denounced the 'blacklists'.[19] As is well known, the unrest, which did not let up, particularly in February in the halls of residence, led on 22 March to the occupation of the administrative building to protest against the arrest of students demonstrating against the Vietnam War and to the formation of the 22 March Movement. Moreover, the *enragés* did not let slip the opportunity to denounce the 'meta-Stalinist' Henri Lefebvre.[20] During February, Lefebvre left for Japan, where he made contact with the students of Zengakuren and had himself replaced at Nanterre by Edgar Morin. Grappin summoned a faculty meeting for 26 March and, despite the interventions of Touraine and Lefebvre, decided to close the faculty in April, on the eve of the Easter holiday. Given that the disturbances resumed in full force after the holidays, he once again requested closure of the faculty on 2 May. We know the sequel. The occupation shifted to the Sorbonne and was brought to a violent end by the police on 3 and 4 May, giving the signal for the sequence of major demonstrations and barricades from 6 May onwards. On Monday, 8 May, Cohn-Bendit and seven other Nanterre students were summoned before the disciplinary committee of Paris University, which, under the chairmanship of Robert Flacelière, director of the École normale supérieure, comprised the deans of the faculties. Four teachers – Lefebvre, Touraine, Guy Michaud, and Paul Ricoeur – came forward to defend the students. Thereafter, France entered into social crisis, as the major appeal, signed by Lefebvre and published by *Le Monde* on 9 May, observed. The following day – 10 May – symbolized it, marked as it was by events as disparate as Herbert Marcuse's lecture at UNESCO, the opening of US–Vietnamese negotiations, and the 'night of the barricades' that set the Latin Quarter ablaze. On 14 May, a meeting of teachers and students declared the Nanterre faculty 'free and autonomous' (according to Ricoeur, Lefebvre was responsible for the formula). By the end of May and in June, during the great strikes, Lefebvre was no longer visible: had Nanterre become inaccessible on account of the public transport strikes? But he was also scarcely to be seen at the Sorbonne or the Odéon, still less perched on a box at Billancourt. According to his own account, he took part in a highly charged evening on television on 13 May, with the leaders of the movement, but in a programme that was never broadcast for want of a 'representative of the working class'.[21]

Obviously, the question of May '68 is not limited to Lefebvre's role during the events. It also, and much more significantly, involves the reception of his ideas by the student audience – or, more precisely, audiences. And this is where we come back to an interpretation completely opposed to that of Ferry and Renaut. In his preface to the new edition of *Métaphilosophie* – the term that serves as a subtitle to this third volume of *Critique of Everyday Life* – Georges Labica remarks that the book, published in 1965, went completely unnoticed at a time when Althusser was publishing his two steamrollers, *For Marx* and *Reading Capital*.[22] However, with respect to Althusserian orthodoxy, which was imposed in terrorist fashion – rather like Bourdieu some decades later – we cannot (as Labica tends to) reduce Lefebvre to a culture of dissidence and heresy. Lefebvre himself vigorously opposed not only Althusser, but anything connected with structuralism, which he condemned irrevocably as a 'technocratic ideology'.[23] Responding to the Althusserian torrent was a multitude of Lefebvrian rivulets. This is what I mean by his various audiences. First of all, there was the quite wide audience for the little 'Que sais-je?' volume on Marxism dating from 1948, which persisted to his advantage with *The Sociology of Marx*, published by Presses Universitaires de France in the 'Sup' collection in 1966, and which immersed itself in Gallimard's 'Idées' collection, where Lefebvre published *Le Langage et la société* and *Everyday Life in the Modern World* in rapid succession. To these would need to be added the more diffuse influence of various journals – in particular, *Autogestion* and *L'Homme et la société*, in whose foundation Lefebvre participated in 1966. But there were other, unquestionably smaller audiences, such as the readers who, following the second volume of *Critique of Everyday Life*, set out to rediscover the revolutionary road in *La Proclamation de la Commune* (1965), by reviving the utopia of a total revolution that was simultaneously political revolution and spiritual revolt. Or again there was the audience – in fact, virtually the same one – brought together by issues of urbanism, which in 1968 took part with Lefebvre in experiments in self-management at the Institut d'urbanisme,[24] and in the activities of the group and journal

Utopie (1967–69), directed by Hubert Tonka, Jean Baudrillard and the architects of the Aérolande group.[25] In other words, while certainly highly diffuse and less doctrinal, was not the influence of the Nanterre sociologist, inspirer of journals and prolific author, equivalent to that of the philosopher cloistered in his ivory tower on the rue d'Ulm?

Even so, was Lefebvre one of the *maîtres-à-penser* of 1968? The question should, it seems to me, be posed differently, in terms that are largely opposed to the analysis developed by Alain Touraine in an interview published in the catalogue of an exhibition organized by the Bibliothèque de documentation internationale contemporaine – 'L'apparition d'une nouvelle sensibilité sur la scène politique' – which seems to me to represent a well-nigh caricatural instance of retrospective reconstruction.[26] In it, Touraine bases his explanations on a rudimentary and gratifying dichotomy between 'irresponsible teachers' and a few clear-sighted ones, present especially in sociology – a sociology marginalized by, and hostile towards, the more noble disciplines. This allows him to foreground his own role, which was indeed important, while suppressing all the contradictions – his initial caution, his ambiguous interaction with the academic and political authorities and the movement, and his then non-existent intellectual influence on students, at any rate until his on-the-spot book *The May Movement* (1968). Need it be said that he does not so much as mention the name of Henri Lefebvre? A link between the ideology of May '68 and what happened in sociology must indeed be made, in the sense that this discipline emerged as one of the crucibles of critical thinking – but without lapsing into a mythologization of the relationship between sociology and protest.[27] Because it was based upon a professional practice, the key theme was the critique of everyday life and the reading of modernity Lefebvre drew from it. For Lefebvre, fundamentally, modernity was not the domination of major economic forces, not even the advent of a state bureaucracy, but what had dehumanized and alienated man. In Lefebvre, the notion of *radical critique*, which lit up these years, and which is the converse of anti-humanism, referred to a notion – upheld ever since the avant-garde experience of the 1920s – of a revolution conceived in terms of totality. The fundamental revolutionary project, which revolved around the notions of festival, rupture in everyday life, and subversion, had the radical reformation of humanity as its ultimate objective. This is where Lefebvre coincided with, if not influenced, the 1968 protest movement and its aspiration to totality. Behind the notion of 'cultural revolution', seizing symbolic power, and wresting a voice – all of them phrases that seek to account for the 'enigma of '68' – Lefebvre detected a novel development that was incomprehensible and unacceptable to all orthodox thinking about revolution: while economic and social 'infrastructures' had not been overthrown, and the foundations of state power remained secure, the intellectual, moral and psychological 'superstructures' had collapsed. And he was not far from thinking that this was the key thing.

This is why, ultimately, if we wish to follow Lefebvre in his reflections on May '68, it is best to revert to his contemporaneous essay, *L'irruption de Nanterre au sommet*, which has been utterly neglected by most historians.[28] In it, Lefebvre proposes an initial classification, distinguishing between three tendencies in the ideology of May '68: those he dubbed 'archaic' – on the one hand the party of order that rejected subversion, and on the other dogmatists of the Althusserian variety; then the 'modernist' tendency – the main recuperator of the movement; and finally the 'possibilist' – more concerned with potentialities than reality, ready to go beyond reality and proclaim the primacy of imagination over reason. Doubtless it was to the final category that Lefebvre assigned himself. But the main interest of the book lies not in its judgement of the events of 1968, but in its analysis of the Nanterre phenomenon, treated in the same fashion as 'new towns' in earlier writings. The Nanterre faculty, opened in 1964, was presented by a number of observers at the time as a kind of focal point for grievances. 'Nanterre La Folie – University Complex': those who went to Nanterre in these years would not forget this signpost at the little station of La Folie, which, before the advent of the RER, linked the small faculty to the great city. At the time, it was not quite finished, the shanty towns had not completely disappeared, transport was inconvenient, and there was a single hall of residence on campus. Numerous were the first-hand analyses along the following lines: 'in this place they have concentrated all the possible contradictions required for an explosion'. In *L'irruption de Nanterre au sommet*, Lefebvre likewise starts out from the 'desolate landscape' of this 'Parisian faculty outside Paris', but does not confine himself to describing the contrast. 'The faculty was conceived in conformity with the mental categories of industrial production and productivity.... The buildings express the project and inscribe it on the ground. It is to be an enterprise, devoted to the production of averagely qualified intellectuals and "junior cadres" for this society'. Is the place cursed? On the contrary, it is a vacuum, 'the anomic, the extra-social social', absence; it is 'where unhappiness takes shape'. 'Far off, the city – past, present, future – takes on a *utopian* value for boys and girls installed in a *heterotopia* that generates tensions and mesmerizing images'. On site, a dual segregation – functional and social, industrial and urban – encloses culture in a ghetto, reduces the function of habitation to a basic minimum, maintains 'traditional separations – between boys and girls, between work, leisure and private life', and renders the least exercise of control and emblematic buildings – the estate, the administrative tower – *symbols* of repression. In other words, going beyond psycho-sociological analysis of rebellion against the father and authority, and the conflict between generations, through Nanterre Lefebvre proposed to read 'crisis that is far more profound, extending from everyday life to the institutions and state that hold everything together' (pp. 115–18).

It was in terms of spatial and urban issues that Lefebvre formulated the problem of 1968, not those of 'wresting a voice' (Michel de Certeau) or a 'breach' (Edgar Morin, Claude Lefort and Jean-Marc Coudray), because it was there – in the 'urban revolution' – that all the contradictions of modernity were operative. In any event, it was in the wake of '68 and during the ten years between 1965 and 1975 that Lefebvre achieved a peak of celebrity and intellectual influence, at the very moment when he was preparing to take retirement in 1973.[29] This decade marks the transition from radical critique to a more reserved stance, which nevertheless remains dominated by the search for a critical Marxism. It might be asked, and has been by various observers, whether despite (or with) the thunder clap of *The Gulag Archipelago*, the 1970s were not the golden age of a certain 'French Marxism' – precisely not structuralism and Althusserianism, but the Marxism of thinkers who were detached from Communism, from Lucien Goldmann to François Châtelet, from Kostas Axelos to Edgar Morin, Claude Lefort and Cornelius Castoriadis. These were the years when, pursuing a comprehensive line of thought already marked by the *Introduction to Modernity* (1962) and *Métaphilosophie* (1965), Lefebvre defended a general theoretical project (*La Fin de l'histoire*, 1970; *Le Manifeste différentialiste*, 1971), punctuated by a new all-out attack on structuralism (*Au-delà du structuralisme*, 1971; republished in part as *L'idéologie structuraliste* in 1975) and an ambitious reading of the 'statist mode of production' (*De l'État*, four volumes, 1976–78). However, this body of theoretical work was less well received than the works of the other non-dogmatic Marxists of the period. It was his thinking on towns and urban questions (*Le Droit à la ville*, 1968; *Du rural à l'urbain* and *La Révolution urbaine*, 1970; *La Pensée marxiste et la ville*, 1972), and especially that key work *The Production of Space* (1974), which earned Lefebvre recognition – strangely unconventional recognition, since it was bestowed less by philosophers and sociologists than by geographers, urbanists and architects. The 1970s were the years of *changer la vie, changer la ville*, both on the Left, with the Common Programme, and on the Right, with the new urban policy inaugurated under Giscard by Olivier Guichard. Thanks to his personal and social networks, and thanks to ministerial research assignments, from the 1960s urban research was in part organized around Lefebvre – for example, in the multi-disciplinary Centre de recherche d'urbanisme or the journal *Espaces et sociétés*, of which he was a co-founder together with Anatole Kopp, Manuel Castells, Serge Jonas and Raymond Ledrut, before breaking abruptly with it in large part on account of Castells' increasingly Althusserian positions. Amid much fanfare, Castells had taken up the 'urban question' in its relations with state capitalism, in particular in a provocative article, 'Y a-t-il une sociologie urbaine?', in 1968.[30]

It was also in this period, or in subsequent years, that Lefebvre's work enjoyed international diffusion via numerous translations. In Germany, in what was still a sort of pre-Habermasian phase and under the impact of the various alternative and autonomous movements thrown up by 1968, he was received as a French equivalent of Marcuse or of the philosophers of the Frankfurt School. This was the epoch which saw the development among historians (Lutz Niethammer) of the theme of a history 'from below', and among sociologists and philosophers of an 'ethnomethodological' reading, resulting in a theory of action. Two books were devoted to Lefebvre at the time, one of which – Thomas Kleinspehn's – deals directly with everyday life.[31] But it was at the end of the 1970s and the beginning of the 1980s that Lefebvre began to achieve legitimacy in the English-speaking world, because he was placed by various specialists in a much wider current, encompassing the whole of the heterodox Marxism that sought to think through its own crisis since the great breaks around 1956 – whether this body of thought was referred to as 'Western Marxism' (Perry Anderson), the 'New Left' (Arthur Hirsh), or 'Existential Marxism' (Mark Poster).[32]

*

At the beginning of the 1980s, with the appearance of the third volume of *Critique of Everyday Life,* completed at the very moment of the Left's electoral victory, Lefebvre found himself in a rather para-doxical position. On the one hand, he was, so to speak, still living under the impetus of the works that made him one of the representa-tives of the non-communist 'French Marxism' I have just mentioned. His latest work seemed to mark a return to philosophy. This was underlined by Olivier Corpet and Thierry Paquot – two of the leading figures in *Autogestion* with whom he was to break shortly after-wards – in one of the main articles on him published in the mainstream French press – an interview in *Le Monde* entitled 'Henri Lefebvre philosophe du quotidien':

> The first two volumes of *Critique of Everyday Life* seemed to be primarily sociological works. They contained a number of concrete analyses, accompanied by a theoretical inquiry into the instruments and cate-gories required to develop a 'sociology of everydayness'. With this new volume, sub-titled 'For a meta-philosophy of the everyday', you appear to change your approach somewhat, moving towards more intensive abstraction, covering a wider field and more basic questions. So what register does your work, and specifically everything that relates to everyday life, pertain to?[33]

It is true that Lefebvre's main titles in the early 1980s marked, not without some Heideggerian echoes, renewed philosophical ambition: *Le Présence et l'absence, Une Pensée devenue monde, Qu'est-ce que penser?, Le Retour de la dialectique.*[34] This ambition could certainly be accounted for by his distance, since retirement, from the professional role of sociologist. But it is doubtless more readily attributable to his wish to resume what, as is indicated by this last volume of *Critique of Everyday Life*, he had defined in his work of 1965 as 'meta-philosophy'. What this had involved, at a time when radical critique was at its peak, was openly asserting that sociology could only perform a critical function if it formed part of a more ambitious examination, philosophical in kind. However, starting out from Marx, it also implied avoiding the alternative between the institutionalization of philosophy, preserving the figure of the sage, and the liquidation of philosophical speculation in the name of a posture that Lefebvre, targeting Althusser, characterized as positivist or scientist. Meta-philosophy was thus defined as a supersession of philosophy and this objective of transgression continued to mark Lefebvre's thinking when he analyzed the prefix 'meta' in *Qu'est-ce que penser?*[35]

On the other hand, the 1981 work must be restored to its proper context – in particular, the Left's arrival in power. Amid the intellectual effervescence of the early Mitterrand years, Lefebvre had hopes of acquiring a position on key social issues where rapid changes were underway – towns, space and so on. Thus he played a role if not as expert, then as an adviser at least, for example, in connection with the Auroux labour legislation. Was not Michel Delebarre, minister for towns, reported to keep a copy of *Le Droit à la ville* on his ministerial desk, not hesitating to cite it?[36] But Lefebvre's thinking became partially inaudible – and not only on account of the ideological assault on Marxism. At the beginning of the 1980s, Lefebvre opted for a paradoxical reunion with a declining PCF, prompting many idiotic remarks. As Olivier Corpet rather disloyally put it in his 1991 obituary: 'Surprising, even saddening a number of his friends, from 1978 onwards Henri Lefebvre initiated what he wanted to be a "critical" reconciliation with the Communist Party'.[37] It was at this point that he published, with the short-lived Éditions Libres-Hallier, a book of interviews with the young Communist militant Catherine Régulier, *La Révolution n'est plus ce qu'elle était*.[38] The title is significant and in its way already signals the commentary on an aphorism of Adorno's that runs through all of Lefebvre's last writings: the moment for the realization of philosophy was missed. But for now, the rapprochement with the PCF, which was all too eager to get its hands on a Marxist thinker in the straitened circumstances of the 1980s, found expression in numerous interviews in the Communist press. At the time of the book's release, following a PCF Congress that was presented as a significant turning-point, Lefebvre, in an interview entitled 'Not remaining a prisoner of the past', recalled that he had 'quit the party from the left', not seeking to conceal his bitterness and scars. The rapprochement was the product of a process of elimination among leftists – 'terribly dogmatic and divided into small groups' – and the 'more insidious [pressure] of social-democracy', which in his eyes was the vector of computerization and multi-nationalization under American influence.[39] Other articles followed, to the point where it might be said that the Communist press was virtually the only one to attend to Lefebvre in the 1980s, especially given that on several occasions he associated himself with appeals by intellectuals for a Communist vote. Readers were reminded of his oeuvre, in particular when the third volume of *Critique of Everyday Life* came out.[40] But his own interventions all revolved around a refusal to 'follow the pack' in regarding the decline of the PCF as irreversible, and the sociological and political necessity of its survival in order to preserve a radical pole capable of rallying new, alternative social movements, urban, ecological and pacifist.[41] For Lefebvre, this belated and ultimately limited reconciliation was wholly consistent with a stance that had always consisted in rejecting orthodoxy: faced with the prevailing consensus, he believed it possible to identify traces, albeit vestigial, of a counter-culture, a power to say no, in surviving Communist practice.

On this basis, his life came to an end. Driven out of his Parisian apartment – he, the thinker of 'habitation' – and not having retired (as was stupidly said) to his house in Navarrenx, it was after Lefebvre's death in 1991 that his thinking underwent a surprising, if limited, revival. Integrating him into some current of Marxism was no longer the issue. The renewal took two complementary forms. First there was a 'spatial turn', which naturally encompassed various aspects of the everyday. Even if Lefebvre had exerted some influence in the previous fifteen years, it was the English translation of *The Production of Space* in 1991 that marked an initial turning-point. It intersected with inquiries by geographers, sociologists, anthropologists – particularly from North America.[42] Mario Rui Martins, Kristin Ross and Stuart Elden, but especially Edward W. Soja, Fredric Jameson and Mark Gottdiener played a key role in introducing Lefebvre's thinking about space into the United States. Contrary to spatial metaphors à la Althusser or Bourdieu, they introduced two key ideas: the first was that everyday life is the equivalent of social space; the second – and doubtless more important – was that they presented Lefebvre as a precursor of postmodernism.[43] A characteristic phenomenon of 'French theory' was the re-export to France and re-acclimatization of a 'new look' Lefebvrianism, in the wake of this Anglo-American 'spatial turn'. First came the issue of *Annales de la recherche urbaine* in 1994, offering a balance-sheet of ten years on urban questions. While Manuel Castells did not even mention Lefebvre's name, a stimulating article by Isaac Joseph, 'Le droit à la ville, la ville à l'oeuvre. Deux paradigmes de la recherche', analyzed research developments alongside the evolution of urbanization during the *trente glorieuses*, comparing the notion of *droit à la ville* – the title of a work by Lefebvre published in 1968 – which he defined as one of the social rights and which still alluded to an urban utopia, and a book by Jean-Christophe Bailly, published in 1992, *La Ville à l'oeuvre*.[44] Likewise in 1994, virtually a complete number of *Espaces et sociétés*, which Lefebvre had helped establish, was devoted to him. Two articles in particular signalled the importation into France of the theme of postmodernity, discerning in it the epistemological openness and lack of dogmatism characteristic of Lefebvre's Marxism.[45] The same type of revival is evident in a recent number of the journal *Urbanisme*, significantly entitled 'Henri Lefebvre au présent', which is more testimonial than analytical in character, even if the aim is to detect a 'subterranean' Lefebvrian presence, including during the years of Marxism's retreat.[46]

*

The notion of a critique of everyday life was cardinal in Henri Lefebvre, especially when it intersected with the theme of space and towns. In addition to Thomas Kleinspehn's book of 1975, it has prompted a fairly large number of works, which vary in value.[47] Is not this final volume in the sequence stamped with a veritable nostalgia? 'Twenty Years After' is the appropriate title with which to summon up the exceptionally turbulent period, politically and intellectually, separating Lefebvre's last two volumes. It was completely dominated by the polysemic theme of 'crisis': not only the two oil shocks of 1973 and

1979, the failure of every revolutionary model, the death of Mao (1976), Sartre (1980) and Althusser, who strangled his wife (1980). There were also possibilities that had become impossibilities: 'At the end of the nineteenth century and the beginning of the twentieth, it was *possible* that the European working class would find itself strengthened, enter onto the political stage, make itself into a political subject and, by various means, become the dominant class'.[48] This was no longer possible. With the third volume of the *Critique of Everyday Life*, the hour of reckoning had struck ('Continuities', 'Discontinuities'). From the standpoint of Lefebvre's personal trajectory, more tragic perhaps is that at many points in this final volume we see that he too, while unable to abandon the organizing framework of Marxism, while unwilling to 'renounce Marx', had a clear sense that it was all up with a number of the notions, concepts or even realities around which a revolutionary system that also aspired to be a revolution in thought had been constructed. Lefebvre comes straight out with it: the notion of the people,[49] labour as the source of value, and the revolutionary project itself are at an end. This is how the dictum that the moment for the realization of philosophy has been missed is to be understood.

It is this general perspective that leads to the most tragic reality to be recorded: the end of an era in thought. Lefebvre's great contribution, on the dual basis of Marxism and the avant-garde experience, was unquestionably to have rendered the everyday, or more precisely the critique of the everyday, an essential field of sociological exploration and philosophical reflection on social change; and to have made it the theoretical basis of the demand to *changer la vie* that inspired the various movements around May 1968, as well as the thinking of the official Left, which adopted it for its own purposes and instrumentalized it. What volume three reveals is that Marxism, indispensable from the 1930s to the 1960s when it came to thinking about the contemporary world, had not succumbed only to the hammer-blows of the 'New Philosophers' ('Marx is dead'). Thinking about the everyday and the critique of everyday life no longer require Marxism: that, after all, is the lesson of Michel de Certeau.[50] If it is possible to reread Marx today, it is in an utterly different, non-synchronous intellectual configuration. In the mid-1990s, even before the Bourdieu wave, a crop of books on Marxism tried to broach it differently from the good old days when it was intellectually dominant. We had a glimpse of this, for example, at the international conference of the journal *Actuel Marx* on the results and prospects of Marxism in September 1995, or in May 1998 on the occasion of the 150th anniversary of the *Communist Manifesto*. Moreover, this renewed interest derives from intellectual universes that are often very different from Marxist thought in the classical sense of the term and is bound up, in France at least, with the renaissance in political philosophy under the influence of Cornelius Castoriadis and Claude Lefort in particular,[51] not to mention the flourishing in the Anglophone world of an 'analytical' Marxism that rejects Hegelian logic and endeavours to reconcile Marx with John Rawls. Has Marx become 'untimely' in the quasi-Nietzschean sense of the term?[52] At least he has not acquired the remote but venerable status of 'nine-teenth-century thinker' enjoyed by Guizot, Tocqueville, Renan or Taine. He still has some bite!

In the presentation of the issue of *Espaces and sociétés* devoted to him, the authors metaphorically evoke the 'ghost of Henri Lefebvre'. Jacques Derrida's attempt to flush out the 'spectres of Marx' is not conducted metaphorically.[53] Via the notion of spectre, he ponders the spirit of Marxism and contests the new dominant discourse that rejoices in its collapse. In this sense, the 'end of history' is a species of spiritualist gesture, intended to conjure the ghost of Marx. Marxism persists as a 'spirit', neither living nor dead; it haunts neo-capitalism on behalf of radical critique and a capacity for self-criticism. *La Fin de l'histoire* is a work by Lefebvre dating back to 1970 ... 'The moment to realize philosophy was missed'. Is this not to state, in true philosophical-poetical or poetical-philosophical style, and even though there is still something to play for, what François Furet had already announced in *Interpreting the French Revolution* in 1978 and which he subsequently analyzed at great length in *The Passing of an Illusion*: the end of the regime of revolutionary historicity, the end of the illusion that revolution is the only modality of historical change?[54]

Notes

1. For the pre-war period, readers are referred to my preface to volume one of *Critique of Everyday Life* (trans. John Moore, Verso, London and New York 1991), pp. ix–xxviii, where I refer to the article by Henri Lefebvre and

Preface

Norbert Guterman, 'La mystification: notes pour une critique de la vie quotidienne', *Avant-Poste*, no. 2, August 1933, pp. 91–107. See also Henri Lefebvre, *Everyday Life in the Modern World* (1968), trans. S. Rabinowitch, Allen Lane, London 1971. Finally, let us signal that, in 1982, in an interview with Oliver Corpet and Thierry Paquot ('Henri Lefebvre philosophe du quotidien', *Le Monde Dimanche*, 19 December 1982), Lefebvre indicated that he was planning to pursue this line of inquiry with a work on rhythms, revolving around the concept of 'rhythm analysis'. The project was realized only after his death, with the publication by Catherine Régulier of *Eléments de rythmanalyse. Introduction à la connaissance des rhythmes*, Syllepse, Paris 1992.

2. See Luc Ferry and Alain Renaut, *French Philosophy of the Sixties: An Essay on AntiHumanism* (1985), trans. Mary H.S. Cattani, University of Massachusetts Press, Amherst 1990.

3. Vincent Descombes, *Modern French Philosophy*, trans. Lorna Scott-Fox, Cambridge University Press, Cambridge 1980 (was the author really unaware that the French title of his work – *Le Même et l'autre* – was the same as the introduction written by Lefebvre to Schelling's *Philosophical Inquiry into the Essence of Human Freedom*, published by Rieder in 1926?); Christian Delacampagne, *A History of Philosophy in the Twentieth Century*, trans. M. B. Debevoise, Johns Hopkins University Press, Baltimore 1999.

4. Some of these concern the preface to volume one. I am especially grateful to Francis Crémieux for the information and corrections he has provided me with on the basis of his personal archives (letter of 17 February 1996). Indicating that, as the person responsible for culture at Radio Toulouse in 1944, it was he (not Tzara) who brought in Lefebvre, he insists, sending me a copy of the Grasset contract for *Critique de la vie quotidienne* (October 1945) and several letters from Lefebvre, that it was manoeuvring and internal battles at the publisher which account for the fact that the book, delivered in February 1946, was only published in 1947. But were not these internal battles, in which Crémieux was directly involved, essentially political in character?

5. This involved a study of the everyday life of a mining community in Caen threatened with the closure of their mine (1960) and another of a wealthy agricultural community in the Oise at the beginning of the Common Agricultural Policy (1961). See Henri Lefebvre, *Writing on Cities*, ed. and trans. Eleonore Kofman and Elizabeth Lebas, Blackwell, Oxford 1996, p. 15, n. 9.

6. David Bellos, *Georges Perec: A Life in Words*, Vintage 1996. See also Derek G. Schilling, *Mémoire du quotidien: les lieux de Georges Perec*, thesis, University of Paris VII, 1997; Michael Sheringham, 'Attending to the Everyday: Blanchot, Lefebvre, Certeau, Perec', *French Studies*, vol. 54, no. 2, 2000; and Georges Perec, *Entretiens et conférences*, ed. Dominique Bertelli and Mireille Ribière, Joseph K., Nantes 2003.

7. See the intervention by Mathieu Rémy (doctoral student at the University of Nancy II), 'Georges Perec et Henri Lefebvre, critiques de la vie quotidienne', Georges Perec seminar, University of Paris VII, 24 November 2001.

8. Guy Debord, *Correspondance, juin 1957 – août 1960*, Fayard, Paris 1999; *Correspondance, septembre 1960 – décembre 1964*, Fayard, Paris 2001; and *Correspondance, janvier 1965 – décembre 1968*, Fayard, Paris 2003.

9. In particular, some rather sordid stories about the young student at Strasbourg who had become Lefebvre's companion. See Debord, *Correspondance*, vol. 2, letters to Béchir Tlili of 15 April 1964 (pp. 284–85) and Denise Cheype of 27 April (p. 287).

10. Debord, *Correspondance*, vol. 3, letter to Mustapha Khayati of 9 June 1965 (p. 40).

11. See Épistémon, *Ces idées qui ont ébranlé la France: Nanterre, novembre 1967 – juin 1968*, Fayard, Paris 1968.

12. This paragraph on May '68 in part resumes a talk given to the research seminar on 'Les années 68: événements, cultures politiques et modes de vie' (IHTP, 17 March 1997) and 'Henri Lefebvre et la critique radicale', *Lettre d'information*, no. 23, July 1997, pp. 1–23.

13. Henri Lefebvre, *L'irruption de Nanterre au sommet*, Anthropos, Paris 1968; republished by Syllepse as *L'irruption...*, Syllepse, Paris 1998 and translated into English as *The Explosion: Marxism and the French Revolution*, trans. Alfred Ehrenfeld, Monthly Review Press, New York and London 1969.

14. Greil Marcus, *Lipstick Traces: A Secret History of the 20th Century*, Harvard University Press, Boston 1990; Bernard Brillant, *Les Clercs de 68*, Presses Universitaires de France, Paris 2000.

15. A collective letter, signed by Lefebvre, condemning repression and sketching an analysis of the crisis afflicting the university, appeared in *Le Monde*, 17 February 1967.

16. See Pascal Dumontier, *Les Situationnistes et Mai 68: théorie et pratique de la revolution, 1966–1972*, Lebovici, Paris 1990, pp. 80–97 and Jean-Pierre Duteuil, *Nanterre 1965–1966–1967–1968. Vers le Mouvement du 22 mars,*

Acratie, Mauléon 1988, p. 129. An English translation can be found under the title 'On the Poverty of Student Life', in Ken Knabb, ed. and trans., *Situationist International: An Anthology*, Bureau of Public Secrets, Berkeley (CA) 1992, pp. 319–37.

17. See Hervé Hamon and Patrick Rotman, *Génération*, vol. 1, *Les Années de rêve*, Seuil, Paris 1987, p. 390.

18. Henri Lefebvre, *Le Temps des méprises*, Stock, Paris 1975, p. 117.

19. See Yvon Le Vaillant, 'Nanterre-la-folie', *Nouvel Observateur*, 21–27 February 1968; Alain Schnapp and Pierre Vidal-Naquet, *Journal de la Commune étudiante. Textes et documents, novembre 1967 – juin 1968*, Seuil, Paris 1969, p. 122; Hamon and Rotman, *Génération*, pp. 400–01; and Duteuil, *Nanterre*, p. 95.

20. Debord, *Correspondance*, vol. 3, p. 259.

21. Lefebvre, *Le Temps des méprises*, p. 120.

22. Henri Lefebvre, *Métaphilosophie*, Minuit, Paris 1965; republished by Syllepse, Paris 2000 (see p. 6 for Labica's remark).

23. Henri Lefebvre, *Position: contre les technocrats*, Gonthier, Paris 1967. We might note that the book was defended by Jean-François Revel in *L'Express* in 1967–68.

24. And also, in the summer of 1968, at the 'critical university' at Pau with workers from Péchiney de Noguères: see Brillant, *Les Clercs de 68*, p. 445.

25. Cf. Hubert Tonka, Thierry Paquot and Annie Zimmermann, 'Utopie, la parole donnée', *Urbanisme*, May–June 1998 (special issue on May '68), pp. 49–52. See also Jean-Louis Violeau, 'L'Internationale situationniste et la ville' (pp. 41–44) and Laurent Devisme, 'Henri Lefebvre penseur de l'urbain' (pp. 45–49).

26. See Alain Touraine, 'L'apparition d'une nouvelle sensibilité sur la scène politique', in Geneviève Dreyfus-Armand and Laurent Gervereau, *Mai 68. Les mouvements étudiants en France et dans le monde*, BDIC, Paris, pp. 82–86.

27. Michel Amiot, *Les Sociologues contre l'État*, Editions de l'EHESS, Paris 1986.

28. It is all the more contemporaneous with the events in that it first appeared in *L'Homme et la société*, no. 8, April/May 1968.

29. Several yardsticks might be employed. One would be translations, of which Rémi Hess has made an inventory: see his *Henri Lefebvre et l'aventure du siècle*, A.-M. Métailié, Paris 1988, pp. 327–34. Another indicator would be

the numerous radio broadcasts in which Lefebvre participated in these years, in particular a 'Radioscopie' by Jacques Chancel on 2 October 1975.

30. Manuel Castells, 'Y a-t-il une sociologie urbaine?', *Sociologie du travail*, no. 1, 1968. See also Castells, *The Urban Question: A Marxist Approach* (1972), MIT Press, Cambridge (MA) 1979.

31. See Kurt Meyer, *Henri Lefebvre. Ein romantischer Revolutionär*, Europa Verlag 1973 and Thomas Kleinspehn, *Der verdrängte Alltag. Henri Lefebvres marxistische Kritik des Alltaglebens*, Focus-Verlag, Giessen 1975. In contrast, the other authors cited by Hess (*Henri Lefebvre*, pp. 305–11) had no posterity and in any event lacked the influence he attributes to them.

32. See Mark Poster, *Existential Marxism in Postwar France: From Sartre to Althusser*, Princeton University Press, Princeton 1975; Perry Anderson, *Considerations on Western Marxism*, New Left Books, London 1976; Russell Jacoby, *Dialectic of Defeat: Contours of Western Marxism*, Cambridge University Press, New York 1981; Arthur Hirsh, *The French New Left: An Intellectual History from Sartre to Gorz*, South End Press, Boston 1981; Michael Kelly, *Modern French Marxism*, Blackwell, Oxford 1982; and Martin Jay, *Marxism and Totality: The Adventures of a Concept from Lukács to Habermas*, University of California Press, Berkeley 1984.

33. 'Henri Lefebvre philosophe du quotidien', *Le Monde Dimanche*, 19 December 1982, pp. ix–x.

34. *Le Présence et l'absence. Contribution à une théorie des représentations*, Casterman, Paris 1980; *Une Pensée devenue monde. Faut-il abandonner Marx?*, Fayard, Paris 1980; *Qu'est-ce que penser?*, Publisud, Paris 1985; *Le Retour de la dialectique. Douze mots clefs pour le monde moderne*, Messidor-Éditions Sociales, Paris 1986.

35. 'L'être humain va toujours *au-delà* de soi': *Qu'est-ce que penser?*, p. 131.

36. See Jean-Pierre Garnier, 'La vision urbaine de Henri Lefebvre', in 'Actualités de Henri Lefebvre', *Espaces et sociétés*, no. 76, 1994, p. 123. Roland Castro, director of the programme for the suburbs in 1989, has acknowledged his debt to Lefebvre (*Civilisation urbaine ou barbarie?*, Plon, Paris 1994).

37. Olivier Corpet, 'La mort du philosophe Henri Lefebvre', *Le Monde*, 2 July 1991, p. 15.

38. Henri Lefebvre and Catherine Régulier, *La Révolution n'est plus ce qu'elle était*, Éditions Libres-Hallier, Paris 1978. There has been much comment, of a frequently abject sort, from the Parisian microcosm on Lefebvre's relations with a very young Communist whom the party had sent on an assignment to

the ageing philosopher. It involves a classical vision of the plot, added to which is the tiresome reputation as a Don Juan that Lefebvre trailed after him all his life. Catherine Régulier, who was to become his wife, remained at his side to the end of his life.

39. 'Ne pas rester prisonnier du passé. Le philosophe Henri Lefebvre a rencontré le XXIIe Congrès du P.C.F.', *L'Humanité*, 2 March 1978.

40. 'L'invité de *L'Humanité*: Henri Lefebvre, sociologue, philosophe', interview with Jacques Bonis, *L'Humanité*, 2 February 1981, p. 13.

41. See Henri Lefebvre, 'Hurler contre les loups', *Le Matin*, 5 July 1984; 'Quo vadis?', interview with Jacques de Bonis, *Révolution*, no. 236, 7 September 1984; 'La société sans le PC?', *L'Humanité*, 19 November 1985. The attempt at social and political radicalism that Lefebvre still sought in the PCF would, we should note, extend to widely criticized support for the hunger strike by Action directe militants, who had (according to him) been arrested for 'political offences': *Libération*, 2 February 1988.

42. See the excellent analysis in Lefebvre, *Writing on Cities*, pp. 42–52.

43. The most recent appraisal is to be found in Stuart Elden, 'Politics, Philosophy, Geography: Henri Lefebvre in Recent Anglo-American Scholarship', *Antipode: A Radical Journal of Geography*, vol. 33, no. 5, November 2001, pp. 809–21. See also Mario Rui Martins, 'The Theory of Social Space in the Work of Henri Lefebvre', in Ray Forrest, Jeff Henderson and Peter Williams, eds, *Urban Political Economy and Social Theory: Critical Essays in Urban Studies*, Gower, Aldershot 1982; and Kristin Ross, *The Emergence of Social Space: Rimbaud and the Paris Commune*, Macmillan, Houndmills 1988. And see especially Edward W. Soja, *Postmodern Geographies: The Reassertion of Space in Critical Social Theory*, Verso, London and New York 1989; Fredric Jameson, 'The Politics of Theory: Ideological Positions in the Postmodern Debate', in *The Ideologies of Theory: Essays 1971 – 1986*, vol. 2, *The Syntax of History*, Routledge, London 1988; Mark Gottdiener, *The Social Production of Urban Space*, University of Texas Press, Austin 1984; *The New Urban Sociology*, McGraw Hill, New York 1994; 'Lefebvre and the Bias of Academic Urbanism', *City*, no. 4/1, April 2000; 'Henri Lefebvre and the Production of Space', *Sociological Theory*, no. 11, March 1993.

44. See 'Parcours et positions', *Annales de la recherche urbaine*, no. 64, September 1994. Cf. Isaac Joseph, 'Le droit à la ville, la ville à l'oeuvre. Deux paradigmes de la recherche' (pp. 4–10) and Manuel Castells, 'L'école française de sociologie urbaine vingt ans après'. Retour ou futur?' (pp. 58–60).

See also Jean-Christophe Bailly, *La Ville à l'oeuvre*, Editions J. Bertoin, Paris 1992.

45. See 'Actualités de Henri Lefebvre', *Espaces et sociétés*, no. 76, 1994 and, in particular, Michael Dear, 'Les aspects postmodernes de Henri Lefebvre' (pp. 31–39) and Pierre Hamel and Claire Poitras, 'Henri Lefebvre, penseur de la postmodernité' (pp. 41–58).

46. See 'Henri Lefebvre au présent', *Urbanisme*, no. 319, July/August 2001. See the articles by Maïté Clavel, 'La ville comme oeuvre'; Michèle Joly, 'Henri Lefebvre à Strasbourg'; 'Rencontre avec Nicole Beaurain'; Laurent Devisme, 'Henri Lefebvre, curieux sujet, non?'.

47. Donatella Carraro, *L'Avventura umana nel mundo moderno: Henri Lefebvre e l' "homo quotidianus"*, Unicopoli, Milan 1981; Philip Wander, Introduction to Henri Lefebvre, *Everyday Life in the Modern World*, Transaction, Brunswick (NJ) 1984, pp. vii–xxii; Catherine Régulier, 'Quotidienneté', in Georges Labica, ed., *Dictionnaire critique du marxisme*, second edn, Presses Universitaires de France, Paris 1985; Alice Kaplan and Kristin Ross, 'Everyday Life', *Yale French Studies*, no. 73, Fall 1987; Alberto Suarez-Rojas, *La 'Critique de la vie quotidienne' chez Henri Lefebvre. Romantisme et philosophie: genèse d'une critique du moderne*, master's thesis, University of Paris X, 1991; Rob Shields, *Lefebvre, Love and Struggle: Spatial Dialectics*, Routledge, London 1998, and 'Everyday Marxism: The Convergent Analyses of Roland Barthes and Henri Lefebvre', in James Dolamore, ed., *Making Connections: Essays in French Culture and Society in Honour of Philip Thody*, Peter Lang, Bern 1999, pp. 135–46 (see also Rob Shields's website: http//www. Carleton.ca/~rshields/lefebvre.htm).

48. Lefebvre, *Une Pensée devenue monde*, p. 233.

49. We shall allow ourselves a risky comparison here between this disenchanted diagnosis and the works of Pierre Rosanvallon on the 'desociologization of the political', the break in the previous link between social classes and political parties, especially in *Le Peuple introuvable*, Gallimard, Paris 1998.

50. See Michel de Certeau, *L'invention du quotidien*, two vols, Gallimard, Paris 1990 and 1994.

51. Cornelius Castoriadis, *The Imaginary Institution of Society*, trans. Katherine Blamey, Polity, Cambridge 1987; Claude Lefort, *L'invention du politique*, Fayard, Paris 1981.

52. See Daniel Bensaïd, *Marx for Our Times: Adventures and Misadventures of a Critique*, trans. Gregory Elliott, Verso, London and New York 2002. And see, *inter alia*, Étienne Balibar, *The Philosophy of Marx*, trans. Chris Turner, Verso,

London and New York 1995; Michel Vadée, *Marx, penseur du possible*, Méridiens Klincksieck, Paris 1993; Henri Maler, *Convoiter l'impossible. L'utopie avec Marx, malgré Marx*, Albin Michel, Paris 1995; and Yvon Quiniou, *Figures de la déraison politique*, Kimé, Paris 1995.

53. Jacques Derrida, *Specters of Marx: The State of the Debt, the Work of Mourning, and the New International*, trans. Peggy Kamuf, Routledge, New York and London 1994.

54. See François Furet, *Interpreting the French Revolution*, trans. Elborg Foster, Cambridge University Press, Cambridge 1981 and *The Passing of an Illusion: The Idea of Communism in the Twentieth Century*, trans. Deborah Furet, University of Chicago Press, Chicago 1999.

Introduction

1

That changes have occurred in everyday life over recent years is scarcely open to dispute. How far have they gone? Have they worsened everyday life or qualitatively improved it? These are matters for discussion.

That new changes are in store, on the way, is incontestable. Whether, as is universally claimed, they will be radical (in other words, take things and people 'by the root'), is another question.

Nineteen eighty-one seems an appropriate moment to cast a retrospective glance over aspects of daily life during the twentieth century – in practice and 'reality', but also in knowledge, philosophy, literature and art.

Are we not faced with an alternative? Acceptance of daily life as it is (as it develops in and through its changes); or refusal of it, a refusal that can be either heroic and ascetic, or hedonistic and sensual, or revolutionary, or anarchistic – in other words, neo-Romantic, hence aesthetic?

Acceptance involves much more than consenting to trivial acts: buying and selling, consumption, various activities. It implies a 'consensus': acceptance of society, the mode of production – in a word, a (the) totality. In this way, people (who? each and every one of us) condemn themselves to not desiring, conceiving, or even imagining possibilities beyond this mode of production!

An assessment of the century in this respect will have to take account of technologies, but also of social relations and their various expressions, political problems and history, daily life being in its way a historical product (possibly the 'product' closest to us, most accessible to our understanding).

Is it merely a question of analysing daily life as of 1981? Of determining what has and has not changed, forecasting what is going to be altered or consolidated in years to come? No. It also involves establishing whether the critical analysis of everyday life can serve as a guiding thread (an Ariadne's thread!) for knowledge of society as a whole and its inflection in a particular direction, in order to give it meaning. To put it another way, does (critical) study of daily life make it possible to resist the dual fascination – with 'reality' and with catastrophe – that seems to grip such thought as survives today?

2

Previously – in other words, a few decades ago – the term 'daily' referred to what was essential for day-to-day living or survival: 'Give us this day our daily bread'. Since then, its meaning and significance have altered. Broader and vaguer, the word 'daily' refers to the set of everyday acts, and especially the fact that they are interlinked, that they form a whole. Implicitly, it is accepted that daily life does not boil down to a sum of isolated acts: eating, drinking, dressing, sleeping, and so on, the sum total of consumer activities. Except when society is defined exclusively by consumption (something that is increasingly rare), there is an awareness that consideration of these isolated acts does not exhaust daily life, and that we must also attend to their context: the social relations within which they occur. Not only because each action taken separately results from a micro-decision, but because their sequence unfolds in a social space and time bound up with production. In other words, daily life, like language, contains manifest forms and deep structures that are implicit in its operations, yet concealed in and through them. In the shops we come across innumerable works devoted to everyday acts: housework, cookery, dressing, sleep, sexuality, and so on. We can even buy 'encyclopaedias' that attempt to assemble these particular aspects. But what is missing in such works is the whole, the sequence. Everyday acts are repeated (reproduced) by dint of this sequence and what it involves.

They are simultaneously individual, 'group' (family, colleagues and friends, etc.), and social. In ways that are poorly understood, the everyday is thus closely related to the modes of organization and existence of a (particular) society, which imposes relations between forms of work, leisure, 'private life', transport, public life. A constraining influence, the everyday imposes itself on all members of the relevant society, who, with some exceptions, have only minor variations on the norms at their disposal.

It is in this sense – broad, rather vague, and as yet not clarified – that daily life has recently entered consciousness and thought, allowing analysis to avoid mundanities about seemingly 'concrete' trifles concerning generations, sexes, incomes, 'household fittings', and so on: familiar details that might be taken for a 'scientific' description or 'phenomenology' of daily life.

In the past, philosophers excluded daily life from knowledge and wisdom. Essential and mundane, it was deemed unworthy of thought. Thought first of all established a distance (an *épochè*) *vis-à-vis* daily life, the domain and abode of non-philosophers. Things have changed. In 1980, the Swiss Philosophy Society organized a European symposium on the subject of 'daily life and philosophy', during which it became clear that today philosophy can be defined by its relation to daily life, by its capacity to grasp it, to understand it, to integrate it into a conceptual whole aiming at totality and universality. Philosophy is thereby seeking to renew itself by overcoming speculative abstraction. And this has been the case since Marx, Husserl, Heidegger, Lukács, and various others. We shall see that 'pure' philosophers, having gripped daily life in their conceptual pliers, still propose to dispose of it by absorbing it, rather than accepting it as it is – or transforming it.

At the same time, the term 'daily' and the 'reality' to which it refers have made their way into newspapers and literature. An increasingly important section of the press revolves around daily life and its 'problems' (to such an extent that the term 'problem' has been trivialized and is becoming well-nigh intolerable). In literature from Joyce to Simenon and Japrisot (a deliberate and somewhat ironic association), novelists seek to capture daily life at ever closer range, in order to derive surprising effects from it. Not to mention American authors who systematically smuggle the extraordinary out of the ordinary (quotidian). Yet daily life is not counterposed in some *binary* opposition to the non-quotidian: the philosophical, the supernatural, the sacred, the artistic. A binary schema of that sort forgets a (the) third term – that is to say, power, government, the state-political. This involves, and even explains, other memory lapses.

3

Preoccupation with daily life has also made its way into what are called the social sciences: history as well as anthropology, sociology, psychology, and so on. Many specialists are discovering in daily life the 'concreteness', the 'reality' they were pursuing, but which, unfortunately, they divided up, in line with their methods, to carve out their 'field'. Some believe that the sciences of human reality converge on this concrete reality. Others, by contrast, reckon that a micro-sociology or micro-psychology is formed at the level of daily life in opposition to macro-sociology or macro-psychology, directed towards the totality. Concern with daily life can also enter knowledge under other rubrics, indirectly or illicitly: 'material civilization', 'habitus', 'praxemes', and so on. Some sociologists are taking up the theme of daily life: without referring to previous research, they call themselves 'new sociologists' after te manner of the 'new philosophers', and announce the advent of a sociology of daily life.[1]

In most of these studies, the critical – hence political – dimension is obscured to vanishing point. The pragmatic and positivist approach, which aims and claims to be scientific, involves endorsement. According to this method, positive knowledge precludes critical thinking. This is a symptomatic attitude. Of what? One records, one ratifies. Knowledge and acknowledgement go hand in hand, in tandem. The scientist – or, rather, the one who knows [*sachant*] – proceeds reflexively: he reflects on what he observes; he reflects it. According to this approach, positive knowledge does not step outside the *fait accompli*: the 'factual', the 'real'. Critical thinking is eclipsed and even eliminated, as is the invariably troubling issue of *possibilities* that are distinct from *reality*.

The theme of the mirror, so common in contemporary writing, perfectly encapsulates what it means: the inability of reflection to perceive anything other than the mirrored or reflected object; neglect of the utter difference between image and object; and finally, confusion between objects in the mirror and the image of the narcissistic 'subject' in front of its own mirror ...

The 'real' and 'reality'? On the face of it, they do not shift; they are unchanging for thought and before it. In truth, if we may still put it thus, 'reality' is constantly moving, sliding, towards something else. For a long time, what philosophers and scientists understood by the term was something profound, secret, hidden: essence or substance, occult qualities, Ideas or things in themselves, transcendence. From this perspective, from Plato to Hegel, the philosopher promulgated the 'true reality', the 'real truth', or the 'deep meaning' – in short, the unity of the real and the true in, by and for the Logos.

What does the word 'real' mean today? It is the given, the sensible and practical, the actual, the perceptible surface. As for daily life, the general opinion is that it forms part of reality. But does it coincide with it? No, for it contains something more, something less, and something else: lived experience, fleeting subjectivity – emotions, affects, habits, and forms of behaviour. We may add that it also includes abstraction. Money and commodities possess an abstract dimension that forms part of everyday reality, which also contains images (a multiplicity of images, without thereby vanishing into the 'imaginary').

Surrealism unquestionably represented a milestone in the displacement of what is called the 'real', in its decentring and recentring. It was characterized by a flight from reality. Moreover, it was in reality that Surrealism discerned the imaginary, discovered the extraordinary and the supernatural. (In this context, see *Le Paysan de Paris* or *L'Amour fou*, with their descriptions of supernaturally charged real objects.) The simultaneous problems of classical idealism and philosophical realism induced a displacement that had been foreseen and heralded by poets. Since then, the 'real' has been represented and valued (or devalued) differently – all the more so since *abstraction* (to which the world of commodities, like that of techniques, belongs) is held, not unreasonably, to be more complex than the 'real', from which it cannot be separated.

Rather than deriving from a 'thing in itself', is not the 'real' usually a *product*, and occasionally a *work*? Sometimes it is the comparatively simple outcome either of knowledge and technical application, or of exchange or history; sometimes an object possessing boundless wealth, horizons, multiple meanings. Account must be taken of these contrasting aspects of 'reality'. Is this reality the opposite of appearances, décor, illusions? Does it not include them as such? Is there still a need for critical thinking to intervene? Unquestionably. All the more so since confusion between the poverty of the object and its wealth, between the product and the work, is common and even organized (by advertising). But at first sight it seems that critical thinking, having become sterile, serves no purpose. Hence its eclipse by a 'reality' that seems eloquent and self-evident.

The abuse of critical thinking, which has lapsed into hypercriticism, must also be acknowledged. For the time being, let us confine ourselves to the catchword of the protest movements: *'changer la vie'*. Originally subversive, it was circulated, trivialized, debased, defused, and touted indiscriminately. Thereafter, if something changed, it was not by virtue of this slogan, but for other reasons: struggles (by, among others, women) and/or techniques. We shall return to the debasement and recuperation that form part of this defeat, as well as to the transformation of daily life during the second half of this century.

A 'retrospective' would be in order here. It would bring out the continuities and discontinuities; what has stagnated and what has changed. This would make it possible to clarify the concept of daily life, deploying and restricting it, for it cannot claim to cover the periods under consideration. It goes without saying that such a project will figure here only in outline. What is more, an 'exposition' reconstructing what daily life consisted in at some particular date would be of aesthetic or anecdotal, rather than theoretical, interest. The important thing is to set out the main features of the transformation of daily life, illuminated in and by the present, with new 'problematics' extending old problems. I must insist straight away on various propositions connected with the facts, that is, the transformations: 'Knowledge of daily life is necessary but not sufficient or self-sufficient. For its objective and stake are not to ratify the existing state of affairs, but to move towards what is possible. Knowledge of daily life is not cumulative, conforming to the usual schema and project of the so-called social sciences, because it transforms itself along with its object …'

A debate at once takes shape, introducing a subjective and even (why not?) emotional dimension into the proceedings.

4

Discourse of the optimist (he also calls himself a 'futurist' or 'futurologist', and is often accused of seeing only what is in front of him). Yes indeed, what changes! Go on, admit it: daily life has changed more over the last few decades than it has since the Gauls and Romans – and for the better. At the beginning of this century, and even up to its mid-point, there were few if any domestic appliances, few cleaning products and detergents. Women had to peel vegetables or do the washing by hand, item by item: what slavery! No fridges, only useless 'larders'. Obviously, there were few if any cars or telephones. Proxemics (do you know this highly scientific term?) remained immutable, distances fixed, communications slow and difficult. Compare the situation today: the amazing variety of tools, machines, techniques at the disposal of daily life, a variety that will increase with computer science and its extensions. Note the growing integration of family life and groups into the life of society and the world ... Isn't what you call daily life going to be absorbed into the intense sociability contained in, and diffused by, communication and information? Unless, with new light having been shed on it, this everyday life reveals novel wealth: the unsaid in what is said; the dramatization, at last unveiled, of human relations; the revelation as spectacle of what had been left in the dark ...

Discourse of the nostalgic (often dubbed 'devotee of the past', he recently had the bright idea of calling himself 'postmodern'). Thank you for reminding us of the blindingly obvious. Isn't it distorting your bedazzled vision? Go on, ask women if their everyday life has changed that much. Do you think a few objects and tools are enough to alter relations between the sexes and the division of labour between them? It is as if these machines you make so much of had made the women's movement possible, prompting them to formulate their demands – their problematic, as the philosophers say – but by no means to resolve it! The reign of the car, kingpin-object, pilot-object, has certainly influenced people and things. For the better? That is far from being proved: at the very least, the disadvantages match the advantages. But enough of these platitudes! In bygone days, there was no TV. But careful: rather than uniting people, can't the media, communications and information technology divide them? Doesn't it depend on the social and political use made of the new techniques? The integration of the private into the social? Do you believe that social life has greatly benefited, been much enriched, since the development of communications? Instead of getting excited, think. Look back a second, if you would, to appreciate what was abandoned *en route*. Paris in days gone by! The Ile-de-France and France of old! Then a building was like a house! The people inhabiting it – the best-off downstairs, the more modestly placed upstairs, and the 'domestics' under the eaves – knew each other, and liked or loathed each other. But they formed a small community within the larger community of the district, in a town that was itself perceived as one big, fine community. Paris, like Lyons or Lille or Toulouse, used to boast an industrious and cheerful populace. Singing was commonplace. Music ruled in towns without any need for DJs. The streets were vibrant. In squares and on boulevards, large circles of people gathered around singers accompanied by accordionists. People learnt the songs, bought the lyrics, and left humming the tune. What have you made of the people, apart from a demagogic theme? Is there still a people in Paris or the towns of France, a 'developed' country? There was unquestionably a certain narrowness in this everyday life: distant things, foreigners, the global horizon went unremarked. Gestures, social customs, rituals of courtesy and urbanity, the way in which women were addressed, the courteousness which concealed a slight disdain, the manner of greeting people – raising one's hat – all this remained traditional, and might seem antiquated. But what a sense of security! The individual felt supported as well as constrained. Relations between neighbours were strong; people helped each other. Events and formal occasions were celebrated collectively. Bread was still hallowed; values – like language the sediment of centuries, derived from long periods of penury and scarcity – had not disappeared. The slightest object could be considered precious, to be preserved or offered up. These rather narrow values simultaneously hemmed people in and protected them. There was no need for a sense of security imparted from on high or from without. Don't put words in my mouth: I'm fully aware that what goes by the name of social security represents progress. But you know as well as I do that it has served the state as a political means for changing an active, responsible populace into a population of welfare claimants, passive folk, who wait for the police when there is a crime or an accident, without stirring. Everyday life has lost the quality and vigour it once possessed, and dissipated, like the space that has been smashed to bits and then sold in pieces. What charms we have lost. In Paris, there were many enchanting places, not only Montmartre but on the heights – Belleville, Ménilmontant – and below, along the length of the Seine – for example, in the direction of the warehouses of Bercy ... As for the Ile-de-France, soon no-one will be able to recount its charm, which survived until the middle of the twentieth century ... But I could go on for ever: I'll stop ...

This debate runs through the century; its origins are more distant. Whether directly or indirectly, it is voiced in innumerable writings or speeches. Is there an answer to this pressing, insistent problematic? A solution? One of the aims of the present work is to avoid its alternatives by opening up a path which is neither that of nostalgia nor that of a futurology enthused by the 'scientific and technological revolution'. Such contradictions between ideas and conflicts in 'reality' can sometimes stimulate thought, and sometimes trap it in a dead end. The first important thing is not to stifle the debate but to follow it through, without imposing a prefabricated solution, be it an unconditional apologia for positive knowledge and technology, or historicism and obsessive recollection of the past.

5

The present work is the third in a series bearing the same title. The first volume appeared immediately after the Liberation in 1946, the second in 1961. These two volumes were complemented by a summary of courses given at the universities of Strasbourg and Paris X (Nanterre), published under the title of *Everyday Life in the Modern World* (1968), and various articles, including a manifesto of 'revolutionary Romanticism' (1957).

Two ways of studying daily life and its alterations might be envisaged: either a periodical publication or a series of works over time attempting regular updates. The first, doubtless preferable, was not feasible for material (editorial) reasons. The second, whatever its drawbacks, indicates a periodization (1946–1960–1968) corresponding to important changes in social practice, as well as socio-political representations and activity. Consequently, these works can today serve as markers, milestones, and even reference points for a balance sheet introducing a new critical analysis. Perhaps this will improve the chances of these works escaping the common fate of our epoch's enormous ideological output, doomed as it is to oblivion.

6

The first volume – entitled *Critique of Everyday Life: Introduction*, and setting out an initial project – was thus published in 1946 amid the optimism (hopes and illusions) of freedom restored. It formulated the concept of the everyday, bringing to developed language and conceptual clarity a practice that was named and yet not recognized – adjudged unworthy of knowledge. This 'elaboration' invented neither the word nor the thing, but overcame the divisions 'philosophy–non-philosophy', 'significant–insignificant', 'ignorance–knowledge'. This is how Marx proceeded with social labour and Freud with sex. The same is true of daily life as of labour: the concept reunites the partial aspects and activities in which limited descriptions and analyses lose themselves. Such a concept is simultaneously abstract and concrete. Daily life would appear to comprise particular cases, individual situations, or general banalities. Here we encounter one of the oldest problems of philosophy and methodology. *Conceptual* theorization resolves it: there is a knowledge of the quotidian. How was it defined at the time?

(a) In the first instance by a certain appropriation of time and space, the body, vital spontaneity and 'nature', an appropriation prone to dis-appropriation or ex-propriation (alienation), whose causes and reasons – historical, economic, political, and ideological – are discovered by knowledge. It none the less emerges that the everyday unfolds and is constituted in a space and time distinct from natural space and time, as well as mental space and time.

(b) With daily life, lived experience is taken and raised up to critical thinking. It is no longer disdained, regarded as an insignificant residue, produced by a necessary methodological reduction, ultimately destroyed. But nor is it overestimated, inflated, counterposed to what is rational. It assumes in theoretical thinking the place it occupies in social practice: there it is not everything, but it is not nothing either. On the other hand, lived experience and daily life do not coincide. Daily life does not exhaust lived experience, for there is lived experience outside it: above and/or below it. Nevertheless, the relation between the experiential and the conceptual is foregrounded. It contains a much larger issue: that of the relations between thought and life – a Faustian question that is scarcely resolved by apologias for life or for pure thought.

(c) *Vis-à-vis* more or less highly specialized, and hence fragmented, activities – thinking, circulating, dwelling, dressing, but also engaging in some particular piece of work – daily life is defined as both a *product* (the result of their conjunction) and a *residue*, when one abstracts from these activities. It receives the remnants, the remains of these 'higher' activities; it is their common measure, their fertile or barren soil, their resource, their common site or ground. This product-residue, result and common ground, can on no account be reduced to the arithmetical or mechanical sum total of these activities. On the contrary, daily life can be understood only if one considers the various activities in the totality encompassing them, that is to say, the mode of production. The latter is not viewed outside or above these multiple activities, but as being realized in and through them as well as in daily life. Daily life is thus the product of the mode of production (in the event, the capitalist mode of production, the case of 'socialism', which cannot be defined as a mode of production, being left to one side). The mode of production as producer and daily life as product illuminate one another.

(d) Daily life also results from conjunctions between cyclical processes and times and linear processes and times – that is, between two very different modalities of the repetitive. The body appears to be a bundle of cyclical rhythms; contrariwise, many regulated activities – a sequence of productive gestures, for example, or social procedures – are clearly linear. In present daily life, the rhythmical is overwhelmed, suppressed by the linear. But the rhythmical cannot disappear; the repetitive cannot be reduced to the results of a combinatory, a prefabricated, imposed linearity. Although such a tendency exists in the modern world, daily life cannot be conceived exclusively in accordance with functional linearity. Likewise, the qualitative cannot completely disappear into the quantitative, nor use into exchange, nor things into pure relations. Daily life includes both aspects, both modes of everyday repetition. (See, below, the paragraph on the 'elements of rhythmanalysis', developing a thesis that remained unexplained in Volume I of the *Critique*.)

(e) Daily life can also be conceived as an encounter and a confrontation between use (use-value) and exchange (exchange-value). Whatever the predominance of exchange-value and its importance in the mode of production, it does not end up eliminating use and use-value – even if it approximates to 'pure' abstraction and pure sign. Labour produces exchangeable goods, commodities; between their production and their consumption, they lead a unique existence that is more abstract than concrete. During this phase, the characteristics of exchange are prevalent: this is the reign of the commodity, its world. While it lasts, the object is *virtually* reduced to a *sign*. Then this mode of social existence is interrupted, and use-value recovers its prerogatives. As well as (social) labour producing exchange-values, we can also stress a certain non-labour (rest, holidays, private life, leisure) that plays a part in the use of products. The time of non-labour forms part of social time, as compensation for the time devoted to production (sold as productive capacity to those who possess the means of production). Like labour, non-labour, or rather the time of non-labour, forms part of the mode of production. It impels the economy – first because it is the time of consumption, and next because vast sectors generating products and surplus-value are constructed on the basis of this non-labour: tourism, the leisure industry, show business, 'culture' and the culture industry. Thus daily life encompasses these modalities of social time, the time of labour and of non-labour alike, the latter in particular being bound up with use. Furthermore, use and use-value are not immutable: they are mobile. For example, the use of space is not reducible to that of any object whatsoever, using and destroying it through consumption. Use of space involves a certain use of time:

transport, the relations between centres and their environs, the use of facilities. In short, there is no absolute priority of exchange, no vanishing of use into exchange, no reduction of use-value to the role of vehicle for exchange-value (all the more so in that in the era to which Volume I of the *Critique* belonged, 'values' in a broad sense, originating in scarcity, and hence use, were still very much with us).

(f) In daily life, what are called natural needs are socially moulded in a way that can transform them to the point of artificiality. In 1946, this social moulding existed, but was not yet very sophisticated and not yet labelled 'cultural'. From this point of view, daily life was defined as the site of a three-term dialectical motion: 'needs– desires–pleasures'. This dynamic was not separated from other elements: labour and non-labour, use and exchange, and so on. In 1946, work was still regarded as the concrete realization of human beings; it featured as one social need among others, and it was even declared that it would soon become the prime social need … under socialism. As everyone knows, and as we shall see later, what occurred was the opposite: compared with not working and leisure, work was discredited; its ethical value gradually faded. In 1946, this process had yet to begin. Work retained the prestige conferred on it by all social classes in the nineteenth century in a quasi-consensus.

(g) Here another aspect of daily life reveals itself: the set of relations of distance – proximity and vicinity or, contrariwise, remoteness – distantiations in time and space. This includes the relations of individuals and groups (families, workshops, corporations) to death in general and to their own deaths (photos, mementoes, commemorations and tombs), as well as the relations between bodies, the relations of the corporeal to the spatial and temporal. At the time of this book (1946), these relations still seemed to be established and solid, because they were traditional. They were soon to alter.

(h) Also at this time, the relations between religious, civic, local, etc., festivals and play on the one hand, and non-holidays, the serious business of life, and daily life on the other – these relations seemed reinvigorated. There was a distinction, but not a division; although it was distinct from daily life, the Festival – its preparation, its celebration, and the traces and memories it left behind – was never far off. Nor was the supernatural, or the extraordinary dimension of the ordinary. Rather than fragmenting it, the time of festivals doubled everyday time.

The complexity of daily life, as it emerges from the preceding summary, cannot be attributed to a linear process, whether historical, philosophical, economic or social. It results from many conjunctions. The realization of the social being known as 'human' found itself thwarted by distortions and alienations that were themselves attributable to a multiplicity of causes – the division of labour, social classes, ideologies and 'values', oppression and repression. But at the time under consideration, there was as yet no rupture between objects and people, their gestures, actions, situations and discourse. All these aspects of daily life were part not only of the mode of production, but of a totality called 'civilization' (a stronger term than 'culture', which was subsequently substituted for it). Fragmentation did not yet obtain; a certain unity persisted, despite wars and despite the disappearance of the major religious, historical and moral referents since the beginning of the century.

It was not yet over. As it manifested itself *at the time under consideration*, daily life harboured a hidden wealth in its apparent poverty. In it were to be found the norms and conventions that determined what is beautiful, true and good for society – in other words, the accepted ethics and aesthetics. Counterposing to them various absolute terms, classical philosophy believed it had invented absolute Truth, absolute Good, absolute Beauty, against which were ranged the False, the Evil and the Ugly. In the course of what are called modern times, the critique of philosophy, acting in concert with the 'human' sciences, has relativized these concepts. Every society, whether old or contemporary, has possessed and still (except in cases of decadence and rapid decay) possesses its norms and values. Nevertheless, dogmatism has not disappeared. On the contrary, it is as if relativism, scepticism and empiricism were creating a need for their opposite – a need for dogmas and absolute truths. Dogmatism is becoming a socio-political fact. The confrontation between dogma and doubt, norms and conventions, fidelity to the established order and rejection of it, occurs in daily life. If these norms are no longer strong enough to impose a representation of the true, the beautiful or the good, it is because the relevant society is decaying or fragmenting. The absence of norms and values demonstrates not that they are no longer important, but that they are disappearing in the course of a 'crisis', a 'mutation', or increasing stagnation.

As Nietzsche said on many occasions, the 'decadent' have chosen what was worst for them. How can this be? When and where was the choice made? Where and when did 'truths' and 'illusions' confront one another? When did the norms, values and conventions that make up a society appear? And how were they imposed? Where do we sense their absence? The dogmatic response is unacceptable: 'This is what you must think …' The only response – poorly explained in the book I am recalling here, but already inherent in critical knowledge – is: *in daily life*. Rather than wishing to destroy existing values as ideological, the 'critique of everyday life' proposed to study their alterations in daily life and the emergence of daily life itself as both reality and value.

The determinations and definitions recalled above converge as aspects of daily life and its concept. Joined to it, closely bound up with the analysis, was a project. It proposed to set free the latent wealth, to bring out the implicit, unexplored content of daily life, valorizing it. It allowed that everyday mundanity, its time and space, contained things that were seemingly incompatible with it – play, the Festival, surprise – and hence the possibility of presenting this profundity and putting it into perspective. With a certain clumsiness of formulation, the project inherent in the conceptualization and theory presented itself thus.

How was this kind of project and book situated in a Marxist perspective, while not allowing itself to be imprisoned in a system? In the first place, it not only intended to complete the lexicon of 'Marxist' terminology by introducing the concept of daily life and various other concepts; above all, it proposed to open up Marxist thought to the realm of possibilities, rather than focusing it on the 'real' (economic) and the factual (historical). The same work also sought to transform the concept of 'revolution'. Revolution was not confined to economic transformations (relations of production), or political transformations (personnel and institutions), but (to merit the title) could and must extend as far as everyday life, as far as actual 'disalienation', creating a way of living, a style – in a word, a civilization. This precludes reducing society to the economic and the political, and modifies the all too famous controversy over 'base' and 'superstructure' by putting the emphasis on the *social*. Relations irreducible to the economic – relations of production and property – are involved in the 'social': namely, the relations between individuals and groups and the totality of those relations – daily life. The aim was to develop and enrich concepts which are employed by Marx, but are unacknowledged or impoverished: *praxis* (*social* practice), the relationship between the individual and the social, *civil society*, and even *mode of production*. In particular, *civil society* was arrived at by a different route from Gramsci: less historical, more contemporary. The much-debated relation between 'base' and 'superstructure' left scholasticism behind and was situated concretely, with daily life including 'superstructural' and 'infrastructural' elements. In short, that book attempted to pose various problems historically but without historicism, and philosophically but without philosophical illusions. As early as 1946, without shouting it from the rooftops, it thus attempted an updating of Marxism – an undertaking that failed for various reasons (historical and political).

To explain the incomprehension and disapproval the book met with, I must stress here some aspects of philosophical thought and 'Marxism' in France, and even in Europe.

Critical knowledge of daily life seems to be *punctual*, that is to say, bearing on various points: needs, activities, products, and so on. Hence a curious misunderstanding. The *punctual* became fashionable only much later, owing to the disappointing character of works about the whole and the totality, after some serious errors (for example, assessment of the 'Third World' as the future and model for the entire world). When this work was published, the whole and the totality were the predominant intellectual concerns (philosophical and scientific), but few people noticed that it arrived at a totality (the mode of production) via an 'element'– daily life – that supplied a path for approaching the whole concretely. That daily life provides a mediation between the particular and the universal, the local and the global, was scarcely understood. Studying daily life (its details) at a given moment bypasses the concept, simulates apprehension of the concrete, goes no further than what is immediate (clothing, housing, etc.), as opposed to grasping the concrete. The limits of this concept

– daily life – are, moreover, those of every concept: none vouchsafes mastery of what it grasps; it opens up a path to practice, but is not a substitute for it. Sometimes a particular concept (for example, art) is born with the end of its referent. Furthermore, knowledge must proceed with caution, restraint, respect. It must respect lived experience, rather than belabouring it as the domain of ignorance and error, rather than absorbing it into positive knowledge as vanquished ignorance. Feelings and emotions, play, festivals, the sacred itself – these are to be treated with tact. The situation is a delicate one: it involves understanding without believing, without endorsing, without taking statements literally. From the outset, the critique of everyday life imparted content to *alienation*, but did not define its status, whether philosophical or scientific or even metaphorical! Understanding lived experience, situating it, and restoring it to the dynamic constellation of concepts; 'explaining' it by stating what it *involves* – this was how the meaning of the work and project was expressed.

7

The originality of the project with respect to traditional philosophy has already been underscored. It regarded daily life neither as the non-philosophical, nor as raw material for some possible construction. It did not regard it as the thing from which philosophy distances itself in order to embark upon either a phenomenology of consciousness, or a logic, or ethics, or aesthetics. It sought to show that the confused character of lived experience, as of daily life, betokened not their poverty but their richness. The slightest object (still) had a direct or indirect relation with art, 'culture', civilization. The project aimed at a revived unity and totality – of the experiential, the philosophical and the political (something that existentialism aspired to a little later, but fell short of). If there was a magical dimension to daily life (rites, formulae, proverbs, traditions), that was also its complexity and its richness. Daily life was taken as an 'object' not in the sense of a static object or a pretext for building a 'model', but as the starting point for a form of action. It did not represent an inferior degree of intellectual or 'spiritual' life. Thus, it was not erected into an 'object' in the epistemological sense, and 'delimiting' it, constituting it as a 'field', was not the issue! All these clarifications are necessary to avoid – albeit belatedly – misunderstandings that were present some decades ago. With respect to philosophy, a metaphilosophical perspective was outlined. This problematic starts out from the exhaustion of the classical problematic – the 'subject–object' relation, or the 'real–ideal' and 'reality–knowledge' relations. Notwithstanding an arguably regrettable tendency to privilege sociology, from the outset the concept of *daily life* welcomed the contributions of economic, political, historical, etc., studies. This justified borrowing from philosophy, in a different inflection, the idea of *totality*, itself integrated into a process of *evolution*, that of the *mode of production* (in the process of being realized as indicated above). Daily life in the totality had nothing in common with the 'primitive', the 'pre-logical' or 'pre-scientific', the infantile. It had before it, around it, above and below it, other 'realities', networks, institutions, including techniques, positive knowledge, and especially the state. In the first volume, the penetration of techniques into daily life (still, at this time, close to 'spontaneity') was demonstrated, as was that of positive knowledge and political action. Even so, no concept – that of the state any more than that of technicity – possesses an ontological privilege with respect to it. They all have their limits. The problem of technique emerged, but was not yet formulated explicitly. Is it a factor which has become autonomous, and could wreak havoc on the world? Is it something destined to be mastered by a cast of technocrats – or by the working class? Must we repudiate enthusiasm for technology (which would later be all the rage, including among Marxists), or, on the contrary, accommodate it? These questions, which would emerge only subsequently, did not feature in the first volume.

It would be incorrect and dishonest to say that the critique of everyday life derives its philosophical positions from either Lukács or Heidegger; but it has not been unknown. It is true that Lukács introduced the theme of *Alltäglichkeit* ['everydayness'] as early as his first works, in *Soul and Form*. Was it he who inspired Heidegger to conceive the theses of *Being and Time* on abandonment and care in the *Alltäglichkeit*? Perhaps. But we should remember that these themes – the appraisal of everyday reality as trivial, given over to care and void of meaning, which directs philosophy to the true life, or authentic existence and authenticity – derive from Romanticism. And, more precisely, from German Romanticism: Hölderlin, Novalis, Hoffmann, and so on. Did not the philosophers, and Lukács in the first instance, turn the claims of the Romantic tradition back against it, supporting them with the modern critique of bourgeois society? After Lukács, Heidegger offered an ontological interpretation of this critique. For both philosophers, daily life, speculatively conceived, amounts to a chaos, a disorder of sensations and emotions, prior to the forms conferred on it by aesthetics, ethics, or logic – in other words, philosophy. Everydayness is a sort of primitiveness. At best, daily life is defined as spontaneity, flux, irruption, and hence as pre-logical. There is no doubt that Lukács demonstrates the presence in literature, and especially in the modern novel, of a protest against the triviality of daily life.[2] According to him, there is thus a tension between the 'problematic hero' and a social practice that has lost the 'immanence of meaning', and likewise becomes problematic in its triviality. Genuinely heroic, the 'subject' resists dissolution or is wrecked against the 'object', reality. In Lukács, however, the 'subject' seeks to rediscover the object. The philosopher never abandoned the philosophical fiction of unity regained – Hegelian reconciliation in supersession and the universal through art and revolution. As Adorno was to object, the negative and the moment of the negative never constitute a relation to the world of the 'subject' for Lukács, but an episode, a transient mood. He underestimated both the critique and the crisis.

As for Heidegger, the characteristic distantiation of being-with-others also implies that, in its *Alltäglichkeit*, *Dasein* finds itself in the grip of those others. It is not itself: others have divested it of its being. Moreover, the other is not someone defined. Anyone can represent it. It is neither this one nor that one; neither some nor all. It is neuter: the *'they'*, *das Man*.[3]

This phenomenology of the ontic thus involves a fundamental, absolute pessimism about the social and the practical. In this respect it is opposed to the Marxist tradition, for which alienation can be countered and overcome. An analogous pessimism is to be found in Sartre, above all in *Being and Nothingness*, a work inspired by a Cartesianized and psychologized Heideggerianism. The other is (only) the degradation of the 'subject', dereliction. For Marx, by contrast, *the other* is both alienation and disalienation (its possibility): alienation in class relations, disalienation in revolutionary potentialities.

Sartre's works contain the sketch of a critique of everyday life: the gaze of the other, bad faith, and the characteristics typical of the 'bastard'. But this critique of daily life remains incomplete, not referred to as such because it remains the prisoner of philosophy and its categories, and consequently condemned to pessimism tinged – but only just – with humanism.

La Conscience mystifiée (1936) already took a stand against the Lukácsian position and its rational optimism, together with the pessimism and nihilism foreshadowed in philosophy with the crisis of rationality. It sought to demonstrate that the anthropomorphism and anthropocentrism of reason were leading thought astray and condemning it to error, a travesty of errantry. It also sought to demonstrate the importance of critical, negative mediation in evolution, in consciousness and society: the moment of appearances and illusions seeking to become reality. This book went a long way in taking account of the negative. The vigour of this moment was displayed to such an extent that unity – of subject and object, the ideal and the real – receded to the horizon, and drew closer only in utopia, which for this reason was creative. Hegelian supersession? While it retains a sense and remains the goal, it can be achieved only through the severe ordeals of an evolution that has nothing linear or preformed about it.

8

A not insignificant point: critical knowledge of daily life does not require a special or perfect language, distinct from everyday discourse. On the other hand, as a familiar precept has it, we should use only such words as possess meaning – and one meaning only. Even when we are distinguishing between the spoken and the unspoken, the unconscious and the conscious, the unknown and the known in daily life – in short, detecting what is contained in the discourse of the everyday – there is no need to invent a different vocabulary, syntax, or paradigm from the one that is present in the discourse. Critical knowledge of daily life is expressed in everyday language and everyone's language: by making explicit what is implicit. This rules out 'proof', but does not preclude the element of play and risk inherent in any conversational discourse.

One postulate of the work (Volume I) that will have to be reconsidered, for it may be that the hypothesis is no longer correct and requires modification, was this: people in general do not know how they live, making the theory of daily life indispensable. This brings it closer to the economic, and even the political! We must be clear as to the meaning of this phrase. 'People' know their needs and their wants through suffering and satisfaction; but they scarcely know how to express them, and still less how to define them. Numerous documents indicate a poverty of vocabulary and clumsiness of expression, but simultaneously the relevance of the testimony. Despite the abundance of information (from mid-century onwards), 'people' today (1981) still possess only scant comparative data. Do they know what they want? Yes, ever more clearly; they are less and less taken in. Do they have a clear knowledge of their situation, their social relations? No. An example: the more important space and place become, the more the mass of people are ignorant of space, for everything conspires to detach them from it – the media, images, transport, general abstraction. Socially, they understand only the rungs immediately below and above them in the hierarchy. That hierarchy precisely has the following function, among others: to obscure whatever would make remote social strata and classes known to one another. Despite innumerable images, or because of the very abundance of representations, the 'poor' can scarcely imagine the everyday life of the 'rich'. They represent it to themselves in accordance with their own lives, as made easier by money. When they are unveiled, power and wealth astound them (as in Luigi Comencini's film *L'argent de la vieille*). Wealth makes Olympians of the rich – inaccessible, outside daily life: above it. There is thus a social 'un-conscious', as well as an 'imaginary'. How are they to be situated? At a deeper level? From the outset, the critique of daily life responded thus: they are the *content of representations*. The dominated represent to themselves the order they belong to solely by means of symbols. To carry this content over into theory is to explain what the symbols say (and dissimulate); it is to explicate the content with words and concepts that escape ideology as far as possible. Unlike psychoanalysis, bringing the (social) unconscious to light reintroduces not only the *relations of production*, but those of *reproduction* (domination and power), as well as *representations* (of a particular social class or stratum for itself, for other classes, for society as a whole). This is the point at which to add that if class struggles, in all their complexity, have their significance and their impact on reality as well as representations, on daily life as well as what is exceptional, class compromises – whether historically proclaimed or not – are no less important. The reproduction of the relations of production and domination is at stake in periods of open struggle and compromise alike.

9

Also to be noted, after so many years, is the happy absence from this work of epistemological concerns. It contains none of what was soon going to obstruct the path of thought for years, to the point of impeding it. A question of generation? No: of orientation. This book was not aiming at a 'pure' or purified scientific knowledge. Knowledge is defined not by its epistemological 'purity', but by its critical import: thought is either critical or it is not (is only discourse). If the concept has limits, critical thinking does not accept them: it tackles what exists, including what is regarded as sacred, untouchable, definitive – the state, the party, the gods, the leader. May that which can resist do so!

Is the concept of 'daily life' operational or not? Yes, since it makes a critical analysis of the 'real' possible. No, for it produces nothing – nothing but a negative proposal as to what is possible: '*changer la vie*'.

From the outset, this orientation conflicted with the one that was soon to be adopted by an intelligentsia driven by the dominant ideology: structuralism and its annexes – epistemology and scientism (which claimed to put an end to ideology). 'Marxism', as they say, would itself capitulate in the face of technocratic ideologies, and divide into two tendencies, two contradictory forms, each with its own arguments: a radical, critical orientation, banking on the negative, which sometimes went as far as hypercriticism; and epistemology, neo-positivism, scientism – in a word, a dogmatism renewed in its vocabulary, but not its make-up.

From the start, the *Critique of Everyday Life* aimed to shatter Marxist orthodoxy and, more precisely, to put an end to the notion of an orthodoxy. In fact, at the time a boundless dogmatism reigned in 'Marxism', which is difficult to comprehend thirty years on. For the dogmatists, absolute Truth pertained to the Party and hence to its leaders, repositories of this priceless treasure. The mere idea of *research* seemed ridiculous, since the Truth was there – already there. At most, those in high places could request – or, rather, command – documents and statistics to confirm established positions, to 'deliver blows' to enemies and 'crush' them. The result? Instead of a development of Marxist thought, through discussion and debate, innovative currents arose outside it. The obvious lacunae of official Marxism, which its 'representatives' did not even perceive, would be made good by philosophies in the usual sense, forming a system (or trying to form one) outside social practice and political action. Hence existentialism; and hence its success!

10

Nearly fifteen years passed. We are now in 1960. Changes – yes, lots of them. Not in the desired direction; on the contrary, in a quite different direction – or maybe inclining towards a loss of direction! The second volume of the *Critique of Everyday Life* sought to combine numerous observations as well as various selective critical studies in one theory. What occurred in the course of these fifteen years? First the apogee, then the decline, of Stalinism, and the failure of the critique of Stalinism inside the Communist movement, particularly in France. How did the contestation that emerged at the time differ from *critique*? In this: that it was intent on being immediately active, without operating through the mediation of what was already established (parties, doctrines, etc.). It also wanted to be radical. It took account of changes in the world and the onset of the crisis affecting the classical concept of *revolution*, substituting for it that of *subversion*.

11

The second volume of the *Critique* did not remain external to the movement. First of all, with official, institutional Marxism falling into discredit, unofficial Marxist thought found an increasingly large audience. In an unforeseen detour, a group such as *COBRA* – artists, writers, architects – which was very active in northern Europe, drew inspiration from the critique of daily life while carrying it further. The desire to transform everyday life made its way through ideologies, philosophies, metaphysical revivals. As early as 1953, the Dutch architect Constant, who inspired the Amsterdam 'provos', invented a new architecture of ambiance and situations, incorporating, as it were, the critique of daily life into space. It was via this detour that the transition was made from critique to contestation, a development involving students and new groups, among them the Situationists. What were the forces of protest directed against? Their objective depended on the groups and individuals. Some, especially among students and intellectuals, resented traditional morality, religion, Judaeo-Christianity. Others took as their target the 'thing', the object – that is to say, the commodity and its attendant ideology. Yet others attacked nationalism, the (in their eyes) neurotic attachment to Motherland and Paternalistic State. Many of them quite simply proposed to destroy capitalism, which they naively believed to be in a critical condition whenever they detected the slightest symptom of economic difficulties, when in fact, economically, the age was one of 'prosperity' and the onset of the 'scientific and technological revolution'. In short, the various forces of protest were not agreed either on the grounds and goals of the contestation, or on the line to pursue. But everyone was in agreement on one imperative: *changer la vie*. Were they demanding their 'share of the cake', of growth and the economic miracle? No. They rejected economic and political reality. They also rejected what was in the ascendant all around them: technocracy, with its dual fetishism of competence and performance; and an ideology that started proclaiming the end of ideology under the sway of knowledge and authority – so that these ideologues merely diffused their own ideologies more successfully (productivism, positivism, logical empiricism, structuralism, etc.). There was no lack of analogies between protest and contestation in France and Europe, and the Cultural Revolution in China: they were ten a penny. The same vigour – and the same failure. Was not this wave of contestation the provisional form of a comprehensive movement directed against fixed hierarchies, established apparatuses, enforced silence, and the ideologies of domination? In France as elsewhere, protesters rejected the productivist ideology that passed for 'pure' knowledge, as well as the reorganization of daily life around the couplet 'production-consumption' – a reorganization that gained ground and was to achieve a quasi-general consensus, except among the protesters. Rejecting, before the ecologists did so, growth, with its brutal implications – harsh technologies, the expansion of towns that remained such in name only – they counterposed the cult of pleasure to that of work. Against an economism void of values other than those of exchange, protest stood for reuniting the festival and daily life, for transforming daily life into a site of desire and pleasure. The protesters were protesting against the fact, simultaneously obvious and ignored, that delight and joy, pleasure and desire, desert a society that is content with satisfaction – that is to say, catalogued, created needs that procure some particular object and evaporate in it. They took radical critique to the extreme by opposing not working to work, which was being promoted as the supreme value. A paradox? Or a demand deriving from the high level of the productive forces and the possibility people sensed of abolishing work through automation of the productive process? In and through imponderables and ambiguities, sound and fury, the problematic of the modern world was taking shape. From 1957 or 1958 onwards, the protesters could legitimately describe themselves as revolutionaries, since they were demanding what the 'regime' and the 'system' (the mode of production) could not but refuse. They put their finger on some sensitive issues. Whether consciously or not, they demonstrated an essential emergent truth: production involves and encompasses reproduction – not only of labour-power and the means of production (classical theses), but of the social relations of domination as well. Thus, re-production took centre-stage. Production as such, and its study, fell to specialists, economists and technologists. As for official Marxism, it stuck to traditional claims about production. However, re-production, exposed by growth at the very heart of capitalist relations of production, could no longer figure as a secondary phenomenon, a simple result of production. Critical analysis of it involved reviving the concept of totality. Where and how was reproduction carried out? In and through the family? The state? The workplace, and it alone? The middle classes? Social practice? All these answers contained a grain of truth, but remained one-sided and incomplete as long as a new analysis of the everyday was lacking.

12

During the period under consideration (1946–61), daily life changed – not in the sense of displaying its latent wealth, but in the opposite direction: impoverishment, manipulation, passivity. Capitalism was in the process of conquering new sectors in these years: agriculture, previously precapitalist in large part; the historic town, which broke up through explosion and implosion; space as a whole, conquered by tourism and leisure; culture – that is to say, civilization reduced and subordinated to growth by the culture industry; finally, and especially, daily life.

The second volume of the *Critique of Everyday Life* contains a thesis that is possibly excessive, that is, hypercritical, but not meaningless. It was developed in co-operation with the oppositional avant-garde. According to this theory, daily life replaces the colonies. Incapable of maintaining the old imperialism, searching for new tools of domination, and having decided to bank on the home market, capitalist leaders treat daily life as they once treated the colonized territories: massive trading posts (supermarkets and shopping centres); absolute predominance of exchange over use; dual exploitation of the dominated in their capacity as producers and consumers. The book thus sought to show why and how daily life is insidiously *programmed* by the media, advertising, and the press. In great detail, and with many convincing arguments, people were having it explained to them how they should live in order to 'live well' and make the best of things; what they would choose and why; how they would use their time and space. These features marked society while wrecking the social. No particular feature – consumption as such, the spectacle and spectacularization, the abuse of images, the overwhelming abundance and redundancy of information – suffices to define this society; all of them are involved in daily life. The upshot is contradictory: undeniable satisfaction and a deep malaise. Rather than a qualitative appropriation of the body and a life of spontaneity, what transpires is a threatening and increasing expropriation by the outside, the quantitative and the repetitive, by disembodied images and alien voices, by the discursive and spectacular moulding of everything that happens. This was the case for 'people' in general, for society as a whole, the middle classes being the axis and support of these operations, their subject and object in so far as these terms still have a meaning. Various privileged products, which really are useful and agreeable – the car, the fridge, the radio, the television – are allocated the following mission: expropriating the body and compensating for this expropriation; replacing desire by fixed needs; replacing delight by programmed satisfaction. The 'real', displaced and situated in a new way in daily life, consequently wins out completely over the ideal. In fact, satisfactions cannot be regarded as negligible: subjective needs, produced for the consumption of objective products, are real; they are reality, which possesses a substance and coherence so often celebrated that it is erected into a criterion of truth.

This indictment, contained in the *Critique of Everyday Life* II, as well as *Everyday Life in the Modern World* and other articles from the same period, laid itself open to attack and was not without its faults. As far as production was concerned, the role of multinationals was hardly mentioned, whereas their intervention in daily life was already visible. Contrary to the Marxist schema predicting the formation and investment of large capital exclusively in what is called heavy industry (iron and steel, chemicals, etc.), many of the most powerful global enterprises established themselves in daily life in this period: detergents and cleaning products, drink and food, clothing. Some curious misunderstandings resulted: blue jeans, produced by these global enterprises – possibly in countries such as Hong Kong and Singapore, whose proletariat was super-exploited – were regarded by young people as a symbol of freedom, novelty and independence. This fashion supplied the critique of daily life with an excellent example of manipulation. A certain Americanism worked its way in – not so much through ideology as via daily life. Critical thinking captured this infiltration only with difficulty, though it detected it here and there.

Inadequately analysed, the production of needs – bureaucratically administered consumption – remained entangled with naturalism; as a result, the efficacy of the media by means of models and images was barely understood. The role and function of the middle classes in subtle changes in daily life, civil society, the state, and their relations, were glimpsed but not clarified. These works did not clearly show how and why programmed everydayness – that of the middle classes – is their reality, and is then transformed by them into 'cultural' models for 'lower' strata and classes. The analytical and critical examination of this manipulation lacked a foundation that would come only later: the theory of representations used by the manipulators, which includes critical examination of symbolisms, the social and individual imaginary, and 'culture'. As a result, the analysis of reproduction, as concealed not *under* but *in* production–consumption, remained incomplete.

13

After the Liberation, the 'people' still had a meaning in France. Peasants, artisans, workers – in short, all those who did not belong to the 'dominant' and 'propertied' classes – still had numerous links, not only in workplaces but also in houses, streets, districts and towns, regions. Over the next fifteen years, this unity began to break up not into clearly differentiated and opposed classes, but into layers and strata. In 1960, the people faded into a historical past, sometimes to be commemorated with a solemnity that allayed suspicion. The beautiful myth of the people as creator and repository of political and philosophical truth, which derived from the French Revolution, became blurred. Social unity fragmented. Although it was subject to the homogenizing instances of law, government and market, as well as the national identity stipulated and codified by the state, it crumbled none the less. This tendency – which was already apparent around 1960, and was destined to become preponderant, even appearing to be rationally self-evident – was not clearly perceived in the works under discussion. They still counted exclusively on positive knowledge: they accepted the hypothesis of the rational efficacy of knowledge, and were not as yet suspicious of what was being infiltrated under that rubric. They certainly wanted to oppose a sort of counter-knowledge to the official scientism, which is integrated into the institutions and integrates people into them, and hence to the relations of reproduction. But this counter-knowledge remained limited and largely ineffectual *vis-à-vis* a knowledge bound up, in one way or another, with power and possessions. It should, however, be added that this attempt at a counter-knowledge also contained a project of counter-power. This was intimately connected with the contestation as it mounted and became generalized during this period. But it was not associated with its violent forms, such as the one which dispensed with any project, calling for immediate action, regardless of the consequences.

This project differed from the one presented in the first volume, because the latter had failed, become impossible. *Changer la vie?* Yes: but it was no longer conceivable or possible to liberate a sort of living core, to display the latent content of daily life. What had become of this core, this rich content? In 1960, they were in the process of disappearing, or had already disappeared. *Changer la vie?* A radical change was necessary, a revolution–subversion. The theory of revolution in and through daily life still sought to develop Marxist theses. It doggedly reminded people that social transformation cannot be confined to political forms and economic relations; that it runs the gravest risks of degeneration if it does not have the creation of a different everydayness as its goal and meaning.

The result, in this way of looking at things, is that subversion must work in tandem with revolution. Regrettably, what happened was that revolutionaries confined themselves to the politico-economic, whereas subversives distanced themselves from it. In short, these two aspects of the transformation of daily life were dissociated. Failure ensued. The critique of everyday life did not attain its goal, even if it was 'fashionable' for a time around 1968.

However that might be, here we must emphasize the *evolution* of the idea and project of *revolution* since its origin. At the outset, it was defined by Marx on the one hand by the *realization of philosophy*, and on the other by the unfettered growth of the productive forces. On the one hand, then, classical philosophy bequeathed to the forces of renewal, the creative capacities of the working class, its principal ideas – freedom, happiness, or quite simply the True, the Beautiful and the Good – for them to realize. On the other, this involved the end of the scarcity that is skilfully planned for the people, and the advent of abundance.

In the event, what happened? On the one hand, philosophy after Hegel and Marx gradually renounced the naive project of renewing the world through truth. The final blaze of this centuries-old project was Nietzsche's *Zarathustra*. Thereafter, philosophy stagnated and then withered away as it tirelessly wrote its own history. It drifted towards scholasticism (Marxist, Kantian-rationalist, or irrationalist). On the other hand, revolution could no longer be defined by growth, given that there was growth in the capitalist mode of production for which the state assumed responsibility; and that what is called the capitalist state succeeded in this task as well as (and sometimes better than) the 'socialist' state. Persisting with this definition, continuing to identify socialist revolution and growth, without even clearly distinguishing between quantitative growth and the qualitative development of society – did this not lead to a crisis of the idea of revolution? Did theory and practice not stand in need of redefinition? Clumsily perhaps, but stressing the main point, the critique of everyday life and related research sought to meet this exigency.

In these works, the study of daily life was carried out in accordance with dialectical procedures. Regarded and presenting itself as such, *positivity* – the programming of daily life – proved destructive of possibilities, even though it had many 'positive' reasons, of the strongest sort, for establishing itself in *reality*. As for negativity – that is, the critical element – it displayed an openness towards possibility. This dynamic internal to knowledge does not make it readily accessible. Around the middle of the twentieth century, it was still possible to capture the imaginary (the extraordinary, the supernatural, the magical, even the surreal, and hence the negativity) at the heart of daily life. A few years later, the imaginary came from without; it was imposed: photography, cinema, television, the world rendered a spectacle. It was now that the imaginary was discovered, and slowly but surely became fashionable. It was also discovered that the imaginary is sometimes identical with the logical (Lewis Carroll). Paradox: the imaginary kills imagination; the fetishism of the imaginary is constructed on the ruins of the imagination. This period of *dis-appropriation*, which provoked the radical protest movement, possessed an appearance that veiled its reality: the art of daily life or daily life regarded as an art and simultaneously 'positively' as a business. Its technical basis? Domestic appliances. A certain major brand launched a famous slogan at the time, which was as effective in advertising terms as it was mystificatory: 'X ... liberates women'. In fact, the positive advantages of this instrumentalization of daily life brought about a consciousness of enslavement. This paradox – another one – will surprise only those who are entrenched in *positivity*: quantified abstraction.

In short, it was under cover of practical innovations and undeniable technical progress that the forms of its own enslavement were insinuated into daily life, in conflict with those of liberation. Otherwise, these forms could not have been imposed. Daily life entered into the circuits of the market and managerial practice (the opposite of self-management), becoming a small business, a family subcontractor, subordinate to the dominant powers. This can extend to the 'self-management' of daily life.

14

The theory of a revolution in daily life was to have some unanticipated repercussions. Critical knowledge was going to spawn hypercriticism – at the extreme, sheer abstract negation of the existing order, rejection of the 'real' treated as a shadow theatre. It must be conceded and stated that this hypercriticism has had some disastrous results – for example, the extermination of humanism, philosophical support of human rights. On the pretext that humanism bore the marks of bourgeois liberalism and suspect ideologies, it was blithely trampled underfoot without anything being put in its place. On the road to hypercriticism, the ultra-leftist intelligentsia demolished all values, for excellent reasons, but in the process destroyed reasons for living. To employ an old metaphor, it sawed off the branch on which it was perched. This was suicidal behaviour. Moreover, the ideological representatives of this intelligentsia rarely took hypercriticism to its logical conclusion, that is, nihilism. Only a few writers – among them, Samuel Beckett – had the 'courage' to do that. Most of the intellectuals affected by hypercriticism accepted a compromise – living, or rather seeking to live, as if society was different from what it was; living outside this intolerable society, and yet within it. People made the best of the situation. In this little game, the so-called advanced intelligentsia gradually lost its credibility; by the same token, it compromised such effectiveness as critical thinking might still possess. This vague nihilism and incessant ambiguity produced a mindless voluntarism, in political action and everyday life alike.

The theoretical critique of work, adopted from Marx and Lafargue (*Le Droit à la paresse* – a text read and approved by Marx), *logically* entailed a rejection of work. Among the themes dealt with by Marx featured the triad, taken from Hegel, of 'need–labour–pleasure'. For certain tendencies, only the last term counted: the triad was dismembered in favour of hedonism. This is defensible when one notes that human beings today exercise only a tiny proportion of their potential for pleasure. In industrial societies, fascinated as they are by leisure, automation and information-processing, work is depreciated. This problematic cannot be overstressed; it accounts for some of the facts attributed to the 'crisis'. Around this time – between 1960 and 1980 – the old proletarian slogan – 'Those who don't work don't eat' – faded and vanished. However, the peremptory refusal of work ('Don't work!' 'Let it all hang out!') compromised a key demand by diverting it in the direction of absurdity. Obviously, this extremism could not speak to 'workers'; it could originate only in a certain middle class and an intelligentsia undeterred by paradoxes. What is more, if some people were saying: 'Don't work!', others – and sometimes the same people – were declaring: 'Stop consuming! Objects, get lost!'. There was, and is, a gulf between such slogans and critical analysis of the 'production–consumption' relation in daily life. Nevertheless, the stress laid on play, on the festival (naively regarded as immune to recuperation by existing society), provided a bridge; it made possible a compromise between the critique of everyday life and ultra-leftist extremism. The domain of the festival was extended: students spoke readily of 'violent festivals'; revolution itself assumed the appearance of a vast popular festival. Notwithstanding some profound disagreements, understanding and agreement were thus reached on various claims about what is possible. The general – and generally accepted – slogan *changer la vie* received a kind of complement, which made it more concrete: 'Make daily life a festival – make your body, time, consciousness and being something that resembles a work of art, something that is not content to give form to a lived experience, but transforms it.' Utopia? Once again, yes: utopia, impossibility. But for what is possible to come to pass, must we not desire the impossible? Thus developed, the theme and slogan *changer la vie* nevertheless remained incomplete, for the project specified nothing about space, the use of time, social relations. On the other hand, it explicitly involved an end to relations of *reproduction*.

15

During the same period, at the opposite pole, scientism was growing in vigour, if not in wisdom and beauty, with variants and implications that have already been indicated on numerous occasions: positivism, empiricism, epistemology, structuralism. The scientistic tendency rejected lived experience as a fact, alienation as a concept, and humanism as a project. Neo-positivism and its Marxist variant had no difficulty showing, or 'proving', that these concepts – alienation, the human – possessed no epistemological status. This seemed decisive to them; moreover, it was perfectly true. The stance of critical knowledge implies that such a problem is a pseudo-problem. These concepts have their reference point in practice and daily life, not in the pure knowledge baptized and consecrated by epistemology. If these concepts – social practice and daily life – lacked epistemological status, those who used them were untroubled by the fact. They declined to be dragged on to the terrain of epistemology, a terrain which seemed perfectly solid to the neo-scientists, but was in fact booby-trapped, mined, unstable. These theoreticians believed themselves to be liberated from all ideology by pure scientific knowledge, whereas they represented the ideology of scientificity or, if you prefer, scientificity become an ideology. Here we encounter one of the most curious paradoxes in an age full of them: the ideology of the end of ideologies. The error of these ideologues remains unforgivable: as from this date (1960 and subsequent years), rather than demanding an epistemological status for them, human rights should have been defended, illustrated, strengthened. Like the philosophers, epistemologists undermined these rights at their foundations, while also undermining those of thought. Indeed, what entity is more vague and more lacking in epistemological status than 'man'? Thought itself! Only mathematical logic, destined to be absorbed into machines, has a status of the kind that ideology strives to impose as primordial. Critical knowledge had no status!

In fact, two conceptions that did not feature in the categories of traditional philosophy were juxtaposed without ever confronting one another in debate – something that was always evaded by the dogmatists. Supporters of the one counted on positive knowledge, and exclusively on it; they defined life by the extension of such knowledge and its application. Even revolution occurred through the application of a positive knowledge contained in Marx and Lenin. Some of the most doctrinaire among them asserted that this knowledge extended from Thales to Lenin. In this tendency, lived experience is minimized; it is distrusted: to live is to know scientifically, and to make such knowledge the criterion of life. Lived experience – spontaneity – was held responsible for the problems and errors of consciousness, including those of political consciousness. Ultimately, lived experience disappeared: it was eliminated. It was reduced to the vacuum created by evicting certain elements from a vast combinatory constitutive of positive knowledge. Epistemological reduction, required for the construction of positive knowledge, focused, in the first instance, on this lived experience.

The opposite tendency, by contrast, counted on absolute spontaneity and on extolling lived experience, which was supposedly enough to transform daily life. Positive knowledge was mistrusted, in favour not so much of the irrational – an outmoded philosophical position – as of what springs up spontaneously, once the obstacles have been removed. Positive knowledge and power were among the obstacles. What this tendency sought to scale down was thus scientificity itself.

Is there room for a conception, an elaboration, which gives the conceptual and the experiential their due, which is not reductionist, but draws them both on to an expanding track, enriching them while critiquing them by one another? Submitting both to a creative activity comparable to that which produces works of art, without thereby aligning oneself with an aesthetic theory? One might suppose so. Meanwhile, confrontation between these hypotheses, tendencies and strategies did not occur. This was characteristic of intellectual life in France in the second half of the twentieth century: controversies were evaded. Instead of open discussions, there were allusions, indirect attacks, and sometimes insults. On one side, we witnessed the arrogance of the 'positivists'; on the other, the rage of the 'negativists', both of them employing *ad hominem* arguments. Similar contradictions ran through Marxism and Freudianism. Marx and Freud set out from a lived experience: social labour for the former; sexual libido for the latter. Both wanted to exalt this lived experience, in order to set it free: hence a revolutionary project on one side, and a project that was subversive in its fashion on the other. Up to now, both endeavours have ended in failure. Why? Among other reasons, it can be asserted that lived experience, thus marked out, has not escaped the sway of positive knowledge, the latter being formulated and codified in accordance with a systematization attributed to the founders.

Up to a certain point, the critique of everyday life followed the same path, with the same twists and turns. At the outset, it proposed to grasp and conceptualize the lived, while extolling it. Yet the very process of conceptualization is not without its drawbacks – among them, the domination of lived experience by the concept. It is clear that the problematic of positive knowledge cannot be avoided. Merely to communicate a project – whether in spoken or written form – it must be conceptualized. Even if the limits of conceptualization are carefully indicated, the process is not risk-free.

16

The Parisian penchant for cliques, clans and conspiracies was to aggravate the conflicts between partisans of *changer la vie* and varieties of scientistic dogmatism, without resolving them. The repositories of positive knowledge regarded themselves as highly superior to those who (as they saw it) were mere ignoramuses. Above all, they thought it would be possible to establish their propositions as definitive truths. Hence misunderstandings and disappointments. Hence also the splitting of Marxist thought into epistemological and critical stances. Hence, finally, manoeuvres on the philosophical and theoretical plane aiming to neutralize these opposed currents by means of one another, in order to dispose of any theory and leave the field free for empirically taken decisions. This brings us to around 1968, high point of contestation and critical thinking, as well as 'prosperity' and the economic miracle, that is to say, growth controlled by the state. In 1968, for the first time, and after various detours that we still do not clearly understand, critical thought again coincided with practice: the rapid rise of the movement, its no less rapid decline, accompanied by the separation of its constituent elements – thought and spontaneity, action and theory.

The critique of everyday life motivated the refusals and demands of the protesters by presenting a project. For the first time, theory was not focused on the past, on history and historical models; moreover, it was not content to propose an economic model. In and through counter-knowledge, it turned positive knowledge against itself, without abolishing it, but by opposing a knowledge of potentialities to ideologies of reality or models. It took its distance from classical positions in such a way as to open up different perspectives.

Another failure. A definitive one? We shall see. Pragmatists make success a criterion: what failed was bad and false. For his part, Nietzsche the anti-pragmatist understood that the decadent sometimes choose what is bad for them, propelling them along the path of decline. Unintended consequences and reverses have their perverse reasons. Moreover, for those who observe the radical labour of the negative, failures are not only failures: since Hegel and Marx, we have known that things also progress by the 'bad side'.

17

Let us jump forward to 1981. What is new? 'Everything,' declares the optimist with whom we are familiar, standard-bearer of realism and champion of modernism: 'Contestation is over. We are already in another era, post-industrial society, the information society ....' 'Nothing,' replies the nostalgic: 'The fundamental relations have not altered, only the discourse and rhetoric. Appearances notwithstanding, it is not the old constrictions that have been smashed to bits, but what remained natural and substantial in relations, proximity, warmth and any – what do you call the thing that has been made so much of since it ceased to exist? – any sociability!'

In 1981, problems are reconsidered and reformulated in terms of *crisis*. Hence many assessments depend upon the way in which this crisis is perceived and appraised. On this crucial point, however, there are significant disagreements, and the 'spectrum', as they say, of analyses and opinions is so wide that it is not easy to see how it remains a spectrum, since there are neither borders nor handle to control it. Some say: there is no crisis, simply a new division of labour on a world scale, as a result of technological progress; and, consequently, a displacement of the centres of production, wealth and power. If that threatens France, let it contrive to pull through with the minimum damage. Eurocentrism could not last for ever, nor could the historical privilege enjoyed by some countries (including ours) ... Others proclaim a total crisis: a crisis of everything that goes to make up a society, culture and values included. Hence a crisis of the Left as well as the Right. A terminal crisis, some go so far as to say, and, in the last analysis, an ineluctable one: catastrophe. A pessimistic conclusion, comes the rejoinder from the other side: the popular movement is fending off catastrophe, and will prevail. A simple economic crisis, declare a lot of realists, which is therefore bound to have political repercussions, good politics making possible the good economics that will lead us out of the crisis. Crisis of the capitalist economy or crisis of imperialism, say certain Marxists, who locate the epicentre of the global upheaval as follows: the relations between 'centre' and 'periphery' have shifted; there are new imperialisms which, although secondary, are active; on the other hand, various countries have embarked upon independent industrialization, and are discovering new roads. Even so, comes the response, the relations of hegemony, domination and dependency remain essentially the same ...

Among those who concede that the crisis is bringing about profound changes, simultaneously affecting labour and its organization, the way of life, modes of knowledge, the scale of recognized values, norms and conventions, many – whether conservatives or reformists – assert that the *enterprise* remains the site of these transformations. It thus supposedly escapes the crisis as a model, a solid, unchanging site amid the various changes. Some maintain that a privileged site of this sort – one that does not exclude productive labour, but incorporates it into a far larger space and time than the workplace and labour-time – is to be found in daily life, which does not escape the crisis but is transformed with it.

As for the crisis in general, a hypothesis is emerging which is rarely discussed, but has arguments in its favour. People always refer to the 'end of the crisis', a solution, a 'way out of the crisis'. They talk about containing or controlling it – which is what the word 'crisis', etymologically construed, suggests. The paradoxical hypothesis is that this 'crisis' cannot be reduced to a phase of instability between two stable periods: quite the reverse, it is becoming the mode of existence of modern societies on a world scale. Neither the thesis of a crisis of economy and society; nor that of a crisis of the bourgeoisie and the working class; nor that of a crisis of the middle classes as relatively stable supports of established institutions; nor the very widespread thesis of a critical period for institutions, values and culture – none of these accounts for the situation, does justice to its gravity or the extent of the problematic. Is not the phenomenon we continue to describe with a term that has become inadequate – crisis – more profound, more radical, than a mere difficult phase for the economy, politics, ethics and aesthetics? Might it not legitimately be thought that the 'crisis' will change these societies root and branch – in their 'anthropological matrix', their historical foundation, their economic 'base', and their superstructural apex? If this is the case, then the crisis is continuing the work of critical thinking, abandoned by thought. It (cor)responds in reality to those who did not want a considered, directed upheaval – something that was possible in 1968. Nothing will withstand this practical critique: the resistance of the existing order will sooner or later be swept aside, dissolved or shattered – even facile nostalgia and derisory optimism, which are complementary ideologies.

What are called modern societies will henceforth live under threat from within and without: threatened with ruin, decay, self-destruction; facing numerous challenges; exposed to unremitting attack. We must get used to the idea that a crisis of this order no longer has anything to do with 'crisis' in the classical sense; that constant invention is required to respond to such situations. Invent or perish! There is no definite or definitive solution, no model to emulate, only a road to open up and construct. This thesis goes beyond currently accepted theses, regarded as bold, on the 'serious crisis' or even 'total crisis'. It indicates the path that must be cut through the ruins. We must also get used to the paradoxical idea that this crisis is not some malady of society, but henceforth its normal, healthy state. A strong organism does not shrink back nervously, avoid risks and dangers, but on the contrary confronts them, acts and reacts accordingly. (It is true, however, that analogies between the social and the organic cannot be pushed beyond certain limits.)

Another, no less paradoxical implication: critical thinking tends to disappear or at least be marginalized, and possibly qualitatively transformed. The 'crisis' takes over the work of critical knowledge, continuation of ancient philosophy, the work that thought sought to accomplish, but which it could not see through to a conclusion. As a critical condition, the 'crisis' is critical thinking *in actu*. This thinking is superseded and realized; outflanked as knowledge, it becomes concrete.

What is left for it to do in its capacity as thought? First of all, to track the radical labour of the negative, the progress of the crisis through the world it engenders while tearing it apart. Possibly, what presents itself as positive (technology, etc.) will turn out to be negative; while the seemingly negative (the wrecking of institutions and values) will prove creative. The dissolution of traditional thinking and critical philosophy occurs on a dual basis: its failure and degeneration into hypercriticism; and the actively critical role of the crisis. This does not betoken the disappearance of dialectical thought and thinking *tout court*. Far from it! It means its renewal in and through a cultural revolution quite different from what has hitherto gone by that name. That said, there is no need to linger over the crisis of the theory of crises, of criticism, of Marxism as a critical theory or theory of crises, and so on.

This perspective does not involve a vision of apocalypse, a catastrophe; but it does not exclude them. The theory of permanent crisis thus replaces that of permanent revolution. The new state of the world, as of the thinking that strives to conceptualize it, could have unforeseen effects over and above such unintended consequences as can be anticipated.

By way of a preliminary question, we might also ask how we should characterize the existence of societies with respect to biological existence and cosmic energy. Is it a genuine problem? We will not know until the end of this study. An unduly famous formula has it that civilizations are mortal. Agreed: but the question posed here is rather different. Can societies survive without a trace of civilization – that is to say, style or, rather, grand style, high culture, and higher values – in a neo-barbarism? The most disturbing thing about organic life and nature is not merely death, but ageing. Everything is mortal: not only civilizations, but ideas, countries and peoples, classes themselves. Are they prey to the same fate as the living individual, reaching their term only through the slow, fatal loss of their vitality, their physical powers? Is daily life a site of decline? Or of attempts at sudden revival? Or sometimes the one and sometimes the other – a site of ambiguity, gambles and wagers?

If social life is subject not only to the organic law of evolution (birth, growth, decline and end) but also to the law of the dissipation of energy; if informational energy itself, and its transmission, are not exempt from entropy, then what are we to conclude as regards daily life? Is it not a site of dissipated energy, lost information, redundancy? This would amount to identifying in daily life an irreversible decline of the social, for which there is no possible cure. This is simply a hypothesis, examination of which we shall not evade. Possibly accepted and consented to in a vague sort of way, such a decline would render modern societies incapable of responding to increasingly numerous and urgent 'challenges', of understanding them, and even of formulating their problematic. From this viewpoint, daily life escapes the threat of obliteration only through its dullness, its ponderousness, its inertia, which make it unbearable.

How are we to dispel a state of confusion which grows from year to year, and certainly forms part of the world as it presents itself – that is to say, as we make it? Can the study of daily life still serve as a guiding thread through the complexities and sediments of modern society? A little later, we shall see that there is also a crisis of modernity. The situation, in the broadest sense of the term, will prove all the more difficult to grasp in that the *neo*, the *retro* and even the *archaeo*, which once, in the glory days of modernity, fought bitterly, are confused today. This also forms part of our world, and is an aspect we must stress right now. Around 1980, a rumour was doing the rounds that everything had changed, that we were entering a different era. The new philosophers, the new architecture, the New Left and New Right, even the *nouvelle cuisine*, sprang up simultaneously. There is indeed something new: but where and what? Illusion or reality? Potentialities, remote possibilities, or the consequences of decisions that have already been taken? There is indeed a neo-bourgeoisie, a new middle class, but they bear a close resemblance to the old ones, with fewer tics and added idiocies. The allegedly new is often only a revival that is unconscious of the fact. Sometimes people also wittingly revive religious, metaphysical and political themes, renovated like old palaces in historic cities: the new tacked on to the old. Some terminological innovations are enough to produce this effect. Fashion and culture have also become mixed up to the point of merging – an old phenomenon, but one that is increasing in scale. Anything that amounts to fashion is regarded as new. Clever advertising makes the neo contain the archaeo, and vice versa. Presentation and verbal packaging conceal the persistence and deterioration of the old in the allegedly new; they also conceal the fact that such exaltation of the archeo prevents the birth of what could spring from the genuinely new. By definition, fashion, even when it results from a cycle (the periodic return of forms), always passes for new. Otherwise, there would be no fashion! The cycle involves obliviousness of its own moments.

Thus, a closer analysis will be indispensable as regards modernity, the neo and the retro, seeking to define what persists under the illusion of the new; what is genuinely new; what is congealed in the old; what is regressing; and what is disappearing. No doubt this analysis will have to go into some points and areas more deeply, without abandoning a comprehensive perspective in the process. It is clear that sexuality and femininity in everyday life cannot be treated in the same way as techniques or the culture industry or the erosion of values.

To summarize: the object of this work is to resume critical analysis of daily life in the year 1981, referring to the previous analyses while trying to avoid their defects, and anticipating the future. The problem has changed. It derives not from a scarcity of material or ignorance of daily life but, on the contrary, from an abundance of material and a kind of excess of positive knowledge. The most cursory glance at publications of all sorts – on towns, on political life as well as private life – immediately informs us of these alterations. But what is their significance? Here our problematic emerges, and can be reformulated thus: is daily life a shelter from the changes, especially when they occur abruptly? Is it a fortress of resistance to great changes, or certain minor but significant changes? Or, contrariwise, is it the site of the main changes, whether passively or actively?

The upshot of these analyses, which remain incomplete, is that daily life cannot be defined as a 'sub-system' within a larger system. On the contrary: it is the 'base' from which the mode of production endeavours to constitute itself as a system, by programming this base. Thus, we are not dealing with the self-regulation of a closed totality. The programming of daily life has powerful means at its disposal: it contains an element of luck, but it also holds the initiative, has the impetus at the 'base' that makes the edifice totter. Whatever happens, alterations in daily life will remain the criterion of change. But that is to anticipate the conclusions of this work.

Notes

1. See especially Michel Maffesoli, *La Conquête du présent: pour une sociologie de la vie quotidienne*, Presses Universitaires de France, Paris 1979, with a preface by Gilbert Durand.

2. See Nicolas Tertullian's remarkable book on the Hungarian philosopher, *Georg Lukács. Étapes de sa pensée esthétique*, Le Sycomore, Paris 1980.

3. See Martin Heidegger, *Being and Time*, trans. John Macquarrie and Edward Robinson, Basil Blackwell, Oxford 1962.

PART ONE

Continuities

1 End of Modernity?

Since the onset of what are called modern times, a standard question has involved the relations between tradition and novelty. It has prompted controversies like that of the Ancients and Moderns at the end of the seventeenth century; and continues to do so. It is not always clear what is at issue in these debates; sometimes that emerges only long after the quarrel – as with the concept of progress in the case of the Ancients and Moderns.

Today, another question is on the agenda: the end of modernity. This was noisily proclaimed as the 1980s approached. At the same time as an irruption of the new, people announced a reversion to tradition, but a reconsidered tradition – a tradition freed from ideology and authenticated by the test of time. The end of modernity heralded a great change, proclaimed from 'on high'.

It was unquestionably in architecture that the announcement caused the greatest stir. Common to technology, art, social practice and everyday life, the architectural is a domain that should not be underestimated or regarded as subsidiary. Developments in architecture always have a symptomatic significance initially, and a causal one subsequently. The Venice Biennale of 1980 was devoted to *postmodernity* in architecture – a slogan launched in the USA two or three years earlier. In what, according to its promoters, did it consist? In a return to monuments, a neo-monumentalism freed from the grip and imprint of political power, whereas monuments were, historically, expressions, tools and sites of the reigning

45

powers. One ought (argued Ricardo Bofill) to go so far as to invert symbols.

So what is this modernity that has been wrecked during the current crisis, and renounced? Its reign dates from the early twentieth century, and ended around 1980. Portents of modernity can be detected earlier, but it did not flourish before the beginning of the twentieth century. Thus, around the 1900s, the 'modern style' made its appearance in France, promoting a kind of baroque: plant forms, curves and interlaces, a femininity indirectly suggested or directly expressed. Modern style soon succumbed to ridicule, and was replaced by modernity, which was more technical, more 'rigorous', sparer, distancing itself from the natural and not afraid to be sophisticated. The distinct lines of concrete replaced volutes. The amusing thing about this story is that the recent challenge to modernity is accompanied by a rehabilitation of modern style, which had in the interim come to be regarded as completely outmoded. It is pleasing. Symbolically represented by the exterior of the metro stations constructed at the turn of the century, it is admired in pride of place in New York's Metropolitan Museum and elsewhere.

Modernity begins with what might be called a silent catastrophe. Let us recall the key features of this singular event. Around 1910, the main reference systems of social practice in Europe disintegrated and even collapsed. What had seemed established for good during the *belle époque* of the bourgeoisie came to an end: in particular, space and time, their representation and reality indissociably linked. In scientific knowledge, the old Euclidean and Newtonian space gave way to Einsteinian relativity. But at the same time, as is evident from the painting of the period – Cézanne first of all, then analytical Cubism – perceptible space and perspective disintegrated. The line of horizon, optical meeting-point of parallel lines, disappeared from paintings. The gaze of the painter and the spectator skirts around objects, circles about them, catches the various aspects of the object simultaneously, rather than perceiving it from some privileged angle, be it a particular side of the object, or its surface or façade. At the same time, tonality in music was dissolved, and replaced by atonality, defined not by the 'dominant–tonic' pair but by the equivalence of all intervals. The classical unity of melody, harmony and rhythm in tonality disintegrated. At the same time, too, all coherent, developed systems broke up: philosophy, the city (the historical town), the family and the figure of the Father, history itself. Truth fell into disrepute. The crisis began with reference systems, that is to say, values and norms. Bizarrely, the First World War would soon foreshadow the end of Eurocentrism. Silent catastrophe prepared a noisy catastrophe: the safeguards had vanished.

What became of daily life in this unique mutation, which was not experienced or lived as such, and went unremarked by those acquainted with it (some of the most lucid of whom would later describe it – for example, Thomas Mann, Robert Musil, Hermann Hesse)? Daily life was consolidated as the site where the old reality and the old representations were preserved, bereft of reference points but surviving in practice. 'One' continued to live in Euclidean and Newtonian space, while knowledge moved in the space of relativity. Comparatively straightforward, Euclidean and Newtonian space still seemed absolute and intelligible because it was homogeneous and had nothing to do with time. As for time, it remained clock-time, and was itself homogeneous. People went on singing tonal melodies, with clear rhythms and harmonic accompaniment. They persisted with habitual perceptions and traditional representations, which were erected into eternal verities when in fact they derived from history, and had already been superseded in scientific knowledge. Daily life was certainly not immutable; even modernity was going to alter it. Yet it was affirmed as a site of continuity, exempt from the curious cultural revolution that set in train the collapse of European values constituted by the logos, active rationality, liberal humanism, philosophy, and classical art. Henceforth, thought and daily life, and thus theory and practice, parted company, taking different and divergent paths: audacity on one side, caution on the other.

From this upheaval emerged the three 'values' that were to make up modernity: technique, labour and language. The components of this triad would meet with different fates and follow distinct trajectories. Technique was gradually to become lord and master; like money and commodities under capitalism, it would take on an autonomous reality, escaping the grasp of thought, society, and even the state. It would spread as general power, simultaneously positive and negative, transforming reality and yet lethal (this includes nuclear technology). As for labour, it would become the rival of technique, privilege and supreme value under 'socialism' at the very moment when technology was discrediting it, because it promised – and doubtless enabled – the replacement of labour. Discourse? Language? They were to supply higher values – of stand-in and substitution – in Western societies. Hence the rise of linguistics and semantics, the incredible abuse of language games (from crosswords to puns and TV games), as well as discursive effects. In the West, and for the West, discourse was no longer a means of communication in the twentieth century, a generic and general tool of consciousness, but the way in which 'man' was installed in the world, and hence his relation to the world. The essence that had been abolished re-emerged in the place assigned to discourse. A particular discourse is 'valid' in and for itself, without reference to any other system than itself. Its apologists maintain that it is sufficient to the extent that it is necessary: it coheres as a function not of some truth or external reality, but of its own coherence. Meanwhile, opponents of this fetishization of discourse, and its unconditional valorization, maliciously observe that it involves the murder of language; language is dissolved along with what conferred meaning on it – that is to say, representations of the true and the real. 'One' – the impersonal speaker, now detached from the 'subject' – says anything, which is passed on to him via the '*one*'. The underlying, rarely stated project – 'Say everything! Voice what remains unsaid in what is said! Achieve uninterrupted speech!' – results not in speech that communicates, but in the dissolution of speaking and writing alike, by releasing uninhibited signification, itself separated from expression. Meaning lies dying. Rhetoric is unleashed. Freed from all ties, signifiers take flight. Thought disappears at the very moment thinkers believe they are thinking freely.

We cannot go into the concept of modernity and its critique in sufficient depth here to settle some rather serious questions. How should we assess what is called modern art, in its full range and diversity – painting, the novelistic literature often regarded as essential, but also music, architecture and sculpture – not forgetting poetry? And first of all, how is it to be situated? For Lukács, modernity and its idolatry accompanied the decline of the bourgeoisie, its decay as a class that was once in the ascendant and sufficiently bold to envisage the universalization of its concepts, values and norms. After Goethe and Balzac, creative potential within the framework of bourgeois society diminished, then disappeared. For the Marxist theoretician, the works of the decline bear its stamp. An increasingly sophisticated technology does not prevent art works or products being of no interest, especially when they claim to be 'interesting', and their only 'interest' is commercial. Let us cut short our evocation of this indictment. By contrast, for another renowned Marxist theoretician, Adorno, modern art possesses aesthetic significance and real value. Certainly, for Adorno, modern art works do not arise outside of their context, and cannot be compared with those of the Renaissance. They nevertheless secrete a profound meaning: they are the negative moments of their age, marking out the transformations of society and the world. Works of 'constructive deconstruction', they offer, if not the Truth, then at least truths about the unfolding process. They render it intelligible, precisely by virtue of those features which, for sectarian criticism, typify decadence: the systematic use of ugliness (from Baudelaire to Beckett), and its transformation into formal splendour through appropriate techniques; the absence of content and meaning, approximating to emptiness and nothingness, but only to skim them ('Twas brillig, and the slithy toves/Did gyre and gimble in the wabe'); or the use and abuse of imagery and discourse in Surrealism, in the return to rhetoric, and so on.

The debate between these two interpretations of modernity will remain inconclusive. It depends in part on the place allotted the negative in dialectical activity. Neither Marx nor Engels, and still less Lenin, accentuates the negative. No doubt Hegel went further than the dialecticians who succeeded him in stressing the profound 'labour of the negative'. If you believe that the negative consists solely in the other, reverse side of the positive; and, consequently, that it creates nothing, since it can only dissolve and decompose the positive to create space for what is to come, then Lukács's peremptory critique of modernity and modern art follows. If, on the other hand, you accept that the negative moment creates something new, that it summons and develops its seeds by dissolving what exists, then you will adopt Adorno's position …

Today, this unresolved controversy is receding with modernity itself. Modernity appears as an ideology – that is to say, a series of more or less developed representations that concealed a practice. Modernity was promising. What did it promise? Happiness, the satisfaction of all needs. This *promesse de bonheur* – no longer through beauty, but by

49

technical means – was to be realized in daily life. In fact, the ideology of modernity above all masked daily life as the site of continuity, by floating the illusion of a rupture with the previous epoch. Now that this illusion has been dispelled and modernity dismissed, discussions about its essence and significance have lost some of their interest. What survives of this period is the general slide from a concreteness derived from nature towards the abstract–concrete as the mode of social existence, something that extends to works of art. The predominance of abstraction in art goes together with the extension of the world of commodities and of the commodity as world, as well as the unlimited power of money and capital, which are simultaneously highly abstract and extremely concrete. The art work thus renounces its previous status: proximity to, and even imitation of, nature. It is detached and released from naturalism. This likewise goes together with the short-lived triumph of the most abstract signs – for example, banking and monetary dummy entries – over what remains of concrete reference systems.

The crisis has brought about the separation of modernity and modernism. If the career of modernity as ideology is over, modernism as technological practice is more than ever with us. For the time being, it has taken over from modernism as regards a possible real transformation of daily life. In short, modernity as ideology now appears as an episode in the development and realization of the capitalist mode of production. In contradictory fashion, this ideology provoked its own specific opposition: the heedless promise of novelty – immediately and at any price – has generated a return to the archaeo and the retro, the optimism of modernity becoming tinged with nihilism. From this great confusion emerges modernism: a clear field for the deployment of technology and the proclamation of the end of ideologies (the ideology of the end of ideology), and yet the advent of new myths to which we shall have to return, such as the myth of transparency in society, the state and political action.

How can we avoid the conclusion that the alternative – modernity or postmodernity – is false? Posed in this way, the question avoids the main thing: technological modernism, its import, its capacity for intervention in daily life; and the related problem, which is simultaneously theoretical and political, of controlling technology. Meanwhile, daily life goes on.

2 Constants

This refers to property, the family, morality, and so on. We hardly need remind ourselves that but a short while ago the family seemed very fragile, reduced to the couple, which was itself provisional, its unspecified mission ending with the increasingly early departure of children, and so forth. But now we are witnessing a consolidation of the family – not that this means a revival of the extended family, the large group of blood relations and collaterals. We shall return to this theme. The family is affirmed not only as a micro-centre of consumption and occupation of a small local space (a place), but as an affective group reinforced by a sense of solidarity, the moral complement of social security. This extends to a fraction of parental elders, without a clear distinction between its two components (blood relations and collaterals). Will it last? The increasing importance of the opposition 'insecurity–need for security' suggests that the decline of a grouping reinforced in daily life will occur only gradually, if at all. Added to this is 'home ownership', a mass phenomenon extending to the working class, and the result of a strategy long planned within the framework of the mode of production. It is sufficient to indicate this commonplace in passing.

Conservatism in daily life contrasts not only with revolution in and through daily life – a project that failed, leading to terrorism, hypercriticism and nihilism. It has causes other than those already mentioned – for example, the reference points that survived the collapse of the old systems. It also has some very strong social bases, such as the professions and the corporatist mentality, ownership and heritage in the traditional sense of the terms. Finally, and above all, a distant but decisive motive is the well-known fact that 'socialism' as we know it renders daily life impossible and unliveable. 'Socialism' seems to have assigned itself other goals and objectives – for example, the boundless growth of the productive forces, or the reinforcement of the state and its strategic power. While it is only too true that capitalism leads to the solitude of the individual or the family group in daily life – via the 'cottage', the car, the telephone and television, and tomorrow, no doubt, the home terminal and microprocessors – socialism obtains the same result by different routes: general mistrust and suspicion, the pressure of state ideology and internalized repression, the ethics and aesthetics of the pseudo-collectivity decreed by the state. Whatever political conclusion is to be drawn from this, it must be registered that in Poland in 1980 workers and the people in their entirety sought to take back control of their everyday life. The state wished to administer daily life, but, to say the very least, did not succeed in its aim. The new organization arose out of this failure. It declares itself self-managing at the level of daily life; and is intent on being such. According to the most clear-sighted Poles, 'Solidarity' is neither theology nor politics in the usual sense: it is 'ordinary life' emerging into the daylight, making demands, calling for help – sometimes incautiously, for it is on the brink of despair. Here, the left critique of the state is closely akin to the critique of everyday life: something we knew already.

That is how this society sinks into its 'crisis'. At the very moment when ideology, proclaiming the end of ideology, heralds the advent of the new, the older, the archaeo, resurfaces. To these – more or less veiled – economic, social and political contradictions, society adds contradictions between its norms and values. The malaise of civilization risks becoming intolerable – not so much for the elite as in daily life. New generations are already torn between the demand for satisfaction and disgust with those who are satisfied; between an expectation of unimagined happiness and a strong sense of being deceived, prompting them to outright rejection. Rejection of what? Of what is offered by way of either traditions or projects of renovation. People reject both repressive morality and any morality advocating sacrifice, whether in the name of religion or of some future revolution; both the work ethic and that of interest properly understood; both the values of altruism and those of calculated egotism. Sometimes people retreat into voluntarism in the name of constructive action, thereby running the risk of being flattened in daily life. This amounts to a failure to respond to the most urgent demands. A desire for uniformity and conformism then mounts like a wave, offering a glimpse of the possibility that one day everything – people and things – could sink into indifference and general equivalence. Unless, that is, a new wave of refusal and protest arises.

3 The World of Commodities

We are only too conscious of the fact that the world as currently established is not the product of revolution. Up until the middle of the century, it was hoped that the workers' movement would liberate all the peoples of the world from the capitalist and imperialist yoke, thus realizing 'humanity' on a global scale. But in their present form the world and planet derive, in the first instance, from the extension of the market and commodities to the entire earth, in an uneven process that has nevertheless swept aside all resistance. This does not mean that popular liberation movements have disappeared – far from it. But the world market exists; and it exerts very strong pressure on all countries.

So what is this commodity which defines the market, and has now conquered the globe or, more precisely, generated the global? The theory of the commodity is far from having been elucidated, still less universally accepted. As popularized in current interpretations of Marxism, this theory defines the product as an object, intended for exchange, which contains or crystallizes a greater or lesser share of average social labour, in conditions of average productivity in the society in question. This determines its exchange-value in currency (money). There is no need to query this thesis here by comparing it with other theoretical systems such as marginalism, and so on. It will suffice to register that it does not get us far: while it makes it possible to understand the economic and social status of the product, it does not enable us to understand the planetary extension of the market and the formation of the world market.

Lukács and various others took the analysis further by showing that, as a commodity, the object produced simultaneously contains and conceals the social relations that made its production possible. As a result, the commodity-fetish, accompanied by its ideology (fetishism in general, which takes the products derived from human activity for realities in themselves), ends up permeating social practice in the capitalist mode of production.

This theory involves the philosophical concept of alienation which, in line with Marx's own thinking, it extends to the economic. The thesis of alienation becomes that of reification. But this theory is also tied up with various implicit or explicit theses of Marx and Marxists as to the fragility of capitalism. Capitalism is supposedly held together only by the superstructural edifice, whose non-correspondence with the relations and forces of production is increasingly marked. Capital benefits from the fact that the relations of production are concealed at the stage of productive activity *under* – or, rather, *in* – products intended for exchange. According to this perspective, this does not render the institutional and ideological superstructures erected upon a fragile and already faltering base more robust. Crises, wars and revolutions will soon carry off this mode of production. One good shove by the working class – and the edifice will collapse!

Now, this does not correspond to what has actually transpired in the twentieth century – that is to say the solidity and flexibility of capitalism, and the skill of its leaders – for which we need a theoretical explanation. What accounts for the vigour of capitalism? The enduring strength of the states constructed by the bourgeoisie? The growth and technological progress in which the capitalist countries have held the initiative? Finally, and above all, how do we explain the formation of the world market and its power?

The theory of the commodity and of fetishism does not account for that market, of which we find only an incomplete study in Marx – one that is restricted to the world market prior to industrial capitalism, stretching historically from the sixteenth to the eighteenth century. In its extreme complexity (flows and currents), and extreme diversity (capital markets, raw material and energy markets, labour and technology markets, markets in finished goods and consumer durables, art markets, markets in symbols and signs, in information, etc. etc.), the current world market requires a different analysis from one that starts out from commodities and exchange. Otherwise, the whole theory collapses.

Take various quantities of different products: *a* of a product X (litres of wine, for example); *b* of a product Y (metres of cloth); *c* of a product Z (kilos of sugar); and so on. Here are these goods in front of me. I can use them (use-value); then they are no longer commodities. For them to be commodities – that is to say, for them to possess an exchange-value and be exchangeable against one another or with other products – it must be possible to write: $aX = bY = cZ = \ldots$ The series of products that have thus become exchange-values is limitless. But is there an end to this series, an ultimate 'good'? Yes: gold, guarantor of money, which is simultaneously found at the end of the chain, and alongside each term as money guaranteed by gold and defined relative to it. One can thus write: $aX = bY = cZ = \ldots = \omega$ (omega designating gold, located at the end of the infinite series). Or again: $aX(\omega) = bY(\omega) = cZ(\omega) \ldots$ Following Marx, gold is called the universal equivalent. In exchange, the materiality of the thing is momentarily erased by its form [*Formwechsel*]. Gold restores materiality to the formal. As a result, commodities are constituted as a non-finite, permanently open, and yet well-defined system of equivalents. The form of the commodity – which is simultaneously abstract and concrete, and whose content is goods and products – determines this system of equivalents. This poses the general question, which we cannot deal with here, of the practical mode of existence of socioeconomic forms.

Also to be noted is that in the unlimited series of exchangeable goods (objects and products), *three* goods enjoy a special role and a happy or unhappy privilege: sex, labour and information. In some respects they approximate to gold, in the sense that they are ubiquitous yet clearly situated. These activities, which are exceptional yet conform to the norm for exchangeable goods, the market and commodities, are carried on in daily life and obscure the system of equivalents to the extent of concealing it. Since Antiquity, sex has been sold and bought: prostitution – marriage. Recently, this business has entered directly into the circuits of exchange (sex shops, etc.). Moreover, sexual fantasy and imagery have widely penetrated the discourse of advertising and daily life; the sexual phenomenon in its own right has thus become the supreme commodity – the product that sells other products. The fate of labour is well known: in the modern age, since industrialization, labour features on the market – this was not the case with agricultural, artisanal, intellectual or spiritual activities, which escaped the harsh laws of exchange. The labour-commodity is special in that, by means of tools and machines, it produces all the other commodities (productive activity generating more market value than it is itself worth on the market – an obvious fact disclosed by Marx).

The latest of these privileged commodities is information. It has always existed, but only recently assumed the status of exchangeable product. The vast cycle and expansion of exchange, from primitive bartering onwards, seems to terminate with it. Exchange has conquered the world; or rather, shaped it. At the same time, an immaterial product has emerged from exchange that is abstract and concrete in its way: information. Is not information most deserving of the title of supreme commodity, commodity of commodities? Produced, it has material (technological) conditions; it requires investment and organized labour. It has a production cost. Once it is produced, it is bought and sold. But it is what makes possible all other exchanges: all the flows in which daily life is immersed. In a sense, it was always thus. But today, this strange, immaterial reality is produced in broad daylight. Information as such is as old as social life, in which information has always been transmitted and received. Specifically as a product, information is just starting out. In it, the logic of the commodity – that is to say, of equivalence – joins general logic, logic *tout court*, or consistency in discourse and statements. In fact – and this is extremely important – as a system of equivalents the commodity comprises a logic; it determines a language that modifies and unifies – globalizes – the languages of different societies. It is closely bound up with the general language of quantification. The fact that there is a commodity–world must be recognized and accepted. In its way, this world tends towards a sort of nothingness, through the abstraction of exchange, monetary signs, and the sign in general. But it never attains this limit. It is reinstated materially. Elements of a critical knowledge of it can be found in Marx, and elsewhere than in Marx – in contemporary social practice. It is in this way that the commodity can constitute and determine the global. As a real world, the world market cannot be conceptualized by a 'spiritual' activity pertaining to philosophy – that of Heidegger, for example, which nevertheless explored internationality as a horizon. Nor can it be conceived on the basis of empirical facts: the expansion of trade and the influx of increasingly sophisticated manufactured products. Such facts do not enable us to understand the possibility – the conditions of possibility – of the global. A straightforwardly economic or political theory of internationality underestimates phenomena that are planetary in scope. Only knowledge of the commodity as reality-producing gives us access to the global. This does not mean that it exhausts it – far from it. But it alone makes it possible to situate daily life in the global, and to assess the retroactive impact of international space on its own conditions, on the contradictions it contains.

One or two additional remarks. As a set or system of equivalents, the commodity has served as a model for other systems of equivalents: the contractual system, for example, based on a different form – reciprocity – as well as on the sequences and constraints determined by that form. Thus, modern society is constituted as a system of systems of equivalence. What is more, the state pronounces the general equivalence of these systems of equivalence; it guarantees and implements it. On the other hand, daily life is established thus: everything – the socio-economic-political whole – rests upon it. Ultimately, all moments would be equivalent in daily life. In that case, daily life would dissolve, as it were, like a bad dream. These limits – of daily life and of the sign – are never reached. The moments assert themselves. Each of them possesses a 'value' in the totality; in the absence of such a 'value', there would be no link between the moments of daily life. Yet they all logically tend towards equivalence. Within the system of systems of equivalence, a levelling occurs: not down to the lowest, and still less up to the 'highest' – the summit of society – but to an abstract social average. Assimilation, repetition, equivalence (calculable, predictable, and hence open to rational administration) – such are the characteristics daily life tends towards, characteristics which were already in evidence some years ago, but are becoming more pronounced. Everyday life managed like an enterprise within an enormous, technocratically administered system – such is the first and last word of the technocratic ethic: every moment anticipated, quantified in money terms, and programmed temporally and spatially.

Nevertheless, sexuality, labour and information retain a certain ambiguity and privilege in daily life. Intense instants – or, rather, moments – it is as if they are seeking to shatter the everydayness trapped in generalized exchange. On the one hand, they affix the chain of equivalents to lived experience and daily life. On the other, they detach and shatter it. In the 'micro', conflicts between these elements and the chains of equivalence are continually arising. Yet the 'macro', the pressure of the market and exchange, is forever limiting these conflicts and restoring order. At certain periods, people have looked to these moments to transform existence: to labour, in the name of socialism; to sexuality, in the name of freedom and pleasure, seeking to wrest it from the world of commodities; and finally, today, to information, to dominate and even dispel the world of material products and commodities. The failure of the first two endeavours, and the problems encountered by the third, indicate that there is no guarantee that we can open up a path in this direction. While it is definitely the case that sexuality and labour can, in their own ways (sexuality through erotic exhilaration and the joy of being in love; labour through strikes and rebellions), at least momentarily break the link between exchange-value and daily life, it may be that information-processing has arrived to complete the empire of commodities and the course of daily life. Unless, that is, it affords an opportunity and a conjuncture that are conducive to 'socialization' of a new type, one that would draw the totality on to other paths. Whence a problematic that has already been hinted at.

4 Identity

Among the factors of continuity, national identity – its acquisition and preservation in the course of the 'crisis' – must be accorded due importance. It corresponds, at the summit, to identity in daily life at the foot. Historically established on the basis of the home market and centralized state power, French identity was asserted and confirmed during revolutions and wars. Today, this formal identity, like the realities to which it corresponds – country, fatherland, nation, state – is under threat on all sides. These threats, which might lead to a loss of identity, are the object of numerous complaints. Is not the 'loss of identity' we hear so much about the (or a) contemporary form of alienation, without being named as such? The pressure of the international tends to break up national identity, by dissolving the sense of belonging to a political and cultural community. Likewise from below, if we may put it that way, with differentialist pressures: regions, towns, local communities. Compromised and even shaken, to a certain extent national identity is everywhere in search of itself and seeking to preserve itself. The tremors are inducing veritable panics. Is the groundswell of these terms – loss of identity, search for identity – at all levels, from the individual to the continental, an accident? No, it has a meaning. Where is Frenchness to be found? Is nationalism, whose pronounced return is becoming menacing, a recovery of lost identity or its ideological simulation? Whatever happens, the preservation of identity signifies the use and abuse of commemoration, the return of the historical as a system of reference, and pressure on daily life to prevent its 'destabilization' and preserve it as a locus of identity. This thus implies a tendency towards the reproduction of relations of domination in identity – a process that is not without its obscurities and uncertainties. Even so, we must distinguish in national identity between reality and ideology: the domestic market and the 'national' culture (in France, for example, the traditional rationalism whose national character is obscured amid the crisis – all the more so in that it is related to the European and Western logos, which is itself in crisis). This identity operates in the direction of non-development – in other words, of conservatism. It strengthens resistance to change, even as the urgent need for change in order to modernize national life is proclaimed elsewhere. Is it not weird that people so often refer to '*la France profonde*' in connection with backward corners, out-of-the-way villages, and small towns frozen in archaism? This Frenchness is obsolete, antiquated; yet it is exalted on television and in the press. Are not some harsh truths being masked under manipulative ideologies here? On the surface, France can be characterized thus: advanced ideologies and retarded structures, which are incredibly difficult to shift (constituent bodies and orders, frozen institutions, etc.). As for what is called '*la France profonde*', it is marked by ideologies that are as retarded as its structures.

We know that the major reference systems – the Town, History, the heavenly or terrestrial Father – have disappeared since the beginning of the century, releasing elements that were previously subordinate – among them, technology. Yet at the heart of daily life, tacit or explicit references persist that are more modest than the major systems of the past, but sufficiently solid and proximate to serve as reference points, if not safeguards. The private family, for example, which survives as a public service. This objective basis – mutual aid in a society that is, to say the least, difficult – does not preclude ties of affection; it keeps them in order. Various theoreticians of information and audiovisual techniques maintain that they do not alter the family reception of messages and images in the slightest – and never will. Simultaneously identified with and loathed as a prison, the restricted family survives, identical to itself and part of the general identity. The same goes for religion, a recourse in the face of anxiety, which is held in disrepute but nevertheless remains strong. Finally, and above all, the same goes for property, which is reassuringly solid – a bastion against all the world's onslaughts: it is valorized anew, with its train of institutions and rites, such as wills. These observations have nothing new or surprising about them, but must be included in any picture of what persists in the identity of daily life. Considered thus, private property is not confined to property in the means of production; it is not simply a means of participating in production and surplus-value. Individually or jointly owned flats (half the French population own their own homes), second homes – these serve not merely an economic function, but a function in terms of security, and hence of identity. Their purchase represents an investment: 'Invest in bricks and mortar'. At stake is certainly ownership and wealth, but also an ethical, and even aesthetic, value. The same goes for rural landownership, which maintains a long tradition – more so than the ownership of bricks and mortar. State and society, as they are, create anxiety, and compensate for it – that is to say, a demand for security that is closely bound up with the need for identity and continuity. The owner of a house is there for life, especially if he earned it by the sweat of his brow. He has his place in space. He dwells in the Same, and the 'other' cannot assail him or drag him out. He is installed in the identical, the repetitive, the equivalent. The permanence of property symbolizes, and at the same time realizes, the continuity of an ego. This ego unquestionably lives a better life in its own property than when it is exposed to anxiety in accommodation that might be lost from one day to the next. These commonplace details make up the mundane character and, consequently, the vigour of daily life. Like the personal objects that form the immediate environment around an individual or family group. To be attached to objects, to privilege them affectively, is today, as in the past, to create a shell or a bubble – that is to say, a protective layer against the assaults of a hostile world. This protection is simultaneously apparent and real, lived and valued as such. The more threatening the outside world becomes, the greater the importance and continuity of the interior – that which surrounds or protects subjective interiority. Disdained during the years of protest, things become 'goods' once again; the environment forms an integral and integrated part of the 'person', of their identity. Whether the objects constitute a system, whether they derive from a more or less rationalized and functional combinatory, is an important, but ultimately secondary, issue. Like the technicization and mechanization of familiar objects, studied by Siegfried Giedion in *La Mécanisation au pouvoir*. Far from imposing a new form on social relations, this mechanization, which involves personal existence in technology, strengthens the identity of daily life: it encloses it, rather than opening it. Take, for example, the mechanization of the bath.[1] Capitalist and bourgeois Europe made the transition from public baths, meeting-place and site of social life, to the bathroom, in which each member of the group is isolated. The mechanical function of 'cleanliness' was enhanced at the expense of bodily relaxation and restoration on the one hand, sociability on the other. Antiquity, by contrast, switched from the private bath to magnificently equipped public (thermal) baths.

This far-reaching dynamic of privatization and identification in the private sphere began a long time ago; it is being strengthened; it sep-arates the private from the public, at the risk of causing a backlash – that is, the confusion of the private and the public. The latter, subor-dinate to political power and the state, can go and find the 'private' individual at home and draw him out of his shell like some edible snail. Isn't this what happens with certain objects, including the tele-vision set and the microprocessor? Public and publicity go together.

Domestic appliances have certainly altered daily life. By opening it out on to the world? Quite the reverse: they have aggravated its closure, by reinforcing repetitive everydayness and linear processes – the same gestures around the same objects. Let us note once again that 'household' appliances have not liberated women; they have made liberation movements possible by alleviating daily drudgery. Only then did specific demands regarding divorce, contraception, abortion, and freely chosen maternity emerge. Something new makes its appearance here. These aspirations, which have given rise to con-flicting movements, were inconceivable when birth and death alike were the preserve of God the Father, Creator of Heaven and Earth. This remains the official teaching of the apostolic Roman Catholic Church, and is fiercely defended by it.

5 Everyday Discourse

Indeed, faith – shaken today, because it is prey to all sorts of contradictions – consists above all in this certainty: beginnings and ends, creation and destruction, depend upon the Lord, his goodness and his ire; they must therefore bear a sacred character. Men, and even more so women, have only to accept this magical-metaphysical-mystical dependency. Evolution pertains to the human; the event or advent possesses a metaphysical significance and an ontological sense: it derives from the eternal. This is conveyed by the solemnity of the words attaching to these 'facts', which are not facts as such, because they rupture the factual sequence. Faith of this sort once intervened powerfully in daily life; it governed it. Has it disappeared? No, though it is weaker. Hence a certain continuity, but also something different that insinuates itself into the fabric of daily life: a more concrete freedom, a secularization of the events that punctuate private lives – births, marriages, deaths. This is a contradictory process. Many people who do not practise religion and its rites, who have 'lost their faith', continue to get married in church, have their children baptized, evoke or invoke the divine in discourse. Religion persists through several processes: rites and gestures, but also words, and the sacralization and hence valorization of the crucial moments of existence. This consecration of beginnings and ends paradoxically guarantees the continuity of daily life. At the same time, it intensifies these moments, dramatizes them, and imbues them with a kind of cosmic significance, under the gaze of the 'hidden god'. Religion continues to impart meaning to daily life – no doubt because it has yet to discover a different meaning.

Has everyday discourse changed much in half a century? Not really. In some respects, it has been impoverished, reduced to 'basic French'. In others, it has been enriched. We do not have a language of daily life alongside the language of the commodity, or that of the unconscious or science. Thus there are not several languages, but various uses of the language, of each language. Nevertheless, new words laden with meaning are making their appearance. So, the technocratic elite has its own vocabulary, which is gradually penetrating ordinary language: *target* (an objective) or *niche* (an available space). Other examples include the disturbing *position oneself*, or the curious *way out* for 'mistaken'. New generations have their lexical innovations: *trip* and *flip*, straight out of the Anglo-Saxon countries, or 'having butterflies' to express nerves. This enrichment of vocabulary does not greatly alter everyday discourse, or its tendency to eliminate many terms of the best French as rather ridiculous archaisms. But this occurs together with the opposite tendency. Used by the middle classes, but also by popular strata, traditional sayings have been preserved. People still say: 'It never rains but it pours', 'what will be will be', 'he who laughs last laughs loudest', 'to put one's shoulder to the wheel', 'you've made your own bed, now you must lie on it' ... Proverbial wisdom has scarcely changed – which is sufficient to demonstrate the continuity of daily life. The semantics of proverbs must take account of a fact that is surprising, to say the least: it seems to indicate that practical situations are altering only very slowly, despite the enormous technical equipment surrounding and penetrating the everyday; despite the pressure of events and other pressures ...

Perhaps this is not the main thing. Lexicon and vocabulary do not determine the peculiar tonality of everyday discourse. Theoretically – philosophically – considered, this discourse is neither true nor false, although it is always presented as veridical. It is constantly organizing the conditions of existence of the group: the family, the office, the workshop, the firm, and so on. Even those who claim to be engaged in what is called plain speaking never say everything they have on their mind or in their heart. Can any social group bear to hear the truth about itself? When the truth emerges, the group risks splintering. The truth is always cruel: however 'spiteful' one considers the everyday nuisance who says what he sees and thinks, once the truth is out, it follows its own course. It most often emerges in daily life during 'scenes', for which it supplies the dramatic interest. For a 'scene' to occur, a discussion, initially muffled and toned down, must escalate, and a dispute or quarrel must loom – spirits with hands like glowing coal, fire in their eyes. The risk is that people will go to the heart of the matter and say what is best left unsaid, or what it is simply not done to say. The reality and truth of relations in daily life, including relations of force, then strike people all at once, and they are appalled not to have understood daily life once the event has finally transformed it. Without stating it, everyday discourse plays on the relation between truth (ineffable, even unknown) and non-truth. What is involved is a saying meagre enough to seem hypocritical, but not meagre enough not bring misanthropy to bear. It is a permanent wager. Daily life and its discourse are thus built on ambiguity, on a carefully arranged compromise. This not very historical compromise constitutes the mode of existence of the everyday – something that understandably displeases most adolescents. 'Scenes' and altercations cannot go on for ever; they exhaust themselves. People then revert to compromise, though the dispute and what is at issue in it will resurface in the near future. For there always is something at stake, even when it is not visible. Quarrels are always filled with unresolved – and often insoluble – problems: so much so that 'compromise' and 'ambiguity' mean 'adaptation and sociability by acceptance'. One must take people as one finds them … This adage of everyday wisdom, and even political wisdom – adopted by Lenin – says precisely what it means. One remedy – or, rather, palliative – is humour, which has nothing in common with irony. The everyday gives rise to its own kind of humour: the humour of the office or workshop, family humour, and so on.

Humour is distinct from the bitter gibe as well as the sarcasm that figures in quarrels; and from the irony that evinces an unforgivable distance. Humour lightens daily life; it takes it lightly; it makes possible a discourse that can consent without capitulating. For humour accepts things: more precisely, it accepts the situation by veiling it, by sometimes covering it with a kind of affection, by remaining within it. It may be that despite humour, or in its absence, the situation degenerates, deteriorates in distressing or sickening fashion, especially when relations of dependency and domination are superimposed upon affective relations and specifically social (community) relations.

Dramatized, daily life explodes and its discourse shatters. Yet it lends itself to dramatization. Did not tragedy aesthetically elaborate what are commonly called domestic scenes – Agamemnon and Clytemnestra – or family disputes – King Lear's daughters, and so on – taking them to a climax? With one essential condition: that the scene is always played out between the powerful. Escalation starts with discourse and discussion, moves on to a dispute and a quarrel, and ends up in a bloody drama. The included middle – the fatal deed – then makes its appearance. Somewhere, there is always a rupture, a

64

possible or actual murder. The everyday always contains comedy and drama, 'roles' that are more or less well played. Theatre pushes mundane drama to the point of Tragedy, and the comedies of daily life to the point of buffoonery. The everyday remains analogous to an improvised performance of a bad *commedia dell'arte* by ham actors. Sometimes a crime of passion, or a moral or political crime, is committed – after which it is buried, in everyday life as at the theatre.

Everyday discourse thus has a stable content, a core or foundation, which is bound up not (as the classical thesis has it) with an unchanging human nature, but with the fact that social relations have for a long time, if not always, been relations of force, authority and power, dependency, inequality in power and wealth. Such relations are tolerable only when they are masked. Stripped of all veils, they would be unbearable. Daily life and its ambiguity, simultaneously effect and cause, conceal these relations between parents and children, men and women, bosses and workers, governors and governed. For its part, critical knowledge removes the screens and unveils the meaning of metaphors. It demonstrates that what makes the functioning of societies possible is neither self-interest on its own, nor violence, nor the imaginary, but the (an) ethics inherent in discourse. At the heart of daily life and its speech we find ethical values, which are supports of social life in that they make it tolerable. Discourse and daily life cover the harshness and brutality of structural relations, the skeleton of society, with a weak but soft flesh. Are not the deep structures of speech and writing procedures – empirically discovered and established procedures – for preserving in one and the same present disparate elements, some of which derive from the past while others are merely potential? Take the sentence and the sequence of spoken or written sentences. This has its foundation in daily life as the reign of what is current – the preservation of its conditions – over past and future alike: the reign of the present, not of presence. Nothing in daily life dies. When someone passes on, people say: 'life goes on ...'. It must indeed go on: the family, the workplace and the firm, the office, the entire society. Roles require continuity. Yet one occasionally wonders whether nothing in the everyday dies because everything is dead already: the repetitive buried under its own repetition, at once unknown and too well known, hidden beneath the surface of the wilted rhetoric of humdrum discourse. Is there an everyday life or an everyday death? Taken to a radical extreme, should not the critique of everyday life declare that life and death tend to merge in modern daily life? But we must know how not to go too far, how not to push critique as far as hypercriticism. Daily life is where 'we' must live; it is what has to be transformed.

The more daily life and its discourse bury life by eliminating death, the more they are consolidated in general ambiguity and compromise: between life and death, presence and absence, thought and non-thought; between the resolve to resolve and thinking that one might think, the creative and the repetitive, desire and non-desire, sublime heights and unfathomable depths. A compromise still obtains between self-loathing and self-love (the *amour-propre* of the Augustinians and Jansenists), between hatred and love both of what is close and of what is remote; and it always has obtained.

As they encounter more obstacles, barriers and blockages than ever in modernity, how is it that so many people have not realized that they were coming up against the boundaries of daily life, boundaries that are invisible, yet cannot be crossed because of the strength of daily life? They come up against these boundaries like insects against a window pane. And yet can people live informally, prepared for anything, in unrestricted, unorganized freedom? Is carrying chaos within oneself sufficient to give birth to a star? Does this not mean that daily life harbours the site, if not the content, of a creation which transforms it, and is to be accomplished? But possibility does not betoken reality.

Hence the strong need to break up daily life, to go off elsewhere, in deeds and not only in words: travel, tourism, caravanning, escapism, drugs and picking people up (the hippie movement), the disdainful attitudes of those who think the world is to be changed through contempt. Hence, also, the fascination evinced by endless discussion of the life of those commonly thought to transcend daily life: Olympians, stars, champions, millionaires, political leaders. And its opposite: readers and spectators then have the satisfaction of discovering that these people live like everyone else; that they suffer from identical illnesses and the same twists of fate. Everyday life is obsessed by what it perceives above it, and readily attributes non-everydayness to it. Through a familiar effect, this induces a new degeneration in daily life: at the extreme, the solitary who dreams of interaction, oneness, crowds. All this has been said many times, but usually from a moralistic standpoint – which is different from the attempt to situate such fascination, as well as its compensations, in daily life by demonstrating its ambiguity and wisdom, artificially complicated to the point of delirium.

While we must call upon fragmented disciplines and sciences such as psychology, history, sociology and so on, to elucidate everyday discourse, and replace it with a conceptual language that makes the transition from the experiential to the conceptual, it would not appear imperative to deconstruct this everyday discourse in order to construct an adequate text. What would that be? Written? Multidimensional? Would it bring to light representations that remain implicit? The underlying and the latent? The depth of lived experience? No doubt. But do we need to invent a jargon? And why invent words? The relation between everyday discourse and the discourse of a knowledge of daily life resembles the relation between the language of the theatre and ordinary language: the same, but different – the same, in another style.

These incursions into and excursions around everyday discourse do not exhaust it. Far from it. They have simply situated it. To proceed with the analysis of continuity in daily life, must we entertain the hypothesis of a latent discourse with psychoanalysts? Yes and no. Yes, in the sense that its elucidation involves making it explicit, unfolding or opening out what is found not below discourse, but in it – beginning with the language of commodities and the gradual extension of equivalents. No, in the sense that there are no grounds for positing a kind of mysterious substance – the unconscious – from which discourse issues while disclosing and veiling it. The everyday content of the discursive form is simultaneously and inseparably individual and social: the social is the content of the individual, invariably unrecognized as such; and vice versa. The elucidation of everyday discourse brings them out of one another and their mutual incomprehension. Providing, that is, it extends to everyday ethics and aesthetics, which exist, if only in the form of denotation – that is, simplistic metaphors and rhetoric: 'How ugly ... But isn't it dreadful! ... Now that – that's nice, that's beautiful. I like that ...'.

Should we adopt from sociology the hypothesis that there are representations which are specific to a society, and pass over into everyday discourse? Yes and no. Such representations exist, but they derive just as much from individuals and their inner depths as from society as such, in a process of constant interaction and conjunction. Contrary to what sociologists (the Durkheimian school) have imagined, representations are not external to individuals. Should we retain the idea of an evolutionary process, a formation, from history? Certainly, but not in the sense of a historical time: we are dealing with a simultaneously subjective and objective time – a subjective time created and measured by the outside in an unremitting confrontation. Finally, should we distrust psychology or draw inspiration from it? Both! Psychologists generally put their trust in psychic 'facts'. Yet everyday discourse and the daily life of discourse involve an ignorance of their own conditions. Nevertheless, these conditions are in them, appear in them: they simply need to be brought out.

Everyday discourse performs an important function: translating into ordinary language – that is to say, decoding in an accessible form – the sign systems and different codes employed in a society, from place signs to codes of courtesy and good manners, to the more or less secret codes of the bureaucracy. Unbeknown to itself, everyday discourse performs this continuous, indispensable labour. On the other hand, it is true that this discourse serves as a vehicle for representations; it consists in a flow of representations. Each word entails a succession of words, attached as 'connotations' to literal denotation. People are only too ready to believe that daily life uses only the denotative: a cat is a cat. In fact, connotations abound and overrun denotation, which does not mean that there is a codified rhetoric of daily life. But in a particular group or milieu, what is connoted is so heavily stressed that it is reduced to the rank of denotation. This is how evaluation, which is most often moral but sometimes aesthetic, works in daily life. What common sense regards as bad or ugly is thus expressed in demonstrative terms, which indicate the thing as if they were pointing to it: 'That's ghastly ...'.

Can we talk in terms of a *system* of representations that is inherent in daily life? This question has been examined elsewhere.[2] In brief, the answer is yes and no. Representations are displaced and substituted for one another. Accordingly, it is difficult to classify them into systems – all the more so since they contain multiple contradictions. They are neutralized or strengthened: in the latter eventuality, they sometimes conglomerate into cores, strong points. They involve more or less powerful values that strive to predominate and impose a certain coherence. In this way, they furnish materials and cases for philosophical and ideological systems, to which they sometimes approximate. Tendencies towards dogmatism are not foreign to daily existence. This is how practical and representative rationality functions in the modern world. If there is a system, it derives from either positive knowledge, or political power and its influence, or both; it would seem that systems derive not from representations as such, but from their methodical elaboration. Nevertheless, representations, as instruments of communication, can be practically elaborated in systems that are inscribed in 'reality' – for example, in architecture.

A kind of venerable Manichaeanism is still with us, and tends to crystallize into a system in daily life. The old paradigm 'friends and enemies – neighbour and stranger – pure and impure – light and darkness – good and evil ...' continues to govern much discourse and inspire much action. On many occasions, it has even been extended: socialism and Marxism are supposedly enemies, dark forces, impurity, evil and calamity.

Upon analysis, certain standard representations contained in discourse turn out to be highly complex, even paradoxical. In daily life, they are accepted without any difficulty. For example, death-in-life, with its opposite: living death. The dead survive in photographic documents; people recognize them; the absent becomes present once again, and people are moved. One should not speak ill of the dead. They are referred to in words that identify them with misfortune, not nothingness: 'My poor father ...'. A visit to the cemetery with flowers on All Saints' Day reawakens the dead by giving life to memory. As for death-in-life, a more explicit analysis might evoke dead gods who come back to life, the heroes and kings who reappear in history and the theatre. Everyone understands ghost stories. That is to say, death-in-life is the great presence–absence in the most elevated works and daily life alike. Is this not the figure, its strangeness softened by familiarity, which forms the link between everyday life and great works?

A string of relations between the living and the dead is thus woven into the heart of everyday life. The photograph and the mask keep these relations alive. The mask, the replica that clings to the skin, is closely related to the absolute other, the deceased. It reincarnates him, transforming the one who wears it into one of the living dead. Paradoxically, this produces a moment of festival, for death is overcome. This festival shatters daily life – or, rather, extends it by magnifying it – whereas the photograph and the image (the portrait) help to shore up its continuity.

Could we not say the same of representations as of power? The sovereign has always been regarded as immortal: son of the gods, his death immortalizes him. He is prince, king, emperor for life and beyond, because he is close to the Lord and the eternal Father. Thus, among the attributes of power was immortality, simulated by embalming and monumental tombs, and fostered on a daily basis by commemorative ceremonies. Everyone understands it within everyday life. The honesty and fidelity of 'subjects' are registered by the fact that they know themselves to be mortal. But they, too, can sometimes demand their share of immortality, through property and inheritance, mementoes, the cemetery and a plot in the cemetery. We know that in Egypt revolts were staged to democratize the immortality of the pharaohs. Modern cemeteries attest to an analogous democratization.

Despite the bizarre aspects running through it, everyday discourse is generally clear. Why? Because redundancy – that is to say, repetition – is the basis of intelligibility. Information theory teaches that redundancy is measured like information itself, since they are inverse quantities: $R = 1/I$. There is information only if there is no sheer repetition. However, pure information – a total surprise and an utter disordering of the elements of the code, or a highly unlikely combination – would be unintelligible. This occurs in screams, sobbing, which are ultimately inarticulate. Consequently, it is the mundanity of everyday discourse that makes for its intelligibility. It is maintained in redundancy: banalities and commonplaces.

Everyday discourse consists in spoken words; voices emit it. It is written badly. When literary discourse seems to approximate to it, it is in fact transcribed and transformed by being transposed. In everyday discourse, as opposed to literary writings, the denotative predominates. This does not contradict an earlier analysis: connotations feature in daily life only when they are reduced to the denotative, immediately linked as values and implicit evaluations to the words used and objects referred to. This impoverishes yet clarifies the discourse, giving it the appearance of a chain of signifiers such that it can be followed, recalled, even inverted. In daily life, time and discourse, everything, *seems* reversible, unlike historical time and natural time, as well as subjective duration. Daily life and its discourse tend to be installed in a space that has priority over temporality. A (seeming) simultaneity obtains. This sets traps for memory and thought alike. The equivalence 'intelligibility–redundancy' is not unimportant in establishing daily life, or in the domination of the linear over the cyclical, even though the latter persists in the alternation of day and night, hunger and satiation, going to sleep and waking up, and so on. Obviously, the intelligibility of daily life remains 'superficial'. Much more than that: it constitutes the surface skimmed by reflection, the fake mirror shattered by thought. The surface determines depth and height alike.

This predominance and equivalence assimilate daily life and its discourse to logic and logistics. Daily life requires us to be logical; otherwise, we are accused of inconsistency. Most of the statements made in this discourse contain a subject and a predicate linked by the copula. This copula, whose function and meaning pose so many problems for philosophers, poses none for interlocutors in daily life. 'The table is dirty', 'the soup is salty', 'the Hoover is bust', and so on. This logical lack of imagination seems to exclude any dialectic. Yet everyday discourse does not exclude provocations, challenges, argumentativeness, retorts, and consequently insolence, sophistry, even eristics, and so on. This reintroduces into it something that is not reducible to logic.

Symbols and metaphors abound and proliferate in commonplace remarks and informality: 'It's clear', 'it's not clear', 'he's doing me a favour', 'the chilliness of this reception', 'he parted on very cold terms', 'he made some warm remarks', and so on. These basic symbols are flattened out in the prose of everyday life, whereas non-quotidian discourses – of literature, the theatre or poetry – revive and amplify them. Daily life would be reduced to its reversible continuity were this one-dimensionality not continually interrupted, making way for dreams, daydreams, fantasies – everything that is called 'the imaginary' – but above all for the 'scenes' which, as we know, purge it through a rudimentary catharsis – rather as classical crises purged the economy of surplus factors.

In the course of their displacement and conflictual relations, representations collide and clash. They are thus put to the test in daily life. While one adman associates health with the representation of a pot of yoghurt, another, promoting for a different brand, will link the same image with 'velvety smoothness'. Who will decide between them? Consumers. Although they are manipulated, they still have a small margin of freedom: they will choose. 'Choosing' is represented in daily life as a value that manipulation does not destroy, but exalts. It might be that one of the two representations cited above succeeds, or fails. The same goes for political representations: rival candidates for power fight via the intermediary of their representations – in other words, their 'brand images' as developed by specialists in political marketing.

Manipulative and manipulated representations make it possible to disconnect in daily life what is linked and should remain so; and to confuse what should remain distinct. This effect derives from the fact that ordinary representations obscure what is represented, become mixed up or separated, depending on the intention of the manipulator. It has been possible closely to track the effects of such manipulation in urban questions: the way in which the fragmentation of the urban, breaks and ruptures, the separation of functions that were once performed in unitary fashion in historical space, have been made acceptable; or the way in which a confusion between the order of established power and the order of daily life has been perpetuated.

In daily life as a lottery, the actor-player budges only in wagering on his luck and bad luck: he will achieve some particular goal or result through mockery, courtesy, charm, irony, and so on. He always has an objective. But what is really at stake is only rarely represented – and then badly. During the action and discourse, it generally remains unseen: what is going to happen? What is going to emerge? Defeat or victory? Unless what is involved is a specific gamble, a settled bet. Then you place your stake on the table and the game commences. Daily life? It is now suspended, if not ruptured. The relation between play and daily life is a conflictual one. Yet the game does not succeed in vanquishing the everyday; it remains a moment.

6 On Vulgarity

Vulgarity is hard to define. But who can deny its 'reality', especially inasmuch as it consists in a certain way of being 'real' and understanding the 'real'? It is usually contrasted with *refinement*; yet this distinction belongs to the realms of vulgarity. Nothing is more vulgar than refinement and the desire to distinguish oneself (to *be* distinguished). An ethical-aesthetic value judgement, a sociological fact, vulgarity derives not from the popular character of gestures and words, but from the daily life secreted and ordained by the middle classes: a certain 'realism' about money, clothes, behaviour and gratification – a realism that is paraded and imposed – forms part of the 'vulgar'. Daily life is confined to what is; it dispenses with any horizon, any resonance; it congratulates itself on its limits and encloses itself in them. It flaunts needs, their objects and their satisfaction. This is its 'behaviour', a reflex and self-contented conditioning, a way of behaving, which extends to life in its entirety and taints it with its tonality – vulgarity. This casts suspicion on any rupture, prohibiting it, ruling out any alteration by identifying 'what is' with good sense and wisdom. Dull realism, which is vulgar and produces vulgarity, stifles even the sighs of the oppressed creature: dreams, appeals to what is different and other, the protests of those – women, children, deviants – who represent irreducible lived experience in daily life, demanding 'something different'. The extraordinary that pierces through the ordinary, the extra-quotidian that tends to break up daily life ('passions', demands that take the form of prohibitions and curses, interjections and exclamations, abuse and insults) – this vulgarity rejects, denying its existence, ridiculing it, reducing it to the extent of destroying it. Impervious, invulnerable, inaccessible, the vulgar being creates a shell around him, protecting him from all but the most commonplace suffering. From daily life vulgarity retains only the mundane. It is not exclusively attached to discourse, but to something more hidden and more essential. Does not satisfaction have a *cumulative* character? Not like positive knowledge, but in an analogous fashion? Satisfactions are added: as they are produced and reproduced, as they produce and reproduce their objects, needs generate the density of the vulgar. This does not mean that anxiety, imagination or distress wrest the 'subject' from vulgarity; someone who is 'frustrated' can remain vulgar in their concerns.

Vulgarity is not confined to daily life and those who focus on what is trivial in it. Certain 'reflections' that do their best to pass for thought are marred by vulgarity, and bear its stamp just as much as forms of behaviour rooted in habits. The vulgarity of self-satisfied knowledge bears some classic names, which apologias for scientificity and technicity cause people to forget: priggishness, pedantry, ponderousness. In times past, people used to call it 'Philistinism', and Schumann wrote his 'march against the Philistines'. The enormous and enduring success of psychoanalysis does not prevent reflection 'centred' on sexuality lapsing into vulgarity; there is something profoundly vulgar about the attention paid to 'sexual matters', 'sexual relations', sex in general or 'sexuality'. Today, after Nietzsche, a doctrine merits support only if it proposes a new (superior) type of man, society, civilization. Freud brought to language, concepts and theory a 'reality' that had hitherto been ignored, disdained, and even cursed (this is always worth recalling, to avoid misunderstandings). Freud's thought does not lapse into vulgarity; but it can lead to it. Here intellectual coarseness coincides with social crudity – the unhappy adolescents who are forever talking about sex, casting a shameful glance at the other sex and the sex of others. This 'reality' is not in any doubt; nor are the daily problems it poses (itself). But a 'reality', or rather 'realism', of this sort is inherent in vulgarity. Should not theorization of this 'reality' be understood *symptomatically*, as an indication of the malaise afflicting Western, Judaeo-Christian society? Capitalist and bourgeois society? Scientifico-technicist society? Symptom and symbol of a failure that extends far beyond sexuality, can psychoanalysis guarantee that an acceptable everydayness will be established on the language and positive knowledge of the 'unconscious'? Is it not precisely this implicit promise, which has never been fulfilled, this failed prophecy, that sets in train the decline of theory? Something from which vulgar Marxism is obviously not exempt ...

Are we according 'vulgarity' a philosophical status here, as Sartre attempted with his portrayal of the 'bastard' or the 'gaze of the other'? Not exactly. We are introducing into the theory of daily life what is generally regarded as a subjective judgement: vulgarity, boredom, malaise. The so-called social or human 'sciences' do not take account of such things. Thus, boredom does not exist for sociologists as a social fact. They are wrong! As for the move from malaise to ill-being philosophically conceived, that is a different operation.

Neither Marx and 'Marxist' thought, nor Freud, psychology and psychoanalysis, escaped the great illusion of the nineteenth century and part of the twentieth: the confusion between living and knowing – even its identification in the name of the Truth. From this deceptive viewpoint, to live is to know; to learn and know is to live. The lived and the conceived are identified. Confused with 'being', centred on the 'real', defining and consequently mastering it, knowledge has a simultaneously methodological, practical and ontological priority. According to the Cartesian precept, social, practical man becomes the master and possessor of Nature through labour and knowledge: the plenitude of his being is defined in this way, and realized. That's how it is for Marx. If I know what I feel and experience, if I access that in 'me' which eluded my 'knowledge' and pursued its course outside or without my consciousness, I create a satisfying, normal situation: assuagement and health. That's how it is for Freud. As if knowledge possessed the capacity not only to grasp the unknown 'object', be it nature or the unconscious, but to realize the 'subject'. The latter would thus be constituted by positive knowledge, lived as such.

A good deal of empty discussion stems from this attitude, which in practice slips into extreme vulgarity. There is a vulgarity peculiar to the specialist who knows what comes within his narrow competence, but is unaware of the world. There is also the vulgarity of the technocrat, who merely improves his customary performance, and is connected with other domains solely through utterly mundane commonplaces.

The attitude that likes to think itself rational, privileging the conceptual to the extent of hypostatizing it, induces a lively reaction, which remains face to face with the thing that motivates it: fetishism of the absurd, a cult of irrationality. Hence a loop and an imprisonment of thought.

Hence, equally, problems without answers and inconclusive debates, during which the debasement of theory into vulgarity continues. Take Marxists: do the superstructures merely reflect the base? If they reflect the base, how can they act, intervene, effectively? What is the base? Productive forces or social relations? Which relations? Take Freudians: does psychoanalysis possess concepts? What are they? Does psychoanalysis apply these concepts, or does the treatment of 'patients' follow a course in which concepts are of no practical relevance? Whence, if not from positive knowledge and the transference, derives the analyst's power over the patient, a power that is in theory beneficial? Does this process occur at the cognitive level, or within the affects? And so on.

So the fate of the philosophies of pure knowledge has not spared 'Marxism'. Revolution through positive knowledge, transmitted by the political party, brought by it to the working class *from without* (Lenin) – this revolution has miscarried. The result is a situation that would appear favourable to neither the theory, nor the political party, nor the working class; the latter cannot constitute itself as an *autonomous*, self-determining 'political subject' solely by means of positive knowledge (of the economic, of its own condition, etc.). Hence the painful *vulgarization* of Marxist thought. We have waited in vain for the 'working class' – which, according to Marx, had not yet attained the status of 'class' (for itself) – to assimilate the simplified knowledge that was offered it. This knowledge remains the preserve, even the (collective) property, of narrower groups than the 'class' – of an elite stratum of professionals, members of the 'political class', linked to the autonomization of political and state apparatuses. This situation is itself bound up with the autonomization of technicity.

The transformation of the social through and in positive knowledge ends up in its opposite, with positive knowledge promulgating its autonomy, thereby consolidating the existing order that is known and recognized as such. Need we recall here that the critique of everyday life proposed another way: starting out from actual experience, and elucidating it in order to transform it – as opposed to starting from the conceptual in order to impose it? And without disparaging or dispensing with the activity of knowledge ...

7 On Various Corruptions

The years following 1968 witnessed a renewal of daily life by sex and sexuality, which proved illusory and rapidly lapsed into vulgarity. This ideology, which did not think it was ideological, was 'scientifically' justified by psychoanalysis. In a crude reduction, the watchword of a new order – *changer la vie* – was narrowed down to sexual liberation, which itself took some crudely simplistic forms: for example, the negation of any difference between the sexes, the assimilation of the masculine and the feminine, undifferentiated, to the 'unisex'. In the event, it was in these years that the sexual entered completely into the world of the commodity, and sexuality became the supreme commodity.

The critique of everyday life in no way excluded sexuality, but it did not accept its vulgarization. The underlying project, doubtless incompletely formulated but inherent in the approach, involved the permeation of the sexual into everydayness, but not as commodity, as localized, functional sexuality. The sexual was to be transformed in the process of transforming daily life. It was thus a question of Eros, not organs, and of celestial Aphrodite, not the terrestrial Aphrodite, the Venus of the brothels. This in no way excluded pleasure, but included it in a larger project, in a higher quest (why deny it?). We should note that Herbert Marcuse's thinking has suffered vulgarization; he has been received not as a philosopher of creative Eros, but as the theoretician of a 'permissive' society without boundaries or values.

The 'specialization' of the sexual, which accompanies technological specialization and production for 'generalized' exchange, has serious, unnoticed consequences. The separation between social practice (referred to as 'culture', bound up with the abstract character of the whole society) and nature extends to a rupture between sexuality and reproduction. The goal and practical objective are legitimate: to allow lovers to experience pleasure without falling into the trap set for desire by 'nature'. Yet this attitude impacts upon the lot and social status of childhood. The couple tends to reject the child, the natural product of coupling. The special child becomes an object of specialism: there are now child professionals – educators, activity leaders, paediatricians, analysts and psychologists. A relation that was previously normal and normalizing between generations and degrees of maturation, between time and life – this old relation is strained and collapsing. Separation prevails and extends to family life; it eats away at unity and replaces what was once a matter of an open totality by fragmentation. Between excessive holism and mutilating disjunctions, this society has hitherto missed the road to renewal, inflecting it towards a remarkable touch of vulgarity: childhood and adolescence are asserted brutally; they are oppressed and they are praised to the skies; they are, for example, used as advertising and marketing devices. As for adults, who push children and adolescents away into autonomy, they become coarser as a result, for want of a lived relation with the future, which is socially and daily represented by differences between the generations.

For the time being, the transformation of daily life by poetic action and creative Eros has thus likewise failed in the face of the power of commodities, supported on one side by technicity and positive knowledge, and on the other by political power. Sex continues to sink into vulgarity; sexual misery persists despite the vast literature devoted to the 'vulgarization' of 'problems'. Must we therefore abandon the project – that is to say, the conception, going back to Plato, of desire that creates in beauty and involves self-transcendence, as opposed to being valorized as desire and the desire to desire? No – even if we must grant that it involves a distant horizon which is possibly unattainable, an ideal, a utopia even. There is no question of abandoning the thesis that the impossible orientates the possible, in life as in thought, so that during the long wait for transformation, freedom inevitably takes the form of transgression. While the bounds prohibiting transgression are reinforced, while various 'great walls' are raised at the frontiers on which the liberators fought, the fundamental thesis on the impossible and the possible still obtains. An elitist conception? No and yes. No, in the sense that it does not impute vulgarity to what is popular. Yes, in the sense that it differentiates between what has value and what does not; and between the habitable surface and the swampy depths, as well as the inaccessible heights.

8 Conservative Schemas

Received representations and commonly used words are insidious vehicles for a morality, an ethics and an aesthetics that are not declared to be such. Customs and social habits sometimes alter without those who are affected registering the fact. It may be that innovations, gradually accepted and virtually unnoticed, conduce to the inertia or corruption of daily life. Here is an exemplary instance, already signalled elsewhere, which is worth stressing given the gravity of its consequences: the substitution of the 'user', figure of daily life, for the political figure of the 'citizen'.

For a long time, representations of the user have been taking root in imagery and ideology, as well as everyday consciousness and practice. At the outset, this seemed to be the expression of a power of protest capable of acting in and on the everyday. It seemed subversive *vis-à-vis* the many services that are external to productive labour, and yet indispensable for the production and reproduction of social relations – *vis-à-vis* what constitutes the social organization of the everyday: transport and communications, urban living conditions and realities, health, and so on. From this standpoint, the user was going to become the essential component of a force as constructive as it was critical, a force that was restoring the use-value which had become so subordinate to exchange-value and exchange that it was nothing more than their prop. In this way, the priority of use over exchange, the commodity and the market was to be overwhelmingly restored in daily life, primarily in questions and problems related to space.

Was such a representation, raised to the status of a concept, 'false' from the outset? This position, unfailingly adopted by dogmatists and sectarians, discounts what actually happened – that is to say, a massive operation of recuperation, a skilful defusing, an appropriation carried out by state-political power over a fairly long period. The *fait accompli* is now with us: the citizen tends to fade in the face of the user. What, formerly, was the citizen for himself and for society, according to its political constitution? He bore a title that was not honorific or bureaucratic, but effective and even decisive: that of member of the political community. The idea of democracy and its functioning was inseparably bound up with the value and significance of this title: to the rights of the citizen (leaving aside here the historical and ideological justifications of citizenship, that is, the rights of 'man' in general). Now, the rights of the citizen have been devalued, taking with them human rights – and vice versa. Not only does the citizen become a mere inhabitant, but the inhabitant is reduced to a user, restricted to demanding the efficient operation of public services. The user figures in social practice as one party, invariably absent and represented, in contractual terms and conditions. He is transported, cared for, maintained, educated, and so on (by whom? The state? The local authority? The private firm in partnership with public bodies?). Obviously, services must function. The problem begins when the state claims to be a 'service state', not a political state. This allows the authorities to restrict the right to strike and to make strikes 'unpopular'. Individuals no longer perceive themselves politically; their relation with the state becomes looser; they feel *social* only passively when they take a bus or tube, when they switch on their TV, and so on – and this degrades the social. The rights of the citizen are diluted in political programmes and opinion polls, whereas the demands of users have an immediate, concrete, practical appearance, being directly a matter for organization and its techniques. In the everyday, relations with the state and the political are thus obscured, when in fact they are objectively intensified, since politicians use daily life as a base and a tool. The debasement of civic life occurs in the everyday, facilitating the task of those who manage everyday life from above by means of institutions and services.

Should the notion of users and the practice that corresponds to it be destroyed? No! But use must be connected up with citizenship, as opposed to separating the two.

Users become mere receptacles of 'culture' – that is to say, a mixture of ideology, representations and positive knowledge. The enormous culture industry supplies specific products, commodities to which users have a 'right', so that the output of this industrial sector no longer has the appearance of commodities but, rather, of objects valorized by them and destined exclusively for use. Like information! This is the consummation of the world of commodities, without objects and products being reduced exclusively to the function of signs and props of what is exchangeable. Use becomes mystificatory.

Are not this gradual appropriation and degradation of some significance in indifference towards the state and everything related to it? The state is of interest almost exclusively to professionals, specialists in 'political science', whereas everyone should feel 'concerned' and seek to understand the operation of 'apparatuses' that are not public services. This indifference leads to amazing leaps, to surprises that are themselves surprising, when the political is fully revealed: moments of international tension or simply struggles on a national scale. In the long term, this degradation threatens a political class constituted on the basis of the passivity of citizens who are no longer citizens. It is said that it affects workers less than the middle class. What is certain is that it is gradually working its way into habits and customs, into stereotypes. These set the tone of everyday discourse and practice, which tend to establish conservative schemas. It is said that the ideology – the ideal – of liberty and humanism is becoming blurred. Does this involve a loss of illusions, or a loss of social activity as well as political existence? The second estimate seems more accurate.

The programming of daily life is thus pursuing its course with remarkable continuity. The exceptions – the marginal, society's rejects – henceforth enter into computations and statistics. As we shall see later, the dual society, composed on the one hand of a hard core of techniques and high-tech products with related services, and on the other of marginal, even underground, circuits – this divided society is now among the prospects that are circulating. However that may be, there are now publications and information which ensure that everyone is aware of all that is to be done. Much more so than in 1960 (era of the publication of the second volume of the *Critique of Everyday Life*), everyone knows how to live in 1981. They know it thanks to a knowledge that does not originate with them, which they have assimilated, and which they apply to their own individual cases, managing their personal affairs – their everyday lives – in accordance with the models developed and diffused for them. They apply these models more or less methodically. In general, problems begin only when a choice has to be made. Too much choice! But the models invariably resemble one another so closely that choice is futile, and it is enough to pick at random: pot luck. Consequently, only those who refuse the models have problems.

Magazines and weeklies, particularly those directed at women and even those that defend the 'cause of women', work out complete daily schedules – buying and selling, shopping, menus, clothing. From morning to evening and evening to morning, everyday time is full to bursting: fulfilment, plenitude. With 'values' – femininity, virility, or seductiveness – but above all with the ultimate value: satisfaction. Being satisfied: this is the general model of being and living whose promoters and supporters do not appreciate the fact that it generates discontent. For the quest for satisfaction and the fact of *being satisfied* presuppose the fragmentation of 'being' into activities, intentions, needs, all of them well-defined, isolated, separable and separated from the Whole. Is this an art of living? A style? No. It is merely the result and the application to daily life of a management technique and a positive knowledge directed by market research. The economic prevails even in a domain that seemed to elude it: it governs lived experience. The leisure industry rounds off the culture industry by offering travel plans and tourism, which are bought like a wardrobe or an apartment you can move into immediately. *Discover* such and such a country, town, mountain, sea! People buy the 'discovery', the change of scene, the departure and escape, which prove disappointing because they no longer have anything in common with the wish (not desire) and the advertisement. In its turn, the tourist industry thus perfects that of organized leisure and culture, fragmented into exchangeable pieces like space. The extra-ordinary sells very well, but it is now no more than a sad mystification. In this way, the image of a pseudo-freedom takes shape, one that is practically organized and substituted for 'genuine freedom', which has remained abstract. Hence a continuity in the simulation of use, and in the simulation of not working by leisure.

Can such a burdensome rationality be accepted without offering some compensation? On its own, it tips over into the irrational. Philosophers maintain the thesis of a 'crisis' of the logos. This has a certain truth to it. But how and why would the European logos, rationality armed and always battle-ready, escape the total crisis? Yet the logos, which has become technicist rationality, has never had so much persuasive force, penetration, capacity. The inversion of the rational into the anti-rational is not performed reflexively, consciously, but affectively. Because they are disappointed, many people involved with techniques turn to the absurd, magic, occultism, underground ideologies and mysteries. The philosophical thesis of the logos in crisis neglects the paradoxical encounter of the rational and the irrational, which are one another's mirages, rather than mirrors. As for those who are affected, those who suffer the technological pressure, they are kept amused with promises. The entirely 'private' and yet completely liberated individual, cosy in his bubble among his appliances, would, as it were, become the equivalent of the world through boundless information. He would have the spectacle of transparency before him. How can we avoid reverting to myths to cast a chill shadow over this pitiless luminosity? How can we not have recourse to the imaginary, the resurgence of the historical past, the evocative fiction of other lives and different things? The more the 'real' asserts itself and closes before us, the more the present becomes imaginary, the more it is filled with barely credible fictions – tales, dreams, utopias – enriching what is actual with mere semblances.

To conclude this account of continuities, it is appropriate here to recall that an organizational – or disorganizational – schema which has been in place for a long time is currently more operational than ever. It has penetrated daily life, this penetration having been foreshadowed and prepared in other sectors and domains – positive knowledge, space, the state, and so on. Capital itself operates according to this mode or model: capital, which is the same everywhere, divided up in investments, organized in a hierarchy from the small to the large. Today, the everyday is subject to this schema, which simultaneously prescribes and imposes: (a) *homogeneity* – that is to say, the tendency towards the same, identity, equivalence, the repetitive and their order; (b) *fragmentation* – that is to say, the dispersion of time and space, labour and leisure alike, and ever more intensive specialization; (c) *hierarchization*, with hierarchical order equally being imposed on functions – more or less significant – and objects – cars, planes, clothes, publications, and so on.

This hierarchical order runs from the trivial to the exceptional, from the communal to the elite, from the ordinary to the luxurious, from the repetitive to the wonderful surprise ... Identified and formulated elsewhere,[3] this schema is implemented in practice with remarkable tenacity. It is implicit in Marx with respect to social labour, which is increasingly homogeneous, fragmented and hierarchically organized. Its generalization is typical of contemporary society, revolution in Marx's sense having neither swept away the capitalist mode of production, nor achieved its own objectives. The application of the schema to daily life makes the latter correspond with what has been realized in zones and activities that are more or less external to daily life, yet connected with it: the use of time, journeys, labour, and so on.

The following paradox was brought to light in the work cited above: Marx's thought prevails even in that which contradicts it, even in its failure. This failure of the Marxist project (whether temporary or lasting is of little importance here) comes within the province of Marx's thought, and confirms it. Is not the same true of the thesis, fiercely resisted by philosophers, which attributes crucial importance to the economic – a thesis, it is too often forgotten, that goes together in Marx with a no less fundamental critique of economics? The mode of production analysed by Marx has unfolded in a way that simultaneously confirms and contradicts his thought. The strategic estimates of the rulers were foreseen by Marx; he nevertheless believed in their rapid failure, in the imminent collapse of the mode of production. This is what has not happened. This mode of production has, in particular, created the developed world market, the 'scientific and technological revolution' (a substitute for social and political revolution), the world state system, a specific space, massive urbanization, a planetary division of labour and, finally, an everydayness. A homogeneous everyday time: the abstract measurement of time governs social practice. Fragmented everyday time: dispersed by abrupt discontinuities, fragments of cycles and rhythms ruptured by the linearity of measurement procedures, activities that are disconnected, albeit subject to a general plan decreed from above. Hierarchically organized everyday time: the unevenness of situations and moments, some regarded as highly significant and others as negligible, according to value judgements which lack justification, which are themselves in crisis.

It is not easy to grasp the paradox, which eludes all reductionist thinking, whereby the homogeneous covers and contains the fragmented, making room for a strict hierarchization. So here is a brief table of the 'factors' that intervene in daily life and realize the general schema in it:

(a) *Homogenizing factors*: Established law and order – Technological and bureaucratic rationality – The logic that claims to be unitary and is in fact applied to all domains – Space managed on a grand scale (motorways, etc.) – Clock-time, articulated repetitively – The media (not so much via their content as via their form, producing the uniform attitude of listeners or viewers, breeding passivity before the flow of information, images, discourse) – The search for consistency and cohesion in behaviour – Training for this behaviour on the model of the conditioned reflex – Stereotyped representations – The world of the commodity, intimately linked to that of contractual commitments – Linearly repetitive tasks (the same gestures, words, etc.) – Spaces filled with prohibitions – The segmentation of basic functions (eating, sleeping, dressing, reproducing, etc.) in standardized daily life, which goes hand in hand with the fragmentation of so-called higher functions (reading, writing, judging and appreciating, conceiving, managing, etc.), and their programmed distribution in time – The multiple inequalities in the formal equality of the law, inequalities that are precisely masked by homogeneity and dispersal – The epistemological fields and divisions implemented in and through positive knowledge – The bureaucracies and bureaucratic feudalisms, each acting in its own fiefdom – The importance of administrative divisions dividing up space between them – The disposition of space, a social product, into an infinitely divisible (optical-geometrical) visibility – The general and continuing tendency to administer everyday life as if it were a small firm – The tendency to appeal to a positive knowledge bound up with norms, and hence reductive of lived experience – The superimposition and mutual reinforcement of forms of alienation that act, so to speak, in concert, to the point of inducing pathological breakdowns – The domination of the abstract, which is concretely materialized socially in generalized exchange, extending to symbols that have degenerated and been reduced to signs – Fake encyclopaedism, accompanied by a proliferation of lexicons, dictionaries, and so on.

(b) *Factors of fragmentation* (within homogeneity): The many separations, segregations and disjunctions, such as private and public, conceptual and experiential, nature and technique, foreigners and fellow citizens, and so on – Spaces specialized to the extent of establishing ghettos – The division of labour – Fragmented space sold in parcels and lots – Splintered centrality, a theory which is spreading over urban reality in the name of decentralization, and will lead to definitive fragmentation – The dilution of the contrast between high (sacred) points and low points in everyday life, and a growing multiplicity of neutral, indifferent instants – Social separation and disconnection between protected workers (employment laws, unions, etc.) and the rest, who are less protected or completely unprotected, and so on.

(c) *Factors of hierarchization*: The multiform hierarchy of functions, labours, incomes, from the bottom (vanishing into the swamp of the rejects) to the top (disappearing into Olympian clouds), a hierarchy that extends to objects: cars, accommodation, jewellery, and so on – A hierarchy of locations, of 'properties', of the qualities recognized in individuals and groups – Society as a stratified, hierarchical morphology, with superimposed levels – The division of time by the media, broadcasting fragmentary representations rounded off by illusory totalizing visions – The hierarchy of knowledge, with the fundamental and the applied, the important and the unimportant, the essential and the anecdotal – Hierarchy in enterprises, workshops and offices (in the bureaucracy, despite – or rather in – the homogeneity of practice and in the ideology of 'competence–performance') – Degrees of 'participation' in power and decision-taking, from scraps of authority to sovereign power, and so on – Bureaucracy, in the service (not conflict-free) of technocracy, which has come to treat daily life and people in daily life as the raw material for its labour, as a mass to 'handle', as a people on benefit, but which nevertheless tends to get its 'subjects' to perform its own work of registration and enrolment, form-filling of all sorts ...

How are we to represent this society in a way that is simulaneously both rational and palpable (visual) as – albeit with a few upheavals – it takes shape? The metaphor of the pyramid, Hegelian in origin, supporting the various strata and classes from a wide base to a very narrow summit, is no longer representative. Why? A split has developed between, on the one hand, society's rejects and the people expelled outside of the main circuits (whole regions, the unemployed with no hope of work, youth, women, artisans overtaken by technology, small firms and businesses, etc.), and, on the other, people who are well-integrated into circuits and networks focused around so-called 'high-tech' production (nuclear energy, computer science, the arms industry, etc.). It is a well-known fact that parallel or secondary circuits, networks and channels are established among those 'outside the system': an underground economy that makes it possible for people to survive, without always avoiding degradation. At the extreme – counterpart of the comings and goings of the elite, who travel around in jets, and go from one luxury hotel to the next – we find the nomadism of poverty, wandering misery. And this on a world scale. We are equally aware that people who work in 'high-tech' industries do not fall outside the system, although not all workers enjoy this good fortune. Thus this cleavage divides the working class, part of which finds itself alongside the fortunate and the 'affluent' (terms that are abused so that they can be turned against those who do not count among the most destitute). The disadvantaged subsist at a lower level of everyday life, whereas the Olympians, at or close to the summit, are elevated above daily life. These Olympians engage in luxurious wanderings, high-altitude nomadism. They do not work in the trivial sense of the term, but are extremely busy: they chair, they organize (managers), they possess, and they administer. The classical terms *bourgeoisie* or *grande bourgeoisie* are no longer quite appropriate to these rulers of the international. The term 'Olympians' seems more fitting. It is nevertheless the case that a distinction must be introduced here. The rejects live at the level of *infra-daily life*; the Olympians in a *supra-daily life*. This makes daily life correspond to a sort of social mean. Is this not the life-world of the middle classes? This hypothesis will be expounded later; it is introduced here to explain the continuity in daily life despite the factors of change.

The preceding analyses have already defined a project and broad lines of action against the results, as well as the operational schemas, of the forces that remain dominant:

(a) *Differences against homogeneity*. We shall have to return to this concept of *difference* in order to refute its recuperation, wherein the right to difference includes and justifies social inequalities. 'As soon as it is experienced, perceived in everyday life and not merely imagined, diversity entails classifications, hierarchies, inequalities,' Alain de Benoist has written in his *Éléments*. However, the right to difference – between men and women, children and adults, countries, regions, ethnic groups – presupposes equality in difference. This can flourish only in a democratic society, which this right helps to define as it is added, along with various other rights, to the old human rights.

(b) *Unity against fragmentation and division*, the pursuit and realization of this unity not proceeding without problems and dialectical contradictions, since it is a concrete unity, not an abstract identity, that is to be conceived and realized.

(c) *Equality against hierarchy*, without levelling society, but strengthening the social as the level that mediates between the economic and the political, which are factors of inequality. This presupposes some radical (root-and-branch) changes.

This long struggle would involve a *dialectical* (not a logico-statistical) conception of:

(a) *centrality* in space and time (multiplicity of centres, mobility, dynamism);

(b) *subjectivity*: collective subjects (not only the workers in an enterprise, the inhabitants of a town or region, but the working class as autonomous), substituted for individual 'egos', and reconstructed in line with new concepts;

(c) *sociality*, as opposed not only to the individual but to the state, on the one hand, and hence to the political, regarded as reductionist; but also, on the other, to the economic, regarded as abstraction (exchange and commodity, money, division of labour, etc.).

Notes

1. See Siegfried Giedion, *La Mécanisation au pouvoir*, Centre Georges Pompidou, Paris 1980, p. 512 ff.

2. See Henri Lefebvre, *La Présence et l'absence. Contribution à la théorie des représentations*, Casterman, Paris 1980.

3. See Henri Lefebvre, *Une pensée devenue monde*, Fayard, Paris 1980.

PART TWO

Discontinuities

1 A First Glance at What Has Changed

Within the continuity, the inertia, of daily life, and its passivity, factors of change – even disruption – of the established order are becoming clear.

Technology makes the end of work possible (in the long run). What seemed abstractly utopian yesterday is now taking shape, is on the horizon: the wholesale automation of material production. As we have seen, devaluation of a seductive, prestigious image – modernity – goes together with an intensification of technological modernism and an expectation of novelty, in a kind of frantic fervour for a different society, the product of computer science, telematics, and so on. This society is to be reached via the scientific revolution pushed to the limit, carried through to its term. Cultural snobbery and enthusiasm for modernity have served their time: this myth is no longer required. Does not the new society, proclaiming the end of ideologies and myths, possess its own ideology and myths? Bit by bit, they are unearthed: the ideology of the end of ideology, of transparency and performance, and the myth of freedom realized by information technology, and so on. Thus, the separation between modernity and modernism undoubtedly already represents a change; it anticipates greater changes. Technological progress is occurring in leaps and bounds: some people (who? – a lot of people) anticipate that it will generate its effects *automatically*, since it involves automation. It is allowed to take its course. Is this an intellectual standpoint? The standpoint of the intelligentsia? Of a political party? No: it is the spontaneous orientation of social practice. Modernity is dated: industrial society, with the abstraction paradoxically produced by material production. By contrast, post-industrial society will be characterized by the production and exchange of non-material goods, which are nevertheless more concrete: information, services, and so on.

But *who* is going to carry this transformation through to a conclusion? *Who* is going to put an end to politics as fiction, politics as spectacle? For example: *who* today is in a position to direct computers towards calculating production costs not in money, but in social time and/or energy, so that exchange will no longer have to proceed via the mediation of the market, money and capital? Is it not the case that the existing economic and political powers intend to use recent techniques to maintain, or even perfect, their domination? The end of work? It is possible, but so is the opposite – the contradictory. *Who* is going to steer work towards its decline or end? Workers want to work; those who employ them and profit from their labour (through surplus-value which can, if you like, be called 'profit' – it does not matter) want to make them work. Men of good will and what are called the left-wing parties demand full employment. Is a reduction in labour-time sufficient to set in train the process of the end of labour? And what are we to make of the expansion of leisure, purchased by labour? Workers – the working class – find themselves caught between threatening technologies they scarcely understand, which have begun to wreak their havoc, and the conservatism that promises a more or less ameliorated status quo. In philosophical terms, what exists is the conditions of possibility, not the conditions of realization, which exceed the mode of production itself! The radical revolution – that of non-work – is foreshadowed in an obscure sort of way through aporias and utopias. It has not as yet been formulated clearly. What might daily life become from the viewpoint of not working? How can we inflect it in this direction? How are we to fill daily life or, more mundanely, occupy it in the event of a massive reduction in labour-time? What should we expect – an expansion of the everyday, or its decline? Up until now, the problem has been of interest only to science-fiction writers (e.g. Simak's *Demain les chiens*), and a few philosophers (we should not forget Lafargue's *Le Droit à la paresse*).

It must be clearly recognized that theoretical – that is to say, conceptual – thinking has only a remote connection with social and political practice here. Is this sufficient reason for abandoning it? For declaring it to be ideological or subjective? Or utopian in reactionary mode? No! Theory detects and states conditions of possibility. Nothing more and nothing less. The problematic formulated here corresponds, however, to Marx's most profound – most profoundly and paradoxically dialectical – thought: the working class can affirm itself only in its negation, unlike other historically superseded classes and the bourgeoisie. The self-determination whereby the working class attains the status of 'subject', transcending the condition of object, involves self-negation: the end of all classes, the end of the wage-earning class, and hence the end of work, the end of the working class itself. Utopia? Delirium? But here 'we' (all of us) are ready to get down to the task. The organization or establishment of a 'party of non-labour' cannot even be imagined. The business of a few utopians thus becomes a problem confronting everyone, a fundamental problematic, a vital issue. Smash the techniques and new machines, or use them and develop their potential? But what is going to happen in the course of this total crisis? For it is no longer a question of 'going slow' (André Breton and René Char), or of 'letting it all hang out' (1968), but of making the transition from work to the end of work, without catastrophe. Pending something different and better, the valorization of work – an important dimension of the consensus – is dissolving. Does the road to the withering away of work entail the despair of workers in the advanced countries, trapped in processes they endure rather than dominate, when control over conditions (self-management) has precisely been put on the century's agenda?

The reader will know that the total crisis, which is shaking the mode of production, set in at the beginning of the twentieth century with a silent catastrophe: the collapse of traditional reference points for – and by – thought; and a consequent collapse of values. Practice and daily life have preserved them. From this crisis emerged technology, labour and discourse – three aspects of the Western logos. This triad freed itself from subordination to a totality, with consequences that had not been foreseen by protagonists of such liberation, both in art (which declared itself to be 'art for art's sake', not without breathtaking abstraction) and in science (which also unfolded for its own sake, in collaboration with technology). In the triad 'technology–

labour–language and discourse', technology then freed itself from any control. All along this dangerous path, critical points were not wanting. The devaluation of labour and discourse in the face of technically applicable knowledge was not the least painful aspect of a process that tends to shatter the continuum. Does not the end of these values already register a rupture?

There are other aspects of this process, and different critical points. *Dwelling*, a social and yet poetic act, generating poetry and art work, fades in the face of housing, an economic function. The 'home', so clearly evoked and celebrated by Gaston Bachelard, likewise vanishes: the magic place of childhood, the home as womb and shell, with its loft and its cellar full of dreams. Confronted with functional housing, constructed according to technological dictates, inhabited by users in homogeneous, shattered space, it sinks and fades into the past. With this rupture – that is the substitution of functional housing for 'dwellings', of buildings for edifices and monuments – what are known as modern town planning and architecture abandoned the historic town, if only as example and model. Towns have undergone an 'implosion–explosion'. Crossing points and traffic have assumed greater importance than inhabited spaces. The façade and space on which the town imposed a style are becoming blurred. As the architects say, the volumetry, and the settlement it determines, impart a different style, ever more sharply marked by the opposition between stability and movement, fixed places and flows crossing through space. This produces some contradictory – even chaotic – results. Some people hold that we must forge ahead on this path, determined by technology. For others, nostalgia wins out over hopes for a future marked by incredible inventions. Continuities and discontinuities are thus interwoven in a confusion that is expressed in spatial disorder. Here we recognize the previously mentioned opposition between nostalgics and futurists. Is there another way, between a harsh, absurd 'reality' and compensations, unavailing protests, and the illusions of subjectivity, lyrical flights of regret? Such a road is all the more difficult to outline in that the culture industry knows how to capture the longings of souls, the attractive moods of consciousness waxing indignant and protesting, in order to transform them into profitable spectacles. Experience indicates that even the ludic and the tragic, regarded as irreducible and immune to recuperation, can be marketed up to a certain point. So that they are insufficient to open up another way – unless they take things to extremes: dangerous games, great risks, holocaust and sacrifice. There is often an element of play in daily life: everyone plays their role, their comic or tragic character, more or less well. Sometimes the ludic grows in intensity. Yet when an element of play mingles with exchange in practice – debate and bargaining, speculation – the operation of equivalents is scarcely troubled by it. On the contrary, this is how it operates and is masked: by establishing itself in daily life. Likewise with the ludic in discourse: puns and wordplay, language effects, even screams and inarticulate sobs. It does not prevent logic imposing coherence, sooner or later. Banking on the ludic to rupture daily life is probably a mug's game. For it is to mask the obduracy of the system of equivalents. And yet, at moments of intense risk, in passion and poetry, daily life shatters, and something different comes through with the work, whether act, speech or object.

In their obscure early stages, the commodity and the spread of commodities stimulated the imagination. It is difficult for us moderns to comprehend, but it is definitely the case – as confirmed by history and, better still, by reading texts and understanding art works – that the great imaginative creations followed an expansion of trade, which established contact between people, countries and towns that were oblivious of one another: think of Homer, the great Greek authors, *A Thousand and One Nights*, Shakespeare, and so on. The establishment of communication gave rise to more or less fantastic, untruthful narratives, and to legends and myths. Thereafter, the commercial mentality stifled creative capacity. At best, it yielded hedonism. As for technology, it is as unconducive to flights of spontaneity as to the imaginary. Contrariwise, the mass introduction of techniques into production and administration has generated astonishing creative capacity when it comes to perfected, sophisticated forms of exchange: credit, capital and technology transfers, currency manipulation. There thus develops a technological utopia with an ideology which justifies it, and responds in affirmative mode to negative, subversive ideologies, based on the critique of the existing order, which demand another life, an absolute difference, immediately. It none the less remains the case that the capacity to create – the imagination – first of all requires a simultaneously ideal and real, ideological and practical, break with what exists. This rupture can extend as far as neurosis, schizophrenia and paranoia.

Recent years have confirmed a surprising phenomenon, whose causes and import are obscure, but which seems in its way to mark a discontinuity. Up until the middle of the nineteenth century, the great artist was associated with excellent health, even if in our time a pernickety and slightly malevolent examination has identified symptoms of neurosis. Men of genius mastered angst: Michelangelo, Leonardo, later Diderot, and still later Stendhal and Balzac. Subsequently, the creator – artist or writer – was no longer content to oppose his subjectivity and problematic to real things, objects and people. He called himself into question and counterposed himself to a reality in which he could not put down roots or aspire to a status. He became a case, and it was from this unique case that he drew his inspiration. Can this semi-pathological state, neurosis and sometimes something even worse, be regarded as creative as such? Doubtless not. Yet the striving that seeks release from anxiety and delivery from angst by mastering it stimulates the creativity which contemporary ideology still seeks among so-called normal people. Classical subjectivity, capable of objectivity, gives way in the artist to a different condition: daily life has become so oppressive and repressive that dissolution (Rimbaud) is the sole means of escaping it. The artist can no longer make do with keeping his distance. As his neurosis gives him creative impetus, he cultivates it. This provokes a break, possibly a gulf, between daily life and creation, reality and the work, the state of the creator and therapeutic techniques, which are inevitably normalizing. These observations – or, rather, self-evident facts – confirm what was previously said about modernity and, above all, the action 'in the negative' of contemporary art. This negativity involves neither revolutionary proposals, nor a subversive project. Yet it is there, before 'us', in the works. Exasperation of the morbid is the one thing that allows the creator to rise above the everyday, if only to understand it and show it. Plenitude, whether of lived experience or of the ideal in the Platonic sense, loses its meaning. Hence another gulf – between production and creation – whereas cultural production, which has become a powerful industry, pretends either to deny this gulf, or to fill it. Kitsch, an industrial product, becomes positively comforting – an art of happiness in security – whereas the art work, born out of anguish that has or has not been mastered, disturbs.

The permanent, persistent things in the social landscape – which are relative, and hence in no sense vestigial, but retain their currency

– stem largely from the strategy of the authorities. Whereas a new world economic order is what is required (no-one is unaware of this fact), strategy prescribes a new division of labour on a world scale, maintaining and aggravating inequalities of growth and development. The rulers are opposed to any destabilization – a fashionable term that says what it means – and hence to any movement. If development occurs (even with the greatest power at our disposal, can we prevent it?), it occurs despite the dominant economic and political powers. They authorize technological innovations only after obtaining guarantees; and no doubt this is the form assumed today by the contradiction that Marx pointed out between the productive forces and social and political relations, as well as the 'law of value' considered on an international scale. These powers have disposed of – that is to say, destroyed or neutralized – attempts at direct democracy, for example in towns and local communities. Positioning itself at a global level, political power everywhere sets about obtaining by all possible means – pressure, repression, enticements and promises – the celebrated *consensus*, which assumes and creates stability. To revive and redeploy (another fashionable word) production and the productive apparatus would first of all require massive injections of technology, with consequences that are as formidable as they are unpredictable. Certainly, economic policy no longer consists in scrapping technology – something Lenin regarded as inevitable under monopoly capitalism – but in an adroitly balanced mix aimed at leaving the essential structures intact. Adopted or imposed, innovations are worked out in high places, in such a way as not adversely to affect the relations of domination, and even to strengthen them. Yet alterations occur that shake the system.

A hypothesis that has already been formulated concerns the dual character of the changes. Some, at the level of daily life, are imperceptible but cumulative. They are not merely minor events to be situated at the 'micro' level, simple isolated facts; they are added to, or superimposed upon, one another. Hence they end up generating irreversible, decisive alterations. A well-known historical case: the slow transformation of the Roman world into Christendom during centuries of transition long neglected by historians, but whose significance they are gradually discovering, with their efforts directed precisely towards reconstructing daily life during these times. Other changes occur at a macro level; they are abrupt, disruptive, not gradual, and are thus akin to a 'qualitative leap'. They come from on high, not from below: serious events, political decisions, mutations generally regarded as historic. So they occur at the macro level, but in the majority of cases this does not mean that understanding, a project, knowledge exist at this level. An equally well-known case: the French Revolution and its sequels.

Intermediate changes can also happen, deriving either from one of the above modalities and reacting upon the other, or from their interaction and conjunction. In other words, the duality under consideration should not be frozen; nor should the possibilities of change be fixed in models. A minor example: it would appear that today, within the framework of the current mode of production, the market is altering; there are more goods in demand and products for daily use, but in smaller quantities in each instance. So that it is necessary to envisage diversified production, and less mass production. From this perspective, enormous concentrations of machines, with an extreme division of labour and monotonous repetition of fragmented tasks, have supposedly served their time, work on the assembly line included. Digitally controlled machines, as well as computer and remote control of complex processes, could replace repetitive, dangerous operations (which, it is belatedly recognized, can stifle workers' capacity for invention and initiative). Such modifications of productive labour and the relation between men and machines would unquestionably entail recasting relations to labour, daily life and the world. But this process is only in its early stages – something that confirms several earlier remarks.

The crisis, so it is said, invariably ignoring or masking its profundity, affects daily life in surprising ways, at once crude and subtle, obvious and elusive, conservative and subversive, trivial and dramatic. A kind of crisis of consciousness and, above all, of confidence tends to weaken the relation between daily life and the major institutions that administer it. The consensus over the political and daily life alike, which political speeches ritually evoke on occasion, becomes increasingly blurred. Notwithstanding what specialists call 'dysfunctions' or 'perverse effects', the great institutional entities – justice, the Inland Revenue, the army, the academy, social security, the police, and so on – were generally regarded as broadly fulfilling their duties. The consensus that was indispensable for this had gradually faded in France with the Second World War, defeat and Vichy. Restored after the Liberation, severely shaken in 1968, it then regained some vigour and substance. Why? By dint of the growth to which all social classes and strata *consented*, each of them reckoning to be the beneficiary. However, the distribution of the fruits of growth remained extremely unequal; with the end of this relatively trouble-free growth, the bell tolled for the consensus over the established order, presaging the discrediting of those who banked on it 'democratically'. As long as rapid growth, which aimed to be exponential, lasted, 'progress' brought sizeable profits for some, and a certain comfort and improvement in living conditions for others. *We* were able to forecast needs because, in fact, *we* simultaneously produced these needs and the material goods designed to satisfy them.

Since the onset of crisis, the situation has tended to be turned upside down. The disadvantaged, the rejects, abandon the prospect offered them by the technological and scientific revolution – that is to say, unlimited growth. On all sides, people start blaming existing institutions, holding them responsible for all the illusions and depredations. There is more and more discrepancy between the institutional level and daily life. Without critical knowledge or formulated expression of the discontent that is materializing, what is established takes on a pejorative connotation, both factually and symbolically. Bureaucracy, a brutal and inefficient hierarchy, both cumbersome and tactless, is revealed to the public in all its horror; critical thinking is then at hand. Moreover, suspicion is directed at official institutions but is liable to be extended to other organizations – trade unions, for example. The links between individuals and groups, and between these and the nation (perceived and felt identity), loosen, in such a way that democracy as it is experienced, as national and political community, and the state as a set of institutions, become obscured and in need of profound transformation. Rather than being placed in remote entities, social trust, for all that it persists, is invested in what is proximate, in the local, which enjoys various assumptions in its favour: it occupies a well-defined place; it can be reached; one can act on it and on the people in charge of it; it supposedly eludes the manipulations and abuse of power, for it possesses its own capacity for organization, and the people in charge of it are sensible and sensitive. In short, it is close to daily life.

The symptoms of this new situation in daily life, and outside daily life, are multiplying – as if a rupture was brewing in social behaviour or, more precisely, in the behaviour of individuals *vis-à-vis* the social, which is impoverished, alienated, external. So it is that planning, which but a few years ago enjoyed enormous prestige, no longer elicits a consensus, still less enthusiasm. Planning by institutions is criticized, and not without reason, for impoverishing the social. For a certain period, neoliberalism, an official mystification, benefited from this mindset: a Western model, whose contours were very vague, was revalorized and identified with Freedom, while the standing of the socialist model, hypothetically identified with Soviet reality, fell.

In daily life, problems of an economic kind proliferate; they must be taken into account and taken on. This is the level at which people (people in the everyday) deal with managing the crisis. People at the base sense that what is involved is not a short critical phase but a long period, even though hopes of emerging from it shortly have not disappeared. Hence the shift in centres of interest, through a series of minute alterations that have produced a sizeable change in recent years: the importance of micro-decisions and micro-adaptations, and a lack of interest in the totality and theory. The result is that from 1975 onwards a 'reformist' game and stake replaced those of the contestation, without those concerned having a clear idea of where this attitude is leading them ... Rupture? At all events, a transition beyond contestation and conservatism alike. In their way, the interested parties are charting unknown territory. This goes together with the constitution of secondary circuits of substitution and replacement, external to the major established networks. It is as if, in order to avoid the traps, take advantage of the circumstances, and escape the adverse consequences, the people of daily life had anticipated the advent of the dual society: on the one hand, dominant, established circuits; on the other, external circuits, moonlighting, direct exchange and barter, more or less underground contacts. This sometimes creates the impression that 'subterranean' relations are not external to those established in the public light of day, but penetrate and possibly invigorate them.

Such an analysis accepts various typical features of the 'dual society', without endorsing the central thesis: the split between the two fragments of society. It would oppose any appropriation of the concept of difference by this thesis.[1]

The somewhat dislocated consensus leaves room, on the one hand, for constraint, should the state judge it appropriate; and on the other, for various currents, convergent or divergent. These currents of ideas and opinions – that is to say, of representations – are not unrelated to social classes and strata, but they do not coincide with them. A different 'classification' from classification in terms of classes is emerging, although it is not obvious that it is being consolidated structurally; the two classifications coexist, not without methodological and theoretical problems. The multiplicity of currents in opinion, and also in lifestyles, marks out the everyday, without abolishing its concept. Homogeneity does not disappear; it stands in for the vanishing consensus. Uncertainties, fears and scares, which are not dispelled by official security measures, prompt a sort of neorealism in behaviour: people (the people of daily life) start to respect power more than knowledge. When knowledge clashes with power, it loses all prestige in a confrontation that was once prestigious. Yet authority must still be combined with competence. It would seem that the quest for security at any price generates the opposite desire: a taste for risk revives among a section of young people – that is to say, a taste for living without guarantees. At the same time, the tendency to believe in progress, which seemed outmoded, is strengthened: in certain currents of opinion, the hope is that recent technologies will liberate society from established supervision and tyrannical protection. This hope is sometimes translated into a political aim: control of information from below and socialization of the social good that is information technology. What follows is a devaluation of ideologies, which has already been noted on several occasions. Marxism is not exempt from this: although ideology-critique was energetically pursued, and even inaugurated, by Marx, his theoretical thought is regarded as ideology, and sometimes as the prototype of the ideological. Contrariwise, technocratic ideology is not considered ideological, any more than religions, which are taken to provide models for everyday practice. Obviously, we are simply referring to social tendencies and trends here.

The erosion of institutional images is a subject for study (institutional analysis). These studies do not concern the critique of everyday life directly, yet they are of relevance to it in that they disclose modifications in practice, not merely in the discursive or the imaginary. It seems that a certain understanding of social facts is emerging among a wide public, which in no way excludes impoverishment of the *social*, reduced to 'community' and social security or security measures. Quite the reverse: they proceed in tandem. Naivety and credulity are slowly but surely disappearing: 'credibility' is demanded. People seek out the 'authentic', or tokens of it – which still leaves plenty of room for mystification and deception. It is none the less the case that mistrust on the part of the everyday person extends to all discourses. Have we not reached the point in everyday relations where we interpret gestures and facial expressions as much as we grasp the meaning of words? Interest in 'body language' increases with a certain revival of the body and of interest in the body, with the pursuit of its reappropriation – above all, by and for women – at the expense of the image and the spectacle. The predominance of the visual – image, spectacle – over the corporeal is declining without disappearing – something that will slowly but surely alter the relation between daily life and space. Space is no longer defined exclusively in optical, geometrical and quantitative fashion. It is becoming – or once again becoming – a flesh-and-blood space, occupied by the body (by bodies). Judging from certain readily observable symptoms, daily life is tending to become, or once again become, multi-sensory; the quest and desire for a more actual presence are substituted for images as such. Hence a certain revival of the theatre and, on the other hand, the search for richer (three-dimensional) images.

Citizens – not to mention users – have a stronger and clearer sense of the relations of domination to the extent that authority as such impacts on them, the functioning of institutions no longer proceeding 'all by itself'. They detect manipulation through interpretations of 'facts' that are in themselves ambiguous. The conditions for a rupture and real change in life seem to be being created bit by bit, gradually. Yet who wants 'really' to change life, other than by discourse? Everyday existence at home, in the house (which in a majority of cases is no longer one), reflects office life or factory life; and vice versa. What is intolerable in the one reflects what is intolerable in the other. Taken together, they support one another and everyone, dominant and dominated alike, adapts to it.

At this point in the analysis, we can advance some hypotheses. This analysis detects symptoms of a gradual transformation, which is only just beginning. This does not preclude qualitative leaps as a result of global actions: decisions, events, catastrophes. At the political level, in this perspective, we are witnessing a transition from impersonal power – abstract power and sovereignty – to authority; and from the latter to influence – that is to say, a personalization of authority requiring direct contact with 'subjects'. There is also a transition from large established units towards smaller units, 'base cells' connected to local spaces (sites), which contains a risk of dislocation but tends to favour differences over homogenization. Will the crisis generate differentiation or fragmentation? For the time being, the question will remain without a definite answer, since that depends on both social practice and political practice, initiatives from below and decisions at the top. Furthermore, it may be that new contradictions will emerge, and that the crisis will induce both differentiation and fragmentation – that is to say, sites that are rich in relations and sites without relations, forms of solitude. Thus, we simultaneously observe a growing desire for corporeality, which always has something opaque about it, and a longing for transparency, which precludes any opacity in relations. Similarly, increasing interest attaches to results, which require strict individual or collective discipline, and at the same time to Freedom as well as freedoms. But the most significant thing today, when it comes to assessing factors of continuity and/or discontinuity, is to grasp the *importance* accorded to daily life. The dominated, the 'subjects', now represent themselves to themselves in accordance with everyday practice, not ideologies (which do not disappear for all that). In fact, today everyone banks on daily life: politicians as well as professional manipulators, advertisers and propagandists, and also 'subjects'. The level of the totality remains of decisive importance, since it is the level of decision-making. But it is perceived only in its relation to what are called local and limited – in reality, everyday – actions. Without denying it, this situates the theoretical and practical – that is political – importance of the whole, but registers the recent fact that the local, the proximate – that is to say, daily life – allows for action by those 'concerned' and seems to them to be the privileged site, the only site (and in this they are mistaken), in which they can be effective.

2 Recuperation

A question arises. The alterations now under way, which tend towards provoking rupture, encounter contrary – stabilizing and reductive – forces, which tend towards immobility under the pretext of equilibrium. How and why is it that the elements of mobility and renovation have not hitherto had more impact, to use the sociological terminology? How and why have they not broken through the barriers?

Recuperation is not something invented by intellectuals to explain the failure of subversive, innovatory ideas and projects. Its concept – for that is what it is – was fashioned to refer to a (social and political) practice. Moreover, in accordance with the famous Hegelian law, the concept appeared belatedly, when what it referred to had already occurred, been exhausted, and was even tending to fade.

The recuperative operations can be inventoried; they were deliberately targeted at what might have changed, in order to prevent change. The defeat of change can sometimes entail appreciable modifications, which nevertheless fall short of the possibilities and projects. A remarkable instance, to which reference has already been made, concerns the family. Until recently the family was the dominant figure in social relations, but the twentieth century saw it discredited and weakened; it is increasingly out of place in its social location: the junction between the public and the private. In the current mode of production, the enterprise is gradually replacing the family as dominant figure, for the family itself is assuming the shape of an enterprise. Even so, it still differs from the enterprise because of the affective as well as material investment required to educate children. Notwithstanding resistance, this tends to take pride of place; it becomes the crucial link in the transmission of capital, of material and spiritual (cultural) property. In this way, a model of the bourgeois family is constituted. Belatedly: prior to this, the bourgeoisie still followed the aristocratic model, which, in a manner of speaking, it imitated. Yet no sooner has it been constituted than the bourgeois, capitalist model, generated by the mode of production, tends to break down. Why? Because it is oppressive, even for those who benefit from it. It is attacked on all sides: by women's movements; by intellectuals ('Families, I hate you! ...'); by the proliferation of divorce; by the integration of women into economic activity; and perhaps above all by the control that women have won over the physiological process of fertility – a genuinely new power, or rather *counter-power*, and hence a factor of rupture. And yet, in the very process of this disruption, and in contradiction with it, the restricted family is consolidated. Much more than that: the popular (proletarian) family, previously larger than the bourgeois family and more open to the social, is modelling itself on the bourgeois family. Critical ideology – the rejection of institutions, the aforementioned disappearance of the consensus about institutions, the devaluation of the sacred conjugal bond and of the family as a privileged site – this 'advanced' ideology has not disappeared. It persists. But in social practice, the family, with its modern complement and model, the enterprise, remains function-ally and structurally fundamental. Advanced ideology, backward structures! The laws in France reforming the situation of women and their legal status have strengthened the family. On the other hand, inequality between women and men – discrimination – eliminated to a certain extent from the family group, is maintained in the enterprise, workshop or office, and possibly even intensified. Whence the compen-satory reference of these aspects of daily life to one another. Does this unquestionable recuperation of the familial derive from the state? From the strategy of the mode of production? From a spontaneous alteration in values and norms? Or from an unwitting return to tradi-tions? It really doesn't matter. The phenomenon is with us: a case of alteration and recuperation.

There is no lack of subjects for recuperation: the urban question, difference, self-management, have been recuperated or are in the process of being recuperated. What does the process of recuperation consist in? In this: an idea or a project regarded as irredeemably revo-lutionary or subversive – that is to say, on the point of introducing a discontinuity – is normalized, reintegrated into the existing order, and even revives it. Shaken for a brief moment, the social relations of pro-duction and reproduction – that is to say, domination – are reinforced. Rather than analyzing the process – the diversion and circumvention of the initial project – the hypercritics, dogmatists and sectarians prefer to blame those who took the initiative and launched the idea. This is a theoretical and practical error. The fact that a project or concept has been 'recuperated' does not mean that it was not potentially active for a period of time. It means that 'people' (the opponents of the estab-lished order or disorder) did not know how, or were not able, to seize the opportunity, the favourable conjuncture, and carry out the project. Conjunctures pass; opportunities disappear for good. Even before conquering the doctrine of historical evolution, the Greek philosophers were aware of that. Is this not how inventors, generally positioned on the Left, provide ideas for 'reactionaries', that is, the Right? Certainly. But attributing the failure or diversion to the person who suggested the idea is nevertheless a futile and dishonest polemical operation. Like blaming Marx for the borrowings and appropriations – by Keynes and so many others – that allowed capital to survive and win out. In this way, serious responsibilities are masked. Above all, a basic socio-political fact is veiled: for two centuries and more, invention has been the fruit of critical thinking, that is to say, of the Left. The established order has a great capacity for adaptation and integration; it assimilates what is opposed to it. It has demonstrated a surprising flexibility, an unsuspected capacity, which should taken into account, instead of attacking those who invent. Marx, to come back to him – is not in any way responsible for the degeneration and dubious use of Marxism. Another exemplary case is patriotism, a revolutionary invention that was appropriated over the course of the nineteenth century with national questions and their effects on social and political issues. Another example is planning, brainwave of Marxists and Marx himself, which obsessed statesmen the world over throughout the twentieth century. The sole exception is regionalism – for so long a rightist concept, adopted by the Left and even 'ultra-leftism', but one which the Right can still make its motto if left-wing decentralization misfires! Any misunderstanding on this crucial point leads to the loss of a tool for analysing the modern world critically. Hypercriticism has not made such analysis easier, or more profound, or more effective. It has become impossible to make any proposal without it immediately being accused of recuperation, in the name of a bolder project and especially a more radical negativism. This pseudo-radicalism has always confused moments and aspects within the process. First point: what can be recuperated is not, by the same token, recuperative. Second point, which must be stressed: there is nothing – no proposal, no project, no idea – which cannot be recuperated, that is to say, used by different social or political forces from those in whose name it was advanced. Third point: it is unjust as well as absurd to impute recuperation to those who initiate what is subsequently recuperated.

During the period in which contestation raged and blossomed, up to 1975 or thereabouts, recuperation became an official – in other words, political – activity. Private or joint research consultancies took charge of it. In the past, it occurred spontaneously, blindly, at the level of a fairly large group or social class. A reminder: patriotism, which was digested in the way an animal digests food by the right-wing bourgeoisie, its representatives and political supporters, and transformed into chauvinism. Nationalism made it possible for the dominant class to annex other classes or class fractions to itself by neutralizing opposition, before functioning as an 'ideological detonator' (to use Jean-Pierre Faye's expression, adopted by René Lourau)[2] – that is to say, exploding left-wing ideas and ideologies, and flying like an electric spark between two poles – Left and Right – which were suddenly assimilated, prompting novel political phenomena like national socialism. So recuperation has been going on for a very long time, but not in the manner of the years of protest. During this period, which was fairly brief, the tactic of the consultancies directed by technocrats was simple: assigning the protesters themselves the responsibility for studying delicate questions, thus obliging them to make daring ideas and projects assimilable. Once the idea or project had been 'studied' – that is to say, changed into knowledge and discourse – the established order could take from it what suited it, both to disguise and to renew itself by discovering convenient solutions to real problems. Such operations assumed the priority of a certain positive knowledge, constituted as a corpus but still flexible – that of the technocrats. The latter were conscious of their own weaknesses: their dearth of inventive capacity – of 'creativity', to use their own terminology and mythology. With this shrewd move, the technocrats, who did possess powers of realization, stimulated their deficient imagination and compensated for it, while defusing dangerous theses. As a result, tendencies towards discontinuity, towards rupture, turned into factors for non-change. This fate was not reserved for Marxists, but even so they enjoyed a certain privilege. As the main target of these operations, Marxism was looked upon as the most fertile source once it had been appropriated. An exemplary case was the critique of everyday life, encapsulated as '*Changer la vie*'. This formula – which, to start off with, was disturbing and subversive, albeit vague – was then adopted and adapted on all sides, banalized, recuperated by advertising as well as various political parties, and ended up being blunted and flattened into 'quality of life'. This reduced it to signs of transformation and discourse on transformation, before it ended up in so-called concrete proposals concerning holiday periods and working hours. In lieu of changing life, the image of life was changed!

This prompts me to formulate as an axiom a proposition that I have already advanced: nothing is immune to recuperation. Let me end with the example of human rights. The fact that some dangerous forces, even imperialism, have sought to make use of them, and succeeded; the fact that they have supplied ideologies and tactics – these cannot justify abandoning or disavowing them, except out of sectarianism. On the contrary. We must understand the expression 'arena and stake of the struggle' in its strongest sense. Human rights? Through a hard-fought battle they must be wrested from those who seek to use and abuse them. It was a serious political error (a) to regard these rights as political tools permanently in the service of those who are dominant; (b) peremptorily to refute the ideology that has historically supplied their envelope, throwing the baby out with the bath-water; (c) not to give them a different foundation, extricating them from the old humanist ideology; (d) not to open them out by adding a multiplicity of rights, including the right to live in the city, the right to difference, and so on.

What happens when skilfully conducted recuperative operations succeed? Demands, aspirations, intentions are diverted and turned against the initial design. I must insist upon this paradox: confrontations and crises, including wars, as well as the more or less Marxist-inspired theory of these crises, have hitherto served the mode of production. They have allowed its representatives and leaders to introduce something new into the economico-socio-political order. From one recuperation to the next, the sovereign order and subordinate orders have acquired a capacity for integration that is achieved through opposition, demands, contestation. Recuperation has a most remarkable reduction effect – this observation applies not only to ideologies but to practice as well.

In recuperative operations, it is often difficult to distinguish the mix of strategic intention, ideology and practical spontaneity. Let us examine the case of the reoccupation of town centres by the middle classes and a neo-bourgeoisie – in short, by an 'elite'. For a period of time, it was possible that the deteriorating urban centres, which had been abandoned for the smart suburbs, would be taken back over and even reoccupied by the people. This movement could have become decisive and determinant in a strategy of urban revolutions. Latin America in particular was poised for an enormous revolutionary campaign: starting out from the shantytowns and seizing hold of the centres. Yet this movement has been temporarily broken by repression, violence and corruption, but also by recuperation. Neither workers, nor the unemployed, nor expropriated peasants have taken back control of the town centres.

3 Difference

This concept and its correlative, the right to difference, achieved theoretical formulation around 1968. Before this, obviously, a practice, aspirations and demands, attempts at a rational elaboration, existed. Round about this date, theoretical thinking arrived at difference via several convergent paths: (a) the *scientific route*: the concept of difference plays a major role both in mathematical set theory and in linguistics and related sciences; (b) the *philosophical route*, or general reflections on the human species and its possibilities, on anthropology and ethnic groups, on history, and so on; (c) the *methodological route*, the concept of difference featuring in reflections on logic, but also as an articulation between logic and dialectics; (d) the route of *protest*, in relations between sexes, generations, regions, and so on.

The formulation of the concept, and the right it involves, provided theoretical legitimation for some very diverse movements: the demands of immigrants, of women, regional movements, and so on. This theoretical formulation set itself against integration, whether by violence or, more insidiously, by 'acculturation' – a theme originating in American sociology, derived from such pseudo-concepts as 'cultural model'. The theory provided arguments against centralism and imperialisms. It sought to make a breach in ideology and practices subordinated to state power, and hence to the established mode of production. These practices proceed by the disintegration–integration of whatever resists them.

In the women's movements, difference theory sought to open up a way between two common errors: the one that regarded 'women' as a particular group, and even as a class embodying an essence – femininity; and the other that pushed 'women' to resemble men, to affect male behaviour. The way opened up by differentialist theory leads to demanding a status for women, as for the regions and countries concerned: *difference in equality*. It is self-evident that this equality in difference is not envisaged solely at the level of the individual or group, but on a world scale, between peoples and nations. This utterly transforms the old democratic concept of equality by releasing it from egalitarianism and general equivalence, and restoring a qualitative dimension to it. In this perspective, the right to difference must thus be added to human rights not only to complete them, but also to transform them. They no longer concern the entity 'man' but social and daily being, thus extending and deepening the orientation towards practice and concrete reality of the 'rights' proclaimed by the French Revolution, and originally restricted to property and opinion. In this way, we would leave behind the perennial abstract questions and no less abstract controversies about democracy, socialism and humanism. Today, rights can no longer be presented as a closed list of legal or moral principles, but as a series of practical maxims with the capacity to alter everyday life. This involves a project for society, or at least an important component of such a project. And the implication is that such a right and project are not proclaimed and demanded through discourse alone: they must be conquered; they are won in a political struggle.

The same conceptual and theoretical formulation has another meaning and another goal, indissociable from the one that has just been stated: to make Marxist thought more flexible, and to extend it. In Marx, but even more clearly in most of his successors, thinking is reduced to reflection on economic and political reality, on labour and workers, regarded as something 'real'. Thus, this thinking has become arid and scholastic. In considering only a uniform reality, it has assumed and retained a homogenizing appearance. This form of reflection is not on its guard against equivalence – and this despite appeals to the dialectic as well as historical development, and despite attempts to reintegrate national realities and historical specificities.

A case of unjustified mistrust? Misunderstanding? Incomprehension, or inability to tune into the world? 'Differentialist' research and analysis have found scarcely any echo either among official Marxists or among the others. No doubt they do not want to venture on to difficult terrain. This is the theoretically decisive point. Theses on differences cannot be separated from theoretical conceptions of the relation between *particularities* and *differences*, and the transition from the former to the latter.

Particularities are defined by nature and by the relation of the (social) human being to this nature. They consist in biological and physiological 'realities' that are given and determinate: ethnicity, sex, age. Being born white or black, small or large, with blue or dark eyes, is a particularity. So is being born in Africa or Asia. As for differences, they are defined only socially – that is to say, in specifically social relations. Unlike particularity, difference is not isolated: it takes its place in a whole. Particularities confront one another in struggles which run through history, and are simultaneously struggles between ethnic groups, peoples, and classes or class fractions. It is in the course of these struggles that differences are born out of particularities: they emerge, and this involves a certain knowledge and consciousness of *others* in and through conflictual relations – consequently entailing values that achieve relative acceptance. Spontaneous, natural particularities do not purely and simply disappear. Modified and transformed in the course of confrontations, they are integrated into these differences, which cannot be deemed exclusively cultural. The victory of a particularism abolishes difference and replaces it with a return to the natural, the original, affirmed and valorized as such. Could not the history of Greece, for example, be rewritten in this fashion? Starting with ethnic particularities, original groups and confrontations between them and with the 'barbarians', we have a first stage: the conquest of differences. Next there is a splendid period in which perceived and valued differences flourish. Finally, after the Median and Peloponnesian wars, we witness a return to particularisms and, consequently, decline. We could equally rewrite the history of modern democracies thus, with their oscillations between abstract generalities – permitting the coexistence of imperialism without and democracy within – and national particularisms.

The distinction between particularities and differences, and the dynamic it displays, form part of the theory. Neglecting it leads to confusions with serious consequences. To assert particularities as such under the guise of differences sanctions racism, sexism, separations and disjunctions. This is what differentialist theory, its methodology and concepts, precludes.

This theory and these concepts do not discredit class struggle in the name of difference and the right to difference. As if the bourgeoisie was within its 'rights' in affirming itself bourgeois! If we clearly distinguish between *particularities* and *differences*, the clash and confrontation of classes are born from historical particularities; they must produce a society in which, once 'workers' have grasped how they differ from others, they disappear as such with all their old particularities, the scars of alienated labour. This corresponds to Marx's strongest thinking, over and above vulgarizations of it.

This potential society will avoid the homogeneous – abstract and imposed identity – since, according to this schema, it will integrate what its history of confrontations has bequeathed. Equality in difference will be distinct from formal equality inasmuch as it is concrete. This confers a certain post-historical or trans-historical character on differences. And this assumes that history and evolution are not identified on principle, and that a social evolution beyond struggles to the death may be envisaged! This society is conceived neither as an ideal and a utopia, nor as an actual truth. The project of a plural society is also that of a democracy which unfolds its potentialities, rather than immobilizing them in struggles around state apparatuses. Why *plural*, not pluralist? Because the latter term is restricted to political positions and parties. The plural applies to daily life: to ways of living. Thus, on the horizon we find objectives directed against homogenizing powers, the state in that it erases differences and even particularities (rather than aiding their transformation into differences), as well as supra-national strategies and all *indifferent* operations. Taken to its ultimate conclusion, this theory thus introduces a new element into the debate. Assuming that the working class succeeds in conquering hegemony via the democratic route, it should not make its political goal the destruction pure and simple of the old dominant class – something that is regarded as essential in the classical conception of revolution. It should accept it with its acquisitions, in the name of difference, while obviously stripping it of its supremacy and the attributes that made it possible, therewith leading it towards the decline and end of all classes.

112

How and why has the theory of difference been ignored, neutralized, appropriated?

(a) *Politically*, self-evidently, this theory was intended for the Left – that is to say, the tendencies, organizations and parties with the orientation characterized thus, which is in principle innovatory and ultimately revolutionary. But these parties, inheritors of a strong Jacobin heritage which they did not recognize for what it was – that is to say, centralizing and somewhat phallocratic – have until recently failed to understand the right to difference, still less assimilate it. Perhaps they are fearful of its implications as regards women, regions and immigrants. Up until a few years ago, some politicians gave the nod (traditional terminology) to differentialist movements – regional movements, for example – with great caution, and mainly for reasons of popularity – in other words, to use such movements politically. Is this era going to end? We may hope so. Of the politicians said to be on the Left, some genuinely supported 'human rights', but in their legal, fixed form, as immutable, sacred rights, failing to see that the best way to defend them is actively to develop them (right to live in the city, right to difference, etc.). Others have adopted the defence of these rights reluctantly, following the Helsinki accords. Why? Because the critique of human rights and of formal democracy seemed to be part and parcel of Marxism. While numerous politicians rather grandly gave these 'immutable and sacred rights' a wide berth, making do with praising them from a distance, various ideologues worked no less arrogantly to destroy them, together with their legitimating ideology: humanism. Most of these ideologues were oblivious of the fact that the radical critique – too radical for once – of human rights and formal democracy, as well as their legitimating ideology, was already to be found in the Marxist tradition: refutation of supposed fraternity, of liberty for money, of fictional equality, of the political pseudo-community. Many Marxists have failed to understand that political strategy requires the realization of democracy by developing the rights that constitute its foundation. A positive struggle for the right to difference would have enhanced the effectiveness of struggles for and in democracy. When the 'Left' set about reflecting on differences – that is to say, on differential aspirations and demands – was it not already

113

a little late? Had not the concept of difference already been diverted? Was it not already in the process of being captured and dragged to the right? On the other hand, the neoliberal ideology that has inspired political power for years had already done what was required to neutralize differential aspirations – for example, by baptizing the clear idea of decentralization and regional (territorial) self-management 'deconcentration', or (more ridiculously still) 'decongestion', of the state.

All in all, modifications in daily life in the direction of difference have hitherto remained the deed of a few groups of intellectuals, even though the influence of these groups is expanding and gradually prevailing (new household division of labour, at the micro level, that of daily life and private life, etc.).

(b) *Scientifically*, or rather, in accordance with the ideology of scientificity, an attempt has been made to substitute *distinction* for difference – and this in a rather underhand fashion, without discussion or debate, by mischievously confusing them (when in fact these concepts are opposed: the one implying relations, the other stressing that which separates). What is distinction? An abstract principle of classification and nomenclature on the one hand, and a principle of evaluation on the other. It is difficult to differentiate between these two aspects. The concept thus remains ambiguous as between logic and ethics (or aesthetics). The phenomenon theorized by it passes too readily from what is distinct to what is *distinguished*. In this way, it effects separations by accentuating social distances in the hierarchy. It is perfectly possible to detect and analyse distinctions, to make them an object of positive knowledge. Those who proceed thus will use them to 'classify', assuming that the operation has a strictly objective character when in fact it intervenes and modifies the object. One can easily employ distinction to 'classify' hierarchically organized populations sociologically, without troubling to define social 'classes', by appealing solely to the signs by which people distinguish themselves from one another. Here we recognize an old controversy in the social sciences, a methodological issue that seemed to have been superseded. There was a time when sociologists almost completely disposed of objective social relations, those of production and reproduction. They wanted to 'class' an individual in the bourgeoisie, among peasants, in the working or middle classes, only if she expressly declared herself bourgeois, petty-bourgeois, proletarian, and so on. Yet no-one who is blatantly a member of the bourgeoisie has ever been heard to declare: 'I am a bourgeois ...'. On the contrary. To such questions, the capitalist ingenuously replies: 'I work, I'm a worker!' – which is not untrue, or not completely so. Since the sociologists still refused to eschew subjectivism, it was necessary to refine the subjective criteria. In fact, those who distinguish classes according to the criterion of distinction always risk ordering social groups in relation to themselves, without explaining their link with their own group – the intellectuals – and the link between this group and society. To identify 'classes' with 'classification' defuses conflicts by eliminating the contradictions in the discourse of distinction and the distinguished. The two discourses – the discourses of those who distinguish and of those who are distinguished – are juxtaposed and sometimes combined. Thus we end up situating social groups exclusively by strata and layers, in a hierarchy acknowledged and sanctioned by ideology, taking little, if any, account of the major vertical and horizontal divisions with which the society under consideration is shot through.

Why does difference reconnect, as opposed to separating? Because it exists socially only as something perceived, and yet is perceived as such only in relations that are at once reciprocal and extensive. It situates differential elements, derived from particularities and history, in a whole where everyone has their place and which today extends to the global. Difference rallies by relativizing dissimilarities. Its concept makes it possible to let nothing slip and to lose nothing of the past, other than what evolution rejects – that is, exhausted and finished particularities. Distinction, in contrast, reduces the confrontations, aspects and elements of evolution to particularities that are preserved and asserted as such. In other words, the theory of distinction is centred on the real, what has been accomplished and the past, whereas difference is directed towards what is possible. The theory of distinction endeavours to bring the particular into the conceptual and into theoretical language, whereas difference tends towards the universal.

That said, it is only too true that present-day societies – in France, in Europe, in the Western world – may have missed out on difference. They tend to be founded on distinction – that is to say, on the ideology and practice of an important, influential section of the middle classes, with another section inclined towards protest, critical knowledge, and even contestation. In this sense, there is something novel in daily life: the emergence of distinctive criteria and characteristics at every level, and this without abolishing the general tendency to uniformity. Paradoxically, fragmentation does not preclude homogeneity.

It is only too true that the values and signs thus promoted as principles and criteria of distinction conduce to the disintegration of the social, its reduction. This emerges in Pierre Bourdieu's book on the subject, *Distinction*, which offers a remarkable description of the phenomenon, but without a critique of the process, which is treated 'positively', with the trained eye of the scientist. In sanctioning this process through the scientificity of his account, this scientistic sociologist not only ends up liquidating difference and differentialist thinking, but flattens social reality – that is to say, the reality of the social – by excluding several dimensions: the historical in the first instance, but also the values attached to the art works themselves and not the groups, values that are detached and killed by this sociological description. In defining these values exclusively by their social relation conceived as a factor of distinction, positive knowledge abolishes them. One-dimensionality *à la* Herbert Marcuse thus comes to pass in unforeseen ways, in knowledge and reality alike – and in France, too, not only in the USA. This flattening out is not confined to a work that is scientific in intent, but undoubtedly occurs in the reality described – that is to say, the middle classes, or a section of them at least. Such works perpetuate the most questionable aspects of positive knowledge in general, sociology in particular, and Marxism itself (sometimes reduced to a sociologism, sometimes to a historicism, sometimes to an economism or a philosophism). The reduction of the social to class interests and ideologies – albeit those of the middle classes, not the bourgeoisie – tends to destroy the social. What emerges from this reduction is a more or less static essentialism, or a more or less abstract voluntarism. Taken as a criterion, distinction generates an essence for certain strata, which is imputed to them, to which they are attached, and which is constituted with its distinctive conduct in the face of all opposition (in the face of the totality). It is also the case that ambitions or pretensions dressed up as 'distinction' with respect to supposedly inferior social layers can give rise to political aims that are enlisted in the rulers' game.

If someone prefers the *Carnaval de Vienne* and Schumann's music to the songs of Sylvie Vartan or Sheila, so the argument goes, it is in order to distinguish himself from the petty bourgeois who adore the latter – and also to cancel the distance by means of which the bourgeois elite distinguishes itself from other classes. Intrinsically, Schumann and his music are worth next to nothing. The aesthetic value of the music no longer enters into the equation: without saying so, obviously, the tendency is to eliminate it. What a reduction, what an impoverishment, compared with Adorno's remarks (to confine ourselves to one example) on the relation between the musical, the social and the ideological!

The accumulation of facts, data and even statistics proves what it is intended to prove, yet proves nothing. On the contrary: it tells against the 'realism' of a thesis that destroys potentiality in the name of positive knowledge. This thesis positively supports a mystification that sets out from the real, and uncritically sanctions it by abolishing what Hegel rightly considered to be as real as the accomplished facts, and more so – that is, the possible.

(c) *Strategically*. Here the New Right makes its appearance. Roughly, it says: 'The Left has made nothing of difference and differential demands. Left-wing politicians are basically Jacobins. They will not retreat from that even if they pretend to renounce the doctrine of centralization. If they loosen the reins with respect to differences – for example, as far as the regions are concerned – it is the better to ensure the privileges of the centre and state power. They have more chance of succeeding in this operation than the neoliberals, who failed miserably at it. The demands of the dominated, of countries and regions, young people, women themselves, have failed because they have received no more than lukewarm, mainly verbal, support from the Left. Let us learn the lessons of this failure. The socialist and communist Left is allowing theoretical concepts and instruments that were developed in its name, under its influence, and seemingly attached to it, to slip from its feeble grasp. What does it have to offer against homogeneity, the homogeneity of commodities sanctioned by the state? To this wretched, global, daily homogeneity of Western society as fashioned by the bourgeoisie, the boldest counterpose another homogeneity that is no less menacing and menaced, and which, moreover, can converge with it: the homogeneity of work and the worker. The Left envisages and proposes equality only in non-differentiation, in similarity, or rather in abstract identity itself defined by the state. If these left-wingers, politicians and thinkers, have hitherto failed in their endeavours, and will continue to do so, ceding to force of circumstance, is it not because there is some error in their reasoning, their calculations and speculative constructions? This is their error: they have failed to understand the meaning of the difference – that is to say, the *inequality* – between living species, peoples, groups and classes, and individuals. Differences are qualitative; or they are not differences. That differences exist means that there are superior and inferior types. Those who pronounce "difference" assert intellectual, moral and physical inequality between different people. Otherwise, difference boils down to generalities such as "man" and his various, equally abstract "rights" – as abstract as the entity to which they refer, in which all who reflect on the subject have ceased to believe. Only inequality, openly acknowledged and proclaimed, confers meaning, value and concrete significance on differences, which have hitherto been reduced to mere facts or extolled in utopian fashion by a destructive ideology. Inequality, which is always experienced but illusorily rejected, must be accepted precisely as difference. How can anyone deny that the children of the dominant classes and developed countries assimilate culture, science and knowledge better than the others? If one thinks in terms of "civilizations", rather than the levelling concept of "society", how can anyone deny that there are civilizations which are superior and others which are inferior, successful civilizations and failed civilizations? The egalitarian Left challenges this in vain, and condemns culture to decline. What a long way we have come since Marx naively but firmly identified the proletariat as the inheritor of philosophy! What the Left wants to impose could become law and norm only in the course of crises and struggles that would be ruinous for civilization. How distant is the golden age when revolutionaries dreamed of regenerating the old corrupted society in a bloodbath! Particularities, if we want to talk about them, are identified with genetic inheritance. Essential and not relative (relational), they must be carefully preserved. This thesis is based on the social sciences, and especially biology and sociobiology. As a new science, biology restores it centre-stage, with inevitable controversies that go back more than a century: "The chimerical equality socialism strives for is in total contradiction with the absolute inequality that everywhere obtains between individuals," the biologists Schmidt and Haeckel were already saying in 1877.'

Continuing his discourse, the representative of the New Right would say: 'We must go further and deeper than biology. Our new doctrine cannot make do with a foundation that is restricted to a single science. This position is insufficient to refute the Left by replying to the Marxist critique of capitalism and the bourgeoisie. That critique does not lack arguments or good motives, but today it may be regarded as outmoded. The Marxist Left was not wrong when it showed that the world of commodities extends to the planet, is constituted as internationality on the basis of Americanism and the commodity-order in the USA. Marxists were able to demonstrate the reductive and destructive capacity of this commodity-order with respect to all singularity, everything that resists homogeneity, the standardization and automation of social mechanisms. The Left was unaware, or did not want to see, that this tendency has been strengthened in the name of Marxism. Whether willingly or unwillingly allied to capitalism, Marxism proceeds in concert with it towards a system in which techno-economic rationality, resulting in the self-regulation of the system, becomes identical with madness, in a total, totalitarian mercantilism that destroys the life of peoples precisely by suppressing the right to difference – and to power! The complicity of socialism and capitalism is now established. That is where renewal starts out from. The automation of productive labour? You must be joking! We are heading for a gigantic self-regulated mechanism for organizing work more efficiently …'[3]

At this point in the debate, the hypercritic inevitably intervenes. Let us give him the floor. He takes it and delivers his verdict: 'Just like the rights of man and the citizen, difference and the right to difference belong to the ideological inheritance of the middle classes, who today carry great social weight, out of all proportion to their political influence. Whence their attempt to end this discrepancy. In accordance with their position in contemporary society, they make contradictory use of this ideology. Either they criticize the political authorities, or they launch an attack on them with the aim of replacing them. They seek to distinguish themselves from one another, as layers and strata; and still more to distinguish themselves from the working class. Hence the cult of differences, hence the search for differences and distinctions in food, clothing, furniture, space – in short, everyday life. Differences? The proletariat has no time for them; it has nothing to do with these intellectual niceties; it could not care less about regions, about local or national differences. In so far as it is affected by this ideology, its (class) consciousness is confused, and this can lead it into dead ends. Self-management? It risks overshadowing, postponing, the self-determination, the autonomy, of the working class, and leading us towards a self-managed capitalism! Let us be clear! Let us eliminate these ambiguities! Whether on the Left or the Right, you are all making a fundamental error, an error of method and theory. What is important? Contradictions! Conflict! Not differences! … Contradictions and conflict are blunted and attenuated by substituting differences for them. That is why liberalism yesterday and the Right today have recuperated supposed rights, including the right to difference. The bourgeoisie had to pay the price for what it calls the new deployment of its mode of production. It has paid to make the middle classes, intellectuals and technicians – classes secreted by it and kept for years on the fringes of power – partners in its system. Is it or is it not the case that the town centres and city life modelled by capital have just been occupied or reoccupied by the new middle class and the new bourgeoisie, whereas the people and the working class were not able to take control of them? The upshot, moreover, is that the people and the working class can neither take over the centre, nor achieve genuine decentralization – so that, pending a new order – that is, a genuinely revolutionary transformation – they can only endure the operational schema imposed on them from above: eviction as far away as possible from city centres, ghettos and segregation, with state and political control, and it alone, preventing society from splitting …'

Answers (to the hypercritic as well as the representative of the New Right): 'Everything you have both said about self-management as well as rights, including the right to difference, is correct: it can be said, and already has been said. The right to difference does not preclude all ambiguity. It does not possess an implacable logic. Yes, self-managed capitalism is not inconceivable. Yes, human rights have served as a double-edged political weapon, sometimes for imperialism and sometimes for the struggle against imperialism. What does that mean? This is where we come to the main thing: the arena and stake of the struggle coincide. This is a fundamental formula, which is still barely understood. Moreover, the arena and the stake are expanding. The local, the regional, the national and the global are all part of the vast territory on which the political struggle is developing. You of the New Right reject 'rights' as negating what, for you, is difference. You set difference up against rights, whereas the introduction of difference into abstract rights modifies and transforms them. You, the hyper-critic, reject rights because, according to you, they are harmful – the naive, vain right to freedom of opinion, property rights that are all too real. You thus refuse what gives concrete expression to rights in democracy – that is to say, in the struggle for democracy. Rather than the rise of the middle classes, should we not accept that we are wit-nessing the onset of a crisis in society based on the ideological predominance of these composite, heterogeneous classes, under the hegemony of capital? You reject the concept of democracy, which you judge to be empty. You have your reasons. And yet critical reason demands another approach, enlarging the conception – classical on both sides, bourgeois and Marxist – of rights and struggles. Far from blunting their edge and rendering them empty, differential demands compound economic demands and conflicts, enhancing their strength. It is nevertheless true that the links between the differential and the conflictual change over time; the link is always conjunctural. Do you think a French-speaking worker in Montreal can bear to hear his English-speaking, Anglophile or Americanophile boss say: "Talk white!", without experiencing anger? The pressure of Anglo-American capitalism has been increasing in recent years, dispossessing the French Canadian worker of his "identity", this famous identity of which so much is made, and which is itself rich in hidden conflicts and contradictions. Hence the inevitable proclamation of difference – that is to say, of identity rediscovered and developed in and through differ-ence. When national and linguistic – or, if you're fond of this term, "cultural" – oppression compounds economic and political domina-tion, the latter becomes intolerable. Demands then become differential. It may be that the national takes priority over the social, and endeavours to subordinate it. Then, there is disjunction and sep-aration; social demands have difficulty gaining access to consciousness, language and positive knowledge, action. In the course of this conflict, the national and the differential can smother the social. However, social demands have to go via the national, and retain it. They must pass through the differential phase, and retain something from this passage. The stress is forever shifting. It must be added that both of you, New Right and left-wing hypercriticism alike, confuse particularities and differences. Either you do not appreciate the transition from one to the other, with its problems, its conflicts, its relapses, its regressions; or you underestimate it. When the national takes precedence over the social, it is because it relapses into particu-larism, rather than raising itself up to difference. Finally – our last argument – both sides evince an extraordinary incomprehension of Nietzschean thought. You leftists and dogmatists end up saying that Nietzsche represents the landed aristocracy and its vestiges.[4] One might as well say – to take the texts of the very young Marx – that he represented the liberal petty bourgeoisie in Germany. As for you, men of the Right, you retain only the glorification of the will to power from Nietzsche, when we must also, and especially, see in him the inception of a critique of it. Thought, love and poetry commence where the will to power ceases, where it expires ...'

4 The State and Daily Life

Let us now try to see the question of the state, which has already been glimpsed in certain aspects, in its complexity and totality. In fact, the question of the totality is posed here. From the analyses, an inversion of the common, daily accepted viewpoint has already emerged. The state and its administrative and political apparatuses *seem* to be the keystone of society; they appear to hold it in their powerful grip. This is not untrue, as regards either the representation or what it refers to.

Yet this representation is mystificatory. The state is now built upon daily life; its base is the everyday. The traditional Marxist thesis makes the relations of production and productive forces the 'base' of the ideological and political superstructures. Today – that is to say, now that the state ensures the administration of society, as opposed to letting social relations, the market and blind forces take their course – this thesis is reductionist and inadequate. In the course of major conflicts and events, the relations of domination and the reproduction of these relations have wrested priority over the relations of production that they involve and contain. In its way, daily life likewise involves and contains them. This is a curious inversion: daily life and people in daily life still perceive the institutional edifice above their heads. Similarly, the crowd of believers perceive the cathedral, caress its pillars with their eyes and hands, feel the soil under their feet. In daily life, these believers do not realize that they *are* the soil on which the edifice rests and bears down. With all their gestures, words and habits, they preserve and support the edifice. Neoliberal ideology has succeeded in maintaining this deceptive perspective, and has even reinforced it. Only a certain anarchist tradition has corrected it to some extent, but without succeeding in shaking the edifice. Since the *belle époque* of militant anarchism, which was coeval with the bourgeois *belle époque,* and despite the terrorism that prolongs the anarchist tradition, the edifice has been perfected from year to year, answering the terrorism of its opponents with state terrorism.

In so far as change has occurred, it has been for the worse. There is no need to discourse at length to prove the extension of state – that is, police – control. But be careful when it comes to the critique of the state today! The political situation obliges us to reconsider and reintroduce a distinction between *left critique* and *right critique* that seemed outdated. These two critical stances are often mixed up, in a dangerous confusion. The confusion is increased by the fact that for a long time hypercriticism has regarded as right-wing and reactionary any utterance about the state that did not include the demand for its imminent, even immediate, abolition. Furthermore, the difference between these critical attitudes was blurred by the fact that various political plans, tactically identifying themselves with national unity or democratic action, claimed to be situated beyond the division between Right and Left. This distinction is becoming current once more. What does the right-wing critique claim? It incriminates the bureaucratic cumbersomeness of the state appara-tuses, their clumsy interventions, the enormous cost of these interventions, subventions and support for the various 'social rejects', and so on. As for the left-wing critique, it accuses statesmen of striving to reinforce the state, shattering the social by causing it to permeate society in its entirety, being repressive, using information tendentiously – ultimately, of treating the state as an end in itself, not as an instrument in the service of society. This dual indictment, inseparable from other ideological or strategic elements, cannot fail to shake the state at its foundation. The question of the state is trans-formed: it becomes – the state in question!

The contemporary state has three sides: managerial and adminis-trative; security – the state as guardian, guaranteeing security, insuring and reassuring; finally, and above all, the lethal side – army and armaments, police and justice, repression and oppression. There is no point dwelling at length on the organization of the state here. It is sufficient to show that even in daily life an agonizing conflict sets in between security and risk, between fixed determinations decreed from on high (identity) and inevitable evolution. This contributes signifi-cantly to the malaise, the dissatisfaction that is mixed in with satisfaction. Simultaneously protector and oppressor, manager and arbiter, authoritarian and rational, liberator and identitarian, the contemporary state is piling up contradictions under official dis-courses of the utmost coherence. For years the state technocracy and techno-structure have long concealed the enormity of the bureau-cracy and its arbitrariness under the ideology of competence and performance. Hence the critiques, but also the double-sidedness of those critiques. Hence also the vanishing of joy, pleasure and enjoy-ment in the clutches of the coldest of cold monsters. From what quarter will the deliverance we have been awaiting for so long come? The everyday is strictly dependent upon this situation: it unfolds, or rather stagnates, under this dominion, with functionalism and official formalism disguising the enterprises of the will to power. With what determination have statesmen for decades been cutting down anything that sticks out, destroying whatever does not conform to the established norms, striking at some particular social phenomenon – sex, drugs, idleness, and so on – in order thereby to target everything

124

that threatens them. Thus is daily life normalized. Attempts at emancipation are sometimes repressed, sometimes skilfully recuperated and incorporated – these two aspects of the tactics of administrative apparatuses complementing one another. Need I remark in passing that what we are dealing with is administrative apparatuses, not ideological apparatuses, which are at most capable of erecting a smokescreen over real operations? Moreover, the state is capable only of a seeming preservation of national unity and identity, which it exploits shamelessly. In fact and in practice, the state apparatuses press towards rupture and fragmentation, a split society – the work of the state, concealed by it – forcibly maintained in the existing political framework.

Is it not clear, even obvious, that the critique of everyday lived experience must abandon the immediate, and be reconsidered in accordance with state activity and its enormous organizational capacities? It is not enough to blame capitalism, commodities and money, as well as 'bourgeois' society, for being dehumanizing and oppressive. It is no longer sufficient to invoke the transcendence of 'real life' or the 'true life'. It is no longer even necessary to establish the moral, mental or spiritual priority of the surreal, the ideal or the unreal over the real. Appeals to art can prove as disappointing as the appeal to truth against reality. Refutation of the commodity as a world, and of the global as a product of the market, still has a sense. Unfortunately, however, this sense also implies the non-sense of the refutation. For the essential thing today is the state, which increasingly elevates itself above its own conditions in the world of commodities (which simultaneously supports the state in general and tends to shatter each particular state, dissolving it into the global). The role of critical thinking consists here in demonstrating the mortal character of the state: it bears within it the conditions of its own death and, what is more, it leads to death. Once we have proved this, a choice, a bifurcation, seems unavoidable. Either we attempt to go beyond the level of the state, adopting as a practical and intellectual hypothesis its rupture or dissolution; or we seek to install ourselves in the actual, circumventing and diverting the pressure, if necessary using it to motivate micro-decisions. Is the latter option feasible? Unquestionably, if we accept that all the basic elements of the question have been clarified; that today there is nothing blind and opaque, as was once the case with the spread of the market, industry and technology.

But if it is true that changes in daily life occur by two routes, the local and the global, the micro and the macro, perhaps this option is unavailing?

People may think that the splendour of power and the splendour of the state have nothing to do with the humility of daily life. What a mistake that would be! Critical analysis begins with the disenchantment of the state and the sphere of power. They have nothing magical or sacramental about them. Charismatic? This metaphor, which is itself magical, is no longer meaningful in contemporary politics, where power is acquired through tactics and strategy, manoeuvres and campaigns, including advertising campaigns.

The state today is no longer content to 'discipline and punish'. It was the state of the *belle époque* that assumed an ethical function of normalization: weeding out the useless, eliminating the abnormal. Today, the state manages daily life directly or indirectly. Directly, through regulations and laws, more numerous prohibitions, and the tutelary action of institutions and administrations. Indirectly, through taxation, the apparatus of justice, steering the media, and so on. Since the *belle époque* of 'discipline and punish', a sort of inversion has occurred in the situation. Previously, what was not prohibited was permitted. Today, everything that is not permitted is prohibited. This inversion occurred from the de Gaulle era up to the Giscard era, and its consequences were perceived only after the event, and hence too late to oppose them – all the more so in that this extension of prohibition has been able to cloak itself in a pseudo-liberal ideology. It is self-evident that the state alone cannot ensure control over an entire society – that is to say, over groups and human beings whose numbers are often considerable. It thus functions by guaranteeing the imbrication and equivalence of various forms and 'sub-systems' – for example, teaching, medicine and the organization of health, the organization of time and space, and so on. It chiefly relies on the world of commodities, an active form in everyday life, as well as on the contractual system, another active form. A service state? So it is said; so it is claimed. In reality, what we have is a state controlling daily life because it helps to create it. And it even *moulds* it. It fashions it. This does not mean that each 'user' can easily pass from one to another of the sub-systems or forms linked by the state, and whose equivalence the state ensures.

What escapes the state? The derisory, minuscule decisions in which freedom is rediscovered and experienced: taking the bus to this or that stop; speaking or not speaking to a particular person; buying such and such an object; and so on. Starting from these micro-decisions, freedom seeks to gather momentum. While it is true that the state dispenses only with what is insignificant, it is nevertheless the case that the politico-bureaucratic-state edifice always contains cracks, chinks, spaces. On the one hand, administrative activity strains to plug these gaps, leaving less and less hope and possibility of what has been dubbed interstitial freedom. On the other hand, individuals seek to enlarge these cracks and pass through the interstices.

It is not certain that all the state's functions, old and/or new, archaic or historic, innate or acquired, are preserved as such, simply by being strengthened. Some functions fluctuate. We know, for example, that since the advent of so-called multinational firms, state management of the economic and the social has altered. It may be that what is called the national state will become the manager of outmoded national territories and relations of production for global enterprises. Some important decisions are taken at the level of the state – that is to say, at the national and global level, but outside of state institutions. Consultation and dialogue take place between personalities, meetings during which the 'private' – that is to say, the interests of national or international firms – and the 'public' – that is to say, the representatives of the various groups concerned – mingle and clash. State bodies and political leaders participate in decisions with the aim of maintaining the domestic market, strategic coherence, national unity, and the celebrated consensus – in short, the logic of the mode of production. Sparing unforeseen developments or innovations, one function seems set to be strengthened: the administration of daily life, as a general product at once of the economic, the political and the strategic, and even of ideology. So that everything we have hitherto observed risks being a mere joking matter in comparison with what lies in store: the state of total knowledge – the past, present and future of each member (individual or group) registered, described, prescribed by perfectly informed 'services', down to the smallest move, the smallest payment, the most insignificant of social and individual acts. If we let things take their course, this pessimistic science-fiction scenario will gradually become our familiar landscape, because it is convenient to have a technical device at home that seems to take the whole of everyday life in hand. One day it may well be that, sparing the unforeseen or some initiative, an army of bureaucrats, under the orders of a technico-political high command, will treat daily life not as an object or product, no longer as a semi-colony, but quite simply as a conquered country.

5 Space and Time

Before I examine information technology more closely, let me say a little about social time and space. In this domain, the changes were slow but profound. First of all, everything in terrestrial space has been explored, and nearly everything has been occupied and exploited. What remains unoccupied? The ocean depths. Once again, the major states are engaged in disturbing activities; some theoreticians of strategy have suggested that a global conflict could spring from rivalry over the resources of the oceans. As for forests, lakes, beaches, mountains, they have been well-nigh completely 'appropriated'. Is there any need for me to reiterate again that private property means disappropriation? The space of play, where the body rediscovers itself in rediscovering use, becomes an opportunity for profit, with the latter subjecting the potential for enjoyment to itself, and debasing it. Occupation by financial interests and private property signifies control – that is to say, the end of the freedom that is indispensable to full enjoyment. This occupation of special places and spaces has consequences for daily life. In fact, in the depths of despondency, monotony and boredom, the people of daily life have faith in unoccupied places and free time, in free activities – that is to say, play activities. The ludic can be recuperated; and has been to a significant extent. Yet it too remains the 'arena and stake' of a conflict, over a beach, access to the sea, grazing rights, and so on; and such conflicts can sometimes become acute.

In its multiplicity, time can be envisaged either qualitatively or quantitatively – as biological or physical time, as psychological duration, or finally as social time, leaving to one side sidereal time, historical time, and so on.

As natural time, it has a rhythmical character. Rhythm is an integral and determinant part of qualitative time. It also possesses a quantitative character: it is measured – frequency, intensity, energy expended, and so on. But rhythms are multiple and interfere with one another qualitatively: heartbeats, breathing, being awake and asleep by turns, being hungry and thirsty, and so on. The rhythms in question are only the most easily observable – some diurnal, others monthly, and so on. Although they are repetitive, rhythms and cycles always have an appearance of novelty: the dawn always seems to be the first one. Rhythm does not prevent the desire for, and pleasure of, discovery: hunger and thirst always seem novel. Is this a kind of gift of oblivion that protects the rhythmical from obsolescence, but without erasing all memory? In linear repetition, by contrast, the formal and material identity of each 'stroke' is recognized, generating lassitude, boredom and fatigue.

When Marxists have dealt with rhythms, they have considered them solely on the basis of labour. Indeed, originally the gestures and acts of collective labour were rhythmically organized, invariably accompanied by songs: the songs of oarsmen, haulers, harvesters, shepherds, sailors, and so on. A whole 'Marxist' aesthetic is based on the hypothesis of a transformation and artistic transposition of work rhythms becoming ends rather than means, and pleasures as opposed to punctuating productive activity. This thesis ignores a certain number of facts. In the first place, vital rhythms pre-exist organized social labour; hormonal secretions obey different cycles, making it possible to stress the differential character of rhythms. Secondly, the gestures of labour are organized rhythmically only in forms of work that predate industrial labour. The closer productive activity approximates to industrial production using machines, the more linear repetition becomes, losing its rhythmical character. Take, for example, a sequence of operations like hammer-blows to drive in nails, or the production of pieces by a milling machine, or assembling a car. If the sequence of hammer-blows sometimes takes on a kind of rhythm, it is because the worker is seeking to escape linear monotony. From the very beginning of industrial organization, there is a sudden mutual interference between rhythmical vital processes and linear operations. This foreshadows complex processes, and does not support the thesis of a direct transition from practical work rhythms to aesthetic rhythms in music, dance, architecture, and so on. The general problem here is the spatialization of temporal processes. In this respect, the work of art displays a victory of the rhythmical over the linear, integrating it without destroying it. Cyclical repetition and linear repetition meet and collide. Thus, in music the metronome supplies a linear tempo; but the linked series of intervals by octaves possesses a cyclical and rhythmical character. Likewise in daily life: the many rhythms and cycles of natural origin, which are transformed by social life, interfere with the linear processes and sequences of gestures and acts.

Rhythmanalysis, a new science that is in the process of being constituted, studies these highly complex processes. It may be that it will complement or supplant psychoanalysis. It situates itself at the juxtaposition of the physical, the physiological and the social, at the heart of daily life. Elements of rhythmanalysis could find a place here. This knowledge starts from empirical observations – for example, the sea's waves with their extraordinarily complex undulations and rhythms, or music as a unity of melody, harmony and rhythm. Compared with the existing sciences, it is multi- or interdisciplinary in character. It cannot but appeal to wave theories, to the principle of the superimposition of small movements, whereas larger wave movements create interferences. It equally calls upon a physiology of organs and their functioning, considered in time and not only in anatomical space – something that has limited physiology's perspectives for a long time. It would thus study all cyclical rhythms starting from their origin or foundation – nature – but taking account of their alterations through interference with linear processes. The important thing here is the progressive crushing of rhythms and cycles by linear repetition. It must be emphasized that only the linear is amenable to being fully quantified and homogenized. On a watch or a clock, the mechanical devices subject the cyclical – the hands that turn in sixty seconds or twelve hours – to the linearity of counting. In recent measuring devices, and even watches, the cyclical (the dial) tends to disappear. Fully quantified social time is indifferent to day and night, to the rhythms of impulses.

Critical analysis of daily life devotes a lot of space to the difference between the two types of repetitive processes and their conjunctions. It must give even more space to the complete quantification of social time on the basis of the measurement of labour-time and its productivity in industry. Starting from the organization of labour – divided and composite, measured and quantified – quantification has conquered society in its entirety, thereby contributing to the realization of the mode of production. It is likewise on the basis of this quantification that the everyday was constituted, almost completely eliminating the qualitative in time and space, treating it as a residue to be eliminated. The qualitative has *virtually* disappeared. But here, once again, this 'virtually' is very important. This is the sense in which daily life represents the generalization of industrial rationality, the spirit of enterprise, and capitalist management, adopted and imposed by the state and institutional summit. At the limit, absolute quantification, pure rationality, abstraction, would triumph. The 'virtually' means that this limit is unattainable, and that something else is always possible.

'What is urban space? What is a town? How are they composed at different levels – blocks of flats, buildings, monuments – in a word, the architectural and, at another level, the urbanistic?' We are beginning to think that these questions, which are seemingly empirical and a matter for positive knowledge, have a secret affinity with various philosophical questions: 'What is man? What is his relation to being? What is the relation between being and space? How do things stand with the man's being, his evolution, his ascent, or his nothingness?' If we knew how to define 'man', would we not be able to define the urban and the town? Unless it's the other way round, and we must first of all understand the town if we are to define this political animal who constructs cities, living in them or fleeing them. In that case, inquisitive thinking would investigate the urban in the first instance, rather than positive knowledge in isolation or power *in abstracto*. Perhaps the town holds the answer to some crucial questions that philosophers have ignored for years. Unless, vice versa, the mystery of the town betokens the absence of any answer. Do these enormous collections of things, men, women, works and symbols possess an as yet undeciphered meaning? Or do they have no meaning? However that may be, it is in towns and the urban that the everyday – ours – is instituted.

And here we confront a new paradox among so many others. The break-up of the historic town has been going on since the end of the nineteenth century and the beginning of the twentieth; it figures in the collapse of reference points already referred to. Yet one remarkable result of it has been to facilitate a novel analysis of the urban question. Here before our very eyes is the town, situated on the suburban outskirts; it is in pieces, fragments, parts, laid out alongside one another. In this fragmented city, the only thing to be done is to make an inventory of the elements of the whole, bearing in mind that some pieces may be missing here and there, and that the break-up might have distorted them. The elements that were combined into a strong unity by historic towns (a unity that fragmentation eliminates, and which consequently poses a problem) are perceived item by item. Thus, the activity of knowledge proceeds via the negative! Most specialists in urban questions, happy with such a godsend, make do with describing the fragments; they find the post-mortem analysis of the urban conducted by contemporary practice adequate. They refer to what they collect with terms that seem to contain impressive positive knowledge: housing conditions, the built environment, things mineral and vegetable, amenities, and so on. Yet these terms, far from containing knowledge of the urban, merely refer to functions separated by an anatomical operation, by separation of the historical elements of the urban into inert entities. But it is in this *framework* – a very precise term which encapsulates the rigidity or inertia of the result – that the people of daily life have to live.

Those who have not given up on critical analysis and theoretical thinking know that what they have before them is merely the spectre of the town. And this in the dual sense of the French word *spectre*: (a) an *analysis* comparable to that of white light by the prism which splits it up, revealing what is involved in the apparently simple clarity of the sun or light source; (b) a *ghost*, outliving what was once a vibrant urbanity and its unity.

Assembling and combining these separate elements does not restore the lost life of towns. Here, too, *le mort saisit le vif*! Like the humanity to which it offers shelter, the town is alienated. Moreover, spectral analysis is not exhaustive; the outskirts and suburbs exclude certain elements which are indispensable to the urban – for example, the memory and symbolisms that were once integrated into monuments. As is well known but frequently forgotten, any analysis risks killing its object for the sake of seeing and knowing what it contains. An effective analysis of towns in the real world of their break-up must now be subjected to a method whose watchword and procedure have already been set down: situating and restoring. But such an approach cannot be inaugurated and pursued without taking account of the everyday life of the relevant parties: inhabitants, city dwellers, citizens or, again, 'users'. What is outlined is a problematic. A new one? Not completely new, but one that is rarely articulated to its full extent.

The problematic of time and space far exceeds the present account. Research and discovery follow a path full of obstacles and pitfalls. For example, it may be that analysis finds itself faced with blindingly obvious facts – that is to say, faced with the causes of or reasons for certain observable effects, causes or reasons that have nothing occult about them, even though they need to be discovered; so familiar are they that they simply go unnoticed. This is how things proceed in the study of language, where everyone uses forms and structures without necessarily having a knowledge of them as such. Likewise with the study of everyday life and the urban, where what is most familiar is also the least known and the most difficult to make out.

Time as such is irreversible. It is impossible, inconceivable, to go in reverse. Complete repetition of the past can be demanded of the divinity by those who believe in his omnipotence (Kierkegaard). It can be conceived in the absolute, ontologically and metaphysically (the eternal return). Rerunning time is an initiative undertaken by thought, which reconstructs the past of the individual, the group or a particular society with difficulty. Inasmuch as it is reversible, space is distinguished from irreversible time, although space and time are intimately connected. But time is projected into space through measurement, by being homogenized, by appearing in things and products. The time of daily life is not only represented in clocks and watches; it is also represented in photographs and curios-souvenirs. These memory-objects, these palpable, immediate traces of the past, seem to say in daily life that the past is never past. Not explicitly but implicitly, it signifies the reversibility of time. In this fractured, frag- mented time, we can return to the past, since it is there. More so than others, the kitsch object possesses these strange properties: a blending of memory, recollection, the imaginary, the real. The illusion of reversibility gives everyday time an air which might be taken for hap- piness, and does indeed possess a certain happy – or, at least, satisfied – air. Is it not pleasant to escape time, to break out of time – not into the timelessness of the great *oeuvre*, but within temporality itself? But one of the consequences is the elimination of tragedy and death.

People sometimes ask how and why this tragic age lacks a tragic consciousness, why it eliminates the tragic knowledge around which thinking revolves. Here is a partial answer: the appearance and illusion of the reversibility of everyday time, represented by objects that possess this meaning and this privilege. Eliminating the tragic is part of the tragedy of the age. This elimination does not go beyond appearances. Under the masquerade of kitsch, the tragic follows its course. If objects form a system – something we can accept in the case of functional objects, such as utensils and furniture – its meaning is to be found not in what it declares, but in what it dissimulates, which extends from the tragic to the mode of production via the malaise of daily life. The production of daily life, which is opposed to daily life as *oeuvre*, thus includes the production of everyday space and time, as well as the objects that fill up the everyday, the mass of objects intended to fill time and space. This mass is likewise simultaneously homogeneous and fragmented, and hierarchically organized. Regarding this schema – 'homogeneity–fragmentation–hierarchization' – the main point has been made. Since this organizational schema was discovered in connection with space, there is no point returning to it. By means of such organizational forms, operating in various sectors and domains, and even though these forms and schemas do not correspond to any determinate institution, daily life finds itself instituted. Strategy? Yes and no. No, because the result is obtained in accordance with the objective, and hence 'unconscious', modalities of the mode of production. But yes, because the orientation gives rise to multiple tactical operations directed towards an overall result.

Social space (like theatrical, pictorial or architectural space) can no longer seem like the discovery of a pre-existent, 'real' external space, any more than it can seem like the covering over of a natural space by an 'authentic' mental space. These philosophical schemas are no longer admissible. Social space manifests itself as the realization of a general practical schema. As a product, it is made in accordance with an operating instrument in the hands of a group of experts, technocrats who are themselves representative of particular interests but at the same time of a mode of production, conceived not as a completed reality or an abstract totality, but as a set of possibilities in the process of being realized. This theory accounts both for the specificity of the organizational schema (homogeneity–division–hierarchization), and for its historical appearance at a given moment in the evolution of the mode of production. At this moment, a representation of space – which is by no means innocent, since it involves and contains a strategy – is passed off as disinterested positive knowledge. It is projected objectively; it is effected materially, through practical means. There is thus no real space or authentic space, only spaces produced in accordance with certain schemas developed by some particular group within the general framework of a society (that is to say, a mode of production). This theory also accounts for the correspondence between the various spaces: the general space of society, architectural space, everyday space, the space of transport as well as that of furnishing, and so on.

The splintering of time and space in general homogeneity, and the crushing of natural rhythms and cycles by linearity, have consequences at other levels. This state of affairs creates a need for rhythms. The imposition of daily life as we have defined it thus goes together with rhythmical innovations in music and dance, innovations that accentuate rhythm and restore it to daily life. Is it any coincidence that the institution of this everydayness goes together with the enormous success of exotic or ecstatic rhythms, with the increasing role of music in social life, with the search for 'highs' and the extraordinary, in a transgression of all rules extending even to death trances? The festival, which in other respects has been recuperated and commercialized, is restored, together with features that had been done away with: rupture, transgression, ecstasy. In this way, daily life leads to retaliation; because it is becoming normal, rupture takes abnormal, even morbid, forms. We should not be astonished at this, let alone wax indignant over it. Among the Greeks, the Dionysian did not submit to the pure idea of beauty. The Bacchantes, roaming through the countryside, yelling, diabolical, tearing the living beings they came across to pieces, were not obliged to be 'beautiful'. Even then, it was not a matter of a rupture with daily life, but a return to cosmic forces …

In and through music and dance, time becomes irreversible once again. The festival unfolds once more, headed towards its end, consuming what it draws its substance from: energy, desire, violence. At the heart of everyday positivity, the negative springs up in all its force.

6 Information Technology and Daily Life

For a long time, technological innovations in the domain of information (cybernetics) were principally applied to administration (administrative information processing). More recently, new technical progress and new economic processes have enabled – or, rather, dictated – their application to production. More precisely, the two applications are distinct and complementary. On the one hand, the processes of productive labour have changed, calling into question the old divisions of labour. On the other hand, computer scientists proclaim the generalization of their theoretical and practical knowledge to society as a whole. In contrast to the pessimism and nihilism, the apocalyptic prophesying that was still predominant among the intelligentsia only a little while ago, the optimistic prophecies of technicians and official circles have invaded the media and publishing.

This merits very serious consideration. Computer science and telematics are certainly going to alter social existence. They have already begun to do so. Communication has been an important – possibly essential – phenomenon in social practice since the beginning of history and prehistory. Will computer science, with its repercussions and related disciplines, go so far as to transform everyday life? To transform the social relations of production, reproduction and domination? That is the issue.

It is all the more significant and interesting in that the new technologies have arrived on time, if we may put it like that, in a kind of pleonasm. Grafting themselves on to it, they extend the process of 'formalization of daily life' referred to above. The increasing predominance of the abstract–concrete has already been analysed in its broad outline, without exhausting the theme (far from it). The abstract–concrete reigns in daily life, in place of the *concrete* (the human: each object and gesture having a meaning because they are practically bound up with a civilization) and the *abstract* (opposed to the concrete and distinct in the imaginary as well as ideology). How is this displacement to be characterized? We have seen how: by the world of exchange and commodities; by legality and the importance of impersonal, sovereign Law; by the value attributed to language and, more generally, to signs. These priorities have been readily recognized by positive knowledge, since it recognizes its own instruments in them. Even so, this recognition has given rise to interpretations and superfluous commentary, with all social acts, including buying and consuming, being construed as the 'effects of signs'. This vast process creates the conditions of possibility for a massive use of new technologies. Supporters of these technologies, their theoreticians – or, rather, their apologists – go so far as to claim that they will constitute a new *mode of production* – the one revolutionaries dreamt of, but to be ushered in by a peaceful, silent revolution. Essentially, this mode of production would consist in the production of immaterial goods, supplanting the production of material products, as well as the ever more complete predominance of services over other activities.

Sign effects? Now is the time to grasp them, define them and appreciate their significance as well as their limits. Contrary to Jean Baudrillard, the point at which the social signification of objects entered into their evaluation – that is to say, exchange-value – was not the appropriate moment for a definition and conclusion.[5] That was only one moment, one episode in a larger, ongoing process. Some theorizations characteristically extrapolate from a reality. They push the tendency inherent in this reality as far as it will go; this makes them worthy of note but, at the same time marks and dates them. In this fashion, we easily end up with a radical critique, but such a radicalism is absurd. Were each social act to respond to sign effects, it would sanction all the social relations conducive to this effect. The seemingly most insignificant objects would be the most active mediators. To eat a piece of bread would be to commune with all the labour and all the conditions of labour that went into the production of this foodstuff. Hence to accept them. Such a thesis is *true*, or at least correct, but it only serves to demonstrate unequivocally how a certain quest for truth can result in absurdity. Mirror effects! Language effects! Sign effects! So many effects that are exploited without searching for the real conditions of effects that are simultaneously both real and unreal. These conditions are discovered in the process that tends towards the abstract–concrete. This process never extends as far as pure abstraction, which would be equivalent to a vacuum and nothingness. It *nearly* gets there. But just as it is about to reach this extreme, the process is, as it were, put into reverse, reincarnated or reincorporated by daily life. Similarly, at the other extreme, it cannot vanish into the substantiality of the concrete and the real; it is returned to abstraction. May we not say the same to apologists for information technology? Nevertheless, it is certainly true that the advent of computer science, which is sweeping aside certain earlier ideologies, poses new problems that are planetary in scope. Must we choose between the terms of the alternative: computerization of society (from above), or socialization of information technology (from below)? Can this contradiction be resolved?

A new ideology is looming on the horizon, which is no less disturbing than those that discovered a pretext, a provenance, or a point of impact in use and exchange, the two modalities of value. A text that might already seem distant, but nevertheless stands out – the Nora–Minc Report (1978) – was presented as strictly objective and scientific. It contained political suggestions and warnings, which were formulated and justified. It signalled various dangers: the role of global enterprises like IBM; brutal state intervention in information. At the same time, this text offered a model of society. Technocratic utopia? Sociological forecast? Both. According to this perspective or prospectus, the information society was inevitably going to be divided into three levels or sectors: (a) the kingly, that is to say, sovereign (royal) powers – those of the state and the head of state – controlling information, but also the energy as well as the foreign affairs of the country, and hence relations with global enterprises and the market; (b) the community sector, reconstructing group existence, and hence the social, which had been obliterated and overwhelmed by the long predominance of an economy producing material goods, as well as by abuses of state power; and (c) the competitive sector or level, given over to competition between individuals, enabling their selection in a constant struggle for places and posts in the hierarchy.

All in all, this report proposed a triadic or ternary (three-level) model of society, whereas other authors (André Gorz, etc.) made do with a bi-partite division (the dual society). Unwittingly, the authors of these various texts introduced the 'homogeneity–fragmentation–hierarchy' schema into their conception of things, while spontaneously trying to limit its damage. For other authors, information technology will lead to a sort of cultural revolution, rather than a political and social mutation. Some go so far as to claim that the state will accept not being the exclusive or dominant actor in the social game, withdrawing in favour of other, well-informed actors; and, in this fashion, will even wither away. These models are based on the hypothesis of a society constructed exclusively on the basis of positive knowledge, therewith implying the death of lived experience, or at least its reduction to the sign effects of information technology.

We must therefore examine these theories closely, and discover whether it is possible to end up in the total administration of daily life through the totalizing action of information technology; the total transparency of the entire society with the end of opacity in lived experience; the reduction of the activity of knowing to information technology; and so on.

(a) *Against unitary theory*

With information technology, must we not very clearly distinguish the scientific theory first of all, the technological applications next, and finally the marketing of appliances, their entry into social practice and their introduction into everyday life?

Scientifically, information is a quantity. It is measured. It is defined by a *cost*: how many signs must be used to transmit a message or a series of messages? How many operations are required to discover in a mass of objects the one corresponding to certain features that have been identified in advance? And so on. This yields a probability and can be expressed by a logarithmic function: H (unit of information, the Hartley) = Σ pi Log $2\frac{1}{pi}$, where pi refers to a probability of occurrence, that of an order of signs to the nth message. The quantity H is cancelled in a first borderline case, where all the messages are known in advance and are repeated purely and simply. Then redundancy, the inverse of H $\left(\frac{1}{H}\right)$, is infinite. This same quantity – information – is maximal when there exist *n* messages that are completely different and, in addition, equally probable (H = Log N). Then redundancy is minimal.

First comment: in the case of major redundancy, there is perfect intelligibility. It has already been noted that information theory demonstrates the identity of the intelligible and the redundant. This is of the utmost importance for understanding daily life and the role of repetition in the seeming clarity of the everyday. Redundancy eliminates the noise mixed up in the message; as for information, it involves surprise, and hence disorder. No differences would amount to dullness. By contrast, excessive difference kills meaning by preventing understanding – that is to say, decoding. Yet complete application of a code involves repetition in perfect intelligibility and, consequently, utter monotony.

A second, no less important comment: the mathematical formula above corresponds to that of energy and its dissipation – that is to say, to the theory of entropy. Information theory developed as thermodynamics. Since information comprises a disorder that involves a certain order, a dissipation (loss) of informational energy occurs through increased entropy. This seems to summon up a 'negative entropy' – that is to say, instants in which energy is revived and possibilities spring up – against the tendency to diminution. We glimpse a *dialectic* of information technology that envelops its *logic* – that is to say, identity, the repetitive, the redundant, the intelligible – by subjecting it to the clash between order and disorder. This aspect seems to have escaped the ideologues who graft their interpretations on to scientific theory and logic alone. Equally, we catch sight of a paradox of information ideology: basing a social order, and constructing a coherent model, on a theory that is in fact a theory of disorder. According to the proposed models, whence derive the sources of the disorder without which information technology cannot operate, albeit with a risk of dissipation?

The theory has no right to want and claim to be unitary – that is to say, to cover the whole field of information, practice included. In the transition from mathematical theory to technologies, we have a first discontinuity. Technological application requires the construction of apparatuses, some of them material (channels, transmitters, receivers), others abstract (conventions, codes and decodes, systems). Software is distinct from hardware. In the transition from technological development to social use, to the production and marketing of hardware, we have a further discontinuity.

The press, whether specialist or not, has for some years now been full of descriptions of technical innovations: microprocessors, optical fibres, networks, and so on. Consequently, it is pointless to dwell at length on equipment and techniques. It is sufficient to distinguish between three levels: science, with an implicit or explicit logic; technological applications – that is to say, hardware; and social practice in its various forms – the treatment of information, software and its extensions – which sets out a different problematic. Any theory that eliminates these discontinuities becomes ideology. Moreover, there is no question of some absolute separation shielding practice from certain implications of the theory – in particular, the entropy of informational energy and the dissipation of information. As for the extension of information theory to other domains (notably biology), the same comments apply. A theory based on information that aims to be general, on the model of classical philosophies, blithely crosses frontiers and borders that are in fact clearly marked out. It may be brilliant, but any such endeavour is bound to misfire.

(b) *Information is a product*

This product derives from a determinate productive activity, whose result is consumed and disappears in the act of consumption. The question: 'Does such a product abolish the difference between use-value and exchange-value? Does it inaugurate the reign of exchange in the pure state, without any material movement? Or, on the contrary, does it re-establish use-value?' – this question poses the issue of information as a commodity that is bought and sold. Before we examine it, there is another question. The confusion between producer and creator, between creation and production, has already entailed many illusions and done a great deal of harm, especially in the domains of art and aesthetics. Some people regard the production of information as creation, conferring on it a privilege that is not warranted by critical analysis.

Historically, communication in general and information in particular possessed an undeniable creative capacity. Bold navigators, explorers, discoverers, including plunderers and pirates, established connections between places and peoples that were oblivious of one another's existence. They did not 'transform' the world; they created it. Setting out from separate sites, they literally constructed the world by connecting them, constituting networks of maritime or terrestrial routes; they arrived at the world market. As we know, this world market has gone through two stages: the first predated industrial capitalism; the second came after it.

In this creative activity by means of communication, it was hard to distinguish violent pillaging and warlike enterprises of conquest from the peaceful exchange of goods – that is to say, products that were initially agricultural and artisanal, and subsequently industrial. The violence was only temporary; its enduring mark and effects are to be found in the networks. The result, however, was that exchange was a male preserve. Women were for a long time part of the goods, rather than agents in this creation, which initially unfolded at the level of inland seas – the Mediterranean and China seas – and then on an oceanic scale, before ending up as a planetary phenomenon. The violent, warlike form of relations came to terms with the logical form of exchange – the world of commodities – despite their opposite meanings; and possibly still does. Men stamped the world thereby created with their own imprint, even though reason – that of communication and exchange – was indifferent to violence, sex and location as such. Without their knowing it, through a mixture of struggles and logic, genetically and historically, warriors developed a relationship (to being? to the world? to nothingness?) in which bold, often brutal initiative, capable of the best and the worst, the supernatural and the humdrum, was allotted to them.

From navigation on seas and rivers, via railways and air transport, to the modern media, has the creative capacity of communication and information increased? There is no question that its productive capacity is growing. Yet it is as if production and creation varied inversely, the one declining while the other expands. Railways introduced more changes and novelties than motorways. This comes down to saying – a by now commonplace observation – that growth and development do not coincide. The product tends to predominate – not without environmental damage, as people say. Creation goes on declining and, in imperialism, production rediscovers its link with violence.

During this enormous lapse of time, extending from the first acts of exchange to modern industrialization and urbanization in a transnational framework, local life, rooted and confined to one spot, is preserved and affirmed in ignorance of the global, which is constituted elsewhere. The same applies to the everyday.

During this time, the creative capacity of communication and information is slowly but surely exhausted. With each new means of communication and information – for example, electricity (the 'electricity fairy!', 'electrification plus soviets!'), and then the telephone, radio, television – people anticipate miracles: the transfiguration of daily life. As if it could come from a means or medium. These means or media can only transmit what existed prior to the mediating operation, or what occurs outside it. Today, communication *reflects* – nothing more, nothing less. What was the result of the multiplication of these means in ever more complex forms? Rather than a metamorphosis of daily life, what occurred was, on the contrary, the installation of daily life as such, determined, isolated, and then programmed. There ensued a privatization of the public and a publicizing of the private, in a constant exchange that mixes them without uniting them and separates them without discriminating between them; and this is still going on.

Should we deny all practical change as the media – that is, communications and information – have multiplied? Certainly not. But that is not the point. The issue is different: 'What is the meaning of this multiplication, this abundance of goods which are no longer material, and claim to be substitutes for traditional spirituality? Does it not in fact risk resulting in the destruction of meaning by signs? Where is it leading, to what new order? But whence will this new order originate? From what and from whom?'

McLuhan's thesis about the creative role of communications can be upheld as far as the oldest forms of communication are concerned – for example, navigation, the phonetic alphabet and printing. When it comes to recent products – the telephone or the car – it evokes very strong reservations indeed. To claim that the creative capacity of communications and information increases with their abundance is (a) a postulate; (b) which is contradicted by the history of time, space and social practice; (c) which is equally contradicted by the principle of the dissipation of energy, whether we are talking about heavy energies or subtle energies like information energy. To justify this facilely optimistic and rationalist thesis today, one would have to demonstrate the springing up in the modern world of possibilities that tend towards their own realization. Yet what we actually observe is that the increasing intensity of communications harbours the reinforcement of daily life, its consolidation and confinement. It also harbours a mounting danger of catastrophe. Is it not demagogic to support this thesis today? Does it not involve negating the negative such as it appears and manifests itself in society?

Information is produced. It is consumed. Information technology confirms the outmoded character of the classical Marxist contrast between base and superstructure. Information is not – or not merely – a superstructure, since it is an – exchangeable – product of certain relations of production. What was regarded as superstructural, like space and time, forms part of production, because it is a product that is bought and sold.

Whence the question: 'Who produces information? How? For whom? And who consumes it?' This form of production is not exempt from the classical theses. On the contrary: it extends them. It involves labour and an organization of labour, production costs, an organic composition of capital, a surplus-value – that is to say, profits for those who are in charge of production. Nevertheless, it may be that the production and consumption of information deviates somewhat from certain classical rules or laws, disrupting them. Hardware, software, firmware – these do not have the same appearance. The processing of information differs from its production, yet forms part of it; the initial producer can inscribe it in its computerized activity – something IBM in particular does. As for databases, what precisely is their function and their place? To a certain extent, they are independent of information production, yet they are indispensable to it. Can they be counted on to operate in favour of a democratic management of information technology? Perhaps. But here another danger arises – the state monopoly of data, with the related risk of a global monopoly of information in a transnational system consolidated by this national monopoly. As a source of information, the database is, moreover, proximate to daily life. The consumption of information also occurs in the everyday. Enormous networks, channels, circuits thus start out from daily life, pass through various levels to the planetary (by means of satellites), and then return towards daily life. Whence problems which, some people maintain, have already been solved by technique or the economic and political powers; while others assert that solutions are still pending on account of their complexity, so that it is not too late to intervene.

Produced and consumed, information is sold and bought. It is therefore a commodity. Any commodity? No. It is not material; as we know, it possesses the peculiar characteristic of causing all other commodities to be bought and sold. This has always been the case – that is to say, since the existence of the exchange of marketable goods outside the gift and barter systems. It has always been necessary to know where a particular product is in order to go and find it, transport it, and finally hand it over in return for a determinable sum of money; and that knowledge derives from communication and information.

Information has always been as essential to exchange and markets as money and the quantification of products. Yet for many centuries, information as such did not appear on the market. Its appearance has a retroactive effect: it brings out the importance of information, as well as networks, channels and circuits, in the past. What is novel about the contemporary world is that there is a world market in information, which positively 'drives' the other markets, through advertising, propaganda, the transmission of positive knowledge, and so on. Is not information, the supreme commodity, also the ultimate commodity? Does it not complete the great cycle of the commodity, its extraordinary expansion – in short, the realization of the world of commodities in that of the mode of production, in the global? There are grounds for thinking so.

Far from ushering in a new mode of production, information technology perfects the existing mode of production – capitalism and its world market – which exerts such pressure on 'socialism' that the latter struggles to escape it. In this way, the extraordinary shift – already referred to – of the concrete towards the abstract, and their combination in the abstract–concrete, is rounded off. This way of looking at things makes sense of the enormous circuit that goes from daily life to daily life via the global. The complexity of the world market, which is part of information technology because the latter implies it and marks it out, needs no further emphasis (a market in finished products, but also instruments of production, techniques, capital, energy, labour, signs and symbols, art works and, finally, information, which envelops the totality and constitutes it as global). Complexity does not betoken coherence and cohesion. Although it is aimed for, coherence is not thereby realized. Information technology can neither resolve nor cancel contradictions: it can only express them – or disguise them. The power of the world market does not suppress all resistance – the resistance of a number of countries, particularly the socialist countries – or inequalities, or conflicts between strategies. Hence this market is not established, stable, coherent, even though it possesses an internal, highly potent logic – that of the commodity as a system of equivalents. It tends to homogenize the world, and at the same time to fragment it, since it reflects the diverse origins and provenance of products, including information. As we know, homogeneity no more abolishes fragmentation than aiming for coherence suppresses contradictions.

If is true that information technology presses the commodity to a conclusion, if it perfects and completes the world of commodities, what emerges from this is not something new. On the contrary: a world is coming to an end, in a slow but unyielding process. How can we get out of it? The crisis, as they say, is shaking the base and foundations as much as the superstructures. Hence the demand for something new, an inventive, radical opening: in particular, a different form of growth, intimately bound up with development.

(c) *The Information Ideology*

This ideology presents information in various ways that share the following feature: they do not advertise themselves as ideological, but as observations or positive knowledge. They also have this in common: they absolutize a feature of the 'real', rather than relativizing it and situating it. Here as elsewhere, the operation which constructs ideology, and differs from those that launch, transmit or seek to realize it in practice, consists in the following: an individual or collective *subject* that is more or less uncertain of itself manages to raise an aspect or element of reality or intelligence to the status of definitive truth via discourse. This what happened with the historical, the economic, the political, structure, language, the imaginary, and so on. This operation is reproduced today with information. Thus, the irruption of the supreme commodity has been presented as an adventure, or even as the great 'human adventure', giving this product a romantic halo. We cannot fail to notice that around us, in persistent modernism, other – more adventurous – adventures are indicated: the exploration and exploitation of oceans, genetic engineering and the results of biology, energy problems, and so on. The notion of adventure can be seductive. But in the case of information, and even in the various other instances, it does not withstand examination. How can we ignore the fact that the economic powers (firms) and political powers (states) reserve the ocean depths for themselves, disputing them; that they explore space for the purpose of appropriating it; and that the same is true of information? This ancient Odyssean image – the adventure – can be demagogically exploited. Does it have a meaning? Yes: it applies to the whole human race which, having become planetary and global, does not know where it is headed and risks going where it has no wish to go – that is to say, towards the abyss.

Not only does information ideology not present itself as ideology, but it proposes either to put an end to ideologies or to transfer the ideological function to information apparatuses, including the production and diffusion of positive knowledge, which was formerly the prerogative of schools and universities. The reduction of positive knowledge to information would have consequences: the end of critical and conceptual thinking, and hence the end of all thinking, or its departure to take refuge in illegality and violence. All the more so given that information apparatuses are in great danger of being administratively and institutionally controlled either by the national state, or by transnational forces which would use this supplementary means to consolidate their order. Not only would positive knowledge be reduced to recorded and memorized facts, but everything concerning the political and politics would go through the channels of official information. This would create the greatest difficulties for any action independent of established power, and possibly result in the disappearance of all counter-power. Contradictions at this level (i.e. between states and firms) offer a last chance in a world that aims for coherence and stability, but falls short of them. Information ideology masks the dangers and the opportunities alike. Politics itself would be replaced by the discourse and ideology of the 'competent' – that is to say, technicians who can produce information and technocrats who give them their orders. This tendency, which can already be observed, forms part of the crisis; it extends it, beyond ethical values and social norms, to political institutions and discourses. It might be thought that it favours the personalization of 'kingly' forms of power, as well as appeals for a new consensus around this personalized power. The paramount danger is this: the unchecked reinforcement of the state and its multiple capacities – in particular, that of seizing daily life in its organs of prehension and repressive comprehension.

Information ideology possesses the dubious merit of prophetically heralding the new society: post-industrial, post-capitalist and even post-socialist. Pre-industrial society was supposedly constituted regionally and territorially – that is to say, as is well known, around energy sources and raw materials. Industrial society proper was supposedly organized around the exploitation of energy forms freed from territorial constraints (electrical energy). As for post-industrial society, it is supposedly already being structured around information that is abstract, yet global and universal.[6]

This technological and technocratic utopia makes light of contradictions, old or new. It is true that recent technologies deploy and strengthen communication networks at the global level; and these thus tend to constitute a single network through the interconnection of national and regional networks, integrating multiple services. But at the same time, such globalization diversifies the network thereby constituted, which depends on sources, data banks, and so on.

Let us avoid making a Gothic novel, as well as a romance, out of information technology.[7] Information ideologues assert that society and the social are being transformed, and that a qualitative leap is about to occur. They also believe that information technology is necessary and sufficient to establish new norms and values. Which ones? The end of opacity and impenetrability – and hence transparency! If we credit these ideologues, the information society will finally realize the Truth. Not in the manner of the philosophers, as thought and abstract system, but as reality and practical system. No more secrecy! Anything that happens, anything that supervenes, will immediately reverberate in the totality with all its details. In short, a universal game of mirrors, finally materialized! An effect of signs, finally totalized! No more shadows, no more dark corners or recesses in this pristine practice. This would be tantamount to the realization of philosophy – not by the working class and revolution, as Marx believed, but through technology. Information, together with its extensions, would lead by the shortest route to a fully planned society, in which the centre would constantly receive messages from each base cell, with the result that culture and information, positively identified, possessing the same structure, would render each individual fully conscious. Of what? Of general constraints![8] Hence we are dealing not only – or not so much – with a technocratic utopia or ideology, but with a scientistic mythology – a paradox, what is more, with the myth of an electronic Agora and the disturbing project of a technological extension of the 'audit' intended for the internal control of workshops, but capable of being extended to political and police control of spaces much vaster than the enterprise ...

These ideologues do not think that they are interpreting the techniques, but that they are estimating them objectively. They refuse to concede that they are presenting, or representing, a tendentious political project. To them, the project seems to follow logically from the technology. Is not technologizing the social and political, as opposed to socializing and politicizing technology, a choice and a decision? A political standpoint that presents itself as objective meaning? This line of questioning does not resolve the problem, but it does preclude accepting as a solution utterances that formulate the problem by distorting it, concealing the contradictions involved.

Those who flaunt the technicist perspective allow space and a function for base cells, for micro-societies and micro-decisions – in other words, for daily life. They simultaneously take it into account and abolish it. Information technology can reduce both knowledge and spontaneity. In this perspective, knowing no longer involves using concepts, but simply receiving and memorizing information. The concept is blurred – the concept of knowledge and knowledge by means of concepts. To all intents and purposes, concepts disappear in the face of the facts. Here we recognize a venerable philosophical debate being peremptorily resolved and terminated.

Yet information is lost. How is this dissipation to be resisted, if not by a project and an idea of knowledge? Take, for example, the affirmation of identity: it proclaims its persistence, its perseverance in being, its resistance to decline and difference alike. In this way, identity becomes abstract, fictive, unreal; in this way, it declines ...

The paradoxes, aporias and problems of information ideology are proliferating. If we accept the distinction between activity that produces material goods and activity that produces non-material goods, we may conclude that the second sector is bound to grow more rapidly than the first. Yet it tends thereby to choke and even paralyse it. Some theoreticians – and not the least prominent – have reached the point of forecasting a crisis of information technology, in a society that is already in a critical condition, and from which the ideology in question promised an escape. It is argued that the capacity of useful labour, producing material goods, will decline once the energy dissipated in the production of material goods rises to half of the power that is available and consumed globally. Hence there is a threshold.[9] It is true that informational energy is a subtle energy, analogous to nervous energy in comparison with the heavy energy of the muscles. But is there no such thing as nervous fatigue? Exhaustion and a physiological threshold in organisms?

This conjures up the possibility of a confrontation between the socio-political and the physiological or organic. According to contemporary biology, relational characteristics – that is to say, relative to the *other*, not simply to an impersonal environment – polarize living organisms and define the organic. So that pleasure and desire enter into the genetic programme, together with the many indices and signs of sexuality: olfactory, auditory, visual. Is there not a conflictual, dynamic relationship between these three terms: the rational, the relational or positional, the informational – a relationship that cannot be reduced to quantification?

It is nevertheless the case that information ideologues take the sum of techniques, apparatuses and applications for a unitary, objective knowledge, for an activity capable of affecting the whole of reality. They make information the higher form of positive knowledge, destined to absorb the lower forms. Yet for theory and knowledge, information technology can today be regarded solely as an element and a moment of the activity of knowledge, as yet undeveloped. Substituted for knowledge, information deletes thought and reduces positive knowledge to that which is amassed, accumulated, memorized without gaps, outside of lived experience. The negative disappears in a perfect positivity. Information ideology – or, rather, idealism, dressed up as positive knowledge and even technological materialism on occasion – acts as a factor of dislocation in the activity of knowledge, in the political, and in daily life.

For centuries, progress in communications and information has unquestionably favoured central power and central political control; this forms part of the lowering of creative capacity to which reference has already been made. What is at stake in computerization is determined thus. The die is not cast, but the dice are rolling on a planetary cloth. In France there are imminent dangers. The machinery of information apparatuses tends to reproduce the characteristics of the French political apparatus; it is statist and centralized.[10]

(d) *Introversion*

Computerized daily life risks assuming a form that certain ideologues find interesting and seductive: the individual atom or family molecule inside a bubble where the messages sent and received intersect. Users, who have lost the dignity of citizens now that they figure socially only as parties to services, would thus lose the social itself, and sociability. This would no longer be the existential isolation of the old individualism, but a solitude all the more profound for being overwhelmed by messages. With all services at its disposal, ultimately, this individual atom or family molecule would no longer need to stir. Those analysts who have not renounced critical thinking have drawn attention to this danger. Some people have even looked to the state to ward it off. A pure dream: it is very difficult for state power not to favour a tendency that leaves the field open for it. What state and political authority can conceive of their own dissolution, and organize the conditions for it? State intervention inevitably drives 'users' to withdraw into their shells. Do not shells of this kind abandon individuals to anxiety, to an anguish bombarded by hubbub? Information ideologues hope that as long as the shell is filled with information, the individual will feel at home in it. Without any evidence, to say the least.

As for hopes for a reconstruction of a three-term unity – 'space–time–labour' – by means of information, they belong to abstract utopianism. Home-based, remote-controlled labour consummates the separation and fragmentation that are already under way. Rather than being surmounted, the schema 'homogeneity–fragmentation–hierarchization' will get worse. Once, private life eluded the social. The new privatization will be invaded by the outside while paradoxically losing all capacity for externalization.

People talk about a new society. Would it not be more accurate to fear a new state, founded on the political use of information, ruling over a population enclosed in bubbles it has inflated, and in such a way that each mouth believes its bubble comes out of it?

Control of information will come neither from excessive centralization, a unitary structure ruling over the whole of society; nor from excessive decentralization, issuing in fragmentation and formlessness. It requires a project for society, avoiding facile solutions the most likely of which, alas, can already be glimpsed: centralized power negotiating a compromise with global enterprises. Paradoxically, control of information involves an intensification of surprise effects and a reduction in redundancy, without succumbing to disorder. Yet such effects can come only from below – on condition, moreover, that the active base does not disrupt the network. In the relatively near future, it is possible to imagine everyone ordering what they want, or being able to pay for things, without having to step outside. Will women prefer to go to the market or into shops, rather than tapping away at home on a keyboard? Possibly yes, possibly no: it is a decision for those at the base.

So there are better things to do than disconnecting informational structures into a multiplicity of levels, nets, cells. This thesis, which remains technocratic, is well intentioned and has the merit of technically demonstrating the advantages of a differential organization of space and time. In the case of a crash or attack, differentiated networks can be substituted for one another. The differentiated structure foreseen by technicians does not extend to sanctioning the *autonomous* operation of partial centres; above all, it does not give the floor to those at the base. Hence it does not result in the introduction of *self-management* into information technology. These more flexible schemas foresee counter-powers, but only in order to 'balance' the real powers and decision-making centres without disturbing them. The question posed cannot be resolved solely by means of technique; it is *political*, and will remain so. In society as in art, technique is not an end but a means. A fundamental commonplace: everything depends on the way in which technique is used, who uses it, and for whom. Controlling information, if that is possible, requires accepting that the base – alveolus or cell – has an active life, an existence and a social form, and hence a capacity for self-determination. Here we re-encounter the general problematic of self-management, rendered somewhat more complex. The relations of self-managed units, enterprises or territories, are already in conflict with the market and the state. These conflictual relations interfere with the relations of these units to information technology. Will self-management be realized and actualized by acquiring a content and meaning in information technology? Or will technological and political pressures reduce self-management to a sham? That is the question. The coherence of human groups, such as the sociologist habitually defines them, is merely a fiction, except possibly in the case of a pressure group. In general, a social group has a concrete existence only if it seeks to control its conditions of existence, of living and surviving, and succeeds in so doing. This is how self-management is defined.

We have reached the stage of turning ideological definitions of information technology back round against them: information does not possess the quality, the capacity, of *conferring meaning* on that which does not possess it; or of restoring it to that which has lost it. On the contrary: information technology could well complete the destruction of meaning, by replacing value by signs, the totality by the combinatory, the living word by the message (in classical terms, the spirit by the letter). With the end of meaning, nothing would have meaning – information no more than anything else. (Would there still be anything else?) Where might a restoration, a rebounding, of meaning come from?

Information can no more create situations than it can create meaning. It can only transmit what is said about situations; it simulates or dissimulates situations, with their conflicts. From the standpoint of information itself, it is impossible not to call upon a source or resource, an eruption of surprises, a social negative entropy, violent or pacifying, innovative and creative. This capacity is discovered in the self-management, the self-determination, of effective centres of power, partially or utterly transgressing the order of power. Here alone, thought and the desire to shatter codes and create new codes coincide. Foundational violence? No, creative transgression, beyond transitions, means and averages, media, modes and models.

Daily life sometimes seems like the thing of substance that prevents forms from vanishing into pure abstraction, approximating nothingness; and sometimes like the place from which the content might arise that will transform forms, including the supreme form: information.

Only daily life can attach to the sites of production and consumption what unites them, and yet tends to become detached from them: information. Hence we are dealing not with a duality, a binary system, or bi-polarity, but with a triadic relationship: production–creation–information.

Notes

1. See André Gorz, *Farewell to the Working Class*, trans. Michael Sonenscher, Pluto Press, London 1982; René Lourau, *Le Lapsus des intellectuels*, Paris 1981, esp. pp. 244 ff.

2. See Jean-Pierre Faye, *Langages totalitaires*, Herman, Paris 1973, pp. 446 ff; Lourau, *Le Lapsus des intellectuels*.

3. See, *inter alia*, G. Faye, *Le Système à tuer les peuples*, Éditions Copernic, Paris 1981.

4. See Marc Sautet, *Nietzsche et la Commune*, Le Sycomore, Paris 1981.

5. See Jean Baudrillard, *For a Critique of the Political Economy of the Sign*, trans. Charles Levin, Telos Press, St. Louis, MO 1981.

6. See John McHale, *The Changing Information Environment*, Elek, London 1976.

7. See Pierre Grémion and Haroun Gamous, *L'Ordinateur au pouvoir*, Éditions du Seuil, Paris 1978.

8. See Simon Nora and Alain Minc, *The Computerization of Society: A Report to the President of France*, MIT Press, London 1980.

9. See the works of Ilya Prigogine, Nobel Prize winner in 1977.

10. See the CORDES Report to the Commissariat du plan, 1978, pp. 147–8.

CONCLUSION

Results and Prospects

1 The Middle Classes

Marx forecast their dissolution, even their disappearance, with the polar system of proletariat and bourgeoisie and the essential contradiction between the two. This simplification bears a date; it marks a phase in Marx's thinking regarded dynamically, as intellectual activity and research, not as a finished theory and system. At the end of what is an unfinished work, *Capital*, Marx was obliged to reconsider the propositions he had previously advanced, in the light of a comprehensive analysis of the mode of production and society dominated by capital and the bourgeoisie. The surviving drafts indicate that Marx did not stick with a binary opposition, but reinstated the triadic character of his analysis; he included land, ground rent and agrarian questions in a three-term totality: land–capital–labour. He was likewise obliged to reinstate trade and the bureaucracy – that is to say, the functions of realization and distribution of surplus-value. In Marx, society as we perceive it appeared in all its complexity – minus, obviously, the modalities of social and political practice that Marx could not possibly have foreseen in his day (for example, the 'welfare state' with its networks of redistribution, income transfers, direct or disguised subsidies): practices that were grafted on to Keynesianism, a diversion of Marxism.

It is nevertheless the case that, on this important point, Hegel was right and Marx was wrong. For a historical period whose duration cannot be predicted, but whose end we can possibly sense today, the state has had its social basis in the middle classes, not in the working class. As a result, it has not withered away, as Marx forecast, but, rather, been consolidated. Sometimes it is erected on a pre-existing middle class; sometimes it produces or generates middle classes, bureaucracy and technocracy – and this often under the guise of democracy, even of the socialization of national life and society as a whole.

We can just as easily say *the* middle class as the middle class*es*. In fact, this socio-economic formation evinces a great diversity of standards of living, lifestyles, integration or non-integration into productive activities and institutions. The technostructure that forms part of the upper middle classes does not mix with the groups responsible for transmitting positive knowledge, or with lower-level technicians. For some years now, there has been a new middle class, comprising technicians and technocrats, without this entailing the disappearance of the old middle class composed of doctors, lawyers, and members of the liberal professions. However, there is a certain homogeneity to the layers situated between the summit and the base of society, allowing us to talk about the middle class.

The numerical expansion of these layers and this class occurs in tandem with economic growth in the capitalist mode of production, and also in socialism. This increase has been particularly marked in the United States. People have even wanted to base a new form of society on the middle classes: values, norms, lifestyles, ethics, aesthetics. Before embarking on a critique of this hypothesis, we should recall how fluid class boundaries are becoming. The most comfortably off section of the middle classes – senior managerial staff – is closely adjacent to the 'managers' and the *grande bourgeoisie*, whereas a gulf separates them from the *haute bourgeoisie*, or the directors of global enterprises. As for junior managerial staff – that is to say, junior technicians – this stratum is scarcely distinguishable from what Lenin pejoratively dubbed the 'labour aristocracy' (wrongly, since this layer or stratum would appear to be both robust and capable of political initiatives).

The numerical rise of the middle classes enables us to understand many facts and phenomena at all levels. In effect, we are faced with a society in which the middle classes are *ideologically predominant* under the *hegemony* of big capital. The result, in particular, is the consolidation of the state and the innovations bound up with it: the fact that, from a certain date onwards, the administrators of society have banked on the domestic market; the more or less successful attempts to incorporate the unions into existing institutions; the difficulties and divisions within the working class; the introduction of new techniques; and so on. People have questioned whether 'passive revolutions' in the Gramscian sense do not derive from the salience of the middle classes, which are indeed passive, objects of politics and not active subjects – which would avoid imputing responsibility to the passivity of the working class. The allegedly 'revolutionary' transfer to the state of activities that previously fell to the dominant class – in particular, supervision of the conditions of surplus-value, accumulation, in short, growth – assumes a support. The state that benefits from this transfer has been able to find such a support only among the middle classes. The thesis, widespread in the United States, of a cultural revolution via the agency of the middle classes does not stand up. Only the existence of the middle classes makes it possible for the welfare state to elevate itself above society; this state finds its resources, its personnel, its passive 'subjects', in its social base. Consequently, it can lay claim to the virtues appropriate to active 'subjects': competence, vigour, honest administration, and so on. That said, these strata and classes possess no creative capacity; they cannot institute either forms or values; consuming the products of the culture industry, they are incapable of creating a culture, still less a civilization worthy of the name; they mark out the road to decline. Whence some major malaises: they serve as an effective tool for barring the way to the working class, which they stifle even as the strategy of power is fragmenting it. They propose or impose *models* of all sorts, political as well as cultural. Mystificatory neoliberalism, which concealed wide-ranging economico-political operations, was enough to satisfy a significant section of the middle classes.

Can it last? No. To present this 'order' as definite or definitive, to believe that classes are being reabsorbed into strata, is sheer mystification. The middle classes possess no unifying principle, although they feature in the general homogeneity. They are divided. Some individuals and groups tend towards the Right, and sometimes towards right-wing extremism; others tend to the Left, even to ultra-leftism. Moreover, they have not been immune from attacks by the state-political power they helped to organize. In France, for example, this power has attempted to make it impossible for universities to intervene politically. But we do not have the space here for a closer study of these middle layers, or their relations with the state and society. It must suffice to consider them in the light of the everyday.

It is within the middle classes – in the middle of this middle – that modern daily life is constituted and established. This is where it becomes a model; starting from this site, it is diffused upwards and downwards. Formerly, modes and models derived from the aristocracy or the *grande bourgeoisie* in its *belle époque*. In the course of what are called modern times, the middle imposes its law. It goes without saying that this law has not been generalized, and that it cannot achieve equivalent universality to the historical compromise between a declining aristocracy and rising bourgeoisie in the eighteenth century. Various categories are exempt from the models (cultural and practical) generated within the middle class: the *haute bourgeoisie*, the establishment at a transnational level, the jet set that moves from palace to palace or lives on yachts – and, on the other hand, the 'lower class', which does not even have access to the everyday. So that we have had to distinguish infra- and supra-daily life from daily life itself. This situates it. The 'lower' and the 'upper' class are in a condition of 'survival', but not in the same way: sub-life for the former, hyper-life for the latter. As a model or mode of consumption (the term mode being construed in its twin sense of irresistible fad and way of being), but also as insertion and integration into the social, daily life thus has a highly determinate place of origin and formation. Together with its modalities: domestic appliances, the use of space and time, computer equipment, the car or cars. This set defines not a style of living but a lifestyle. The term 'style' refers to an aesthetic or ethical bearing in which the middle classes are precisely lacking. As for lifestyle, it is easily defined: it is the everyday itself. The predominance of the middle classes has repercussions in what is called culture – that is to say, ethics and aesthetics. Incapable of creating new values, the middle classes create the opposition between conformism and non-conformism. Ethics is confused with conformism, while aesthetics is inflected towards non-conformism.

Technological illusions, mystifications and utopias are attributable to the predominance of the middle classes in conditions of capitalist hegemony. Among them is the illusion that daily life being established in and through positive knowledge involves the death of lived experience: an insignificant fact. This illusion is exploited in all sorts of ways by power and information technology alike. How many people think themselves very human because they tell others how they should live, from menus to clothing, from housing to educating children! As if a society in which it is necessary to prescribe and describe the daily life that it institutes does not condemn itself solely by virtue of this fact. The myth of transparency and its ideology end thus: the substitution of a melancholy science for lived experience and a gay science; the administration of daily life according to models, modes and modalities that are mimetically connected.

These rather caustic observations do not entail rejection and condemnation of everything originating in the middle classes. Far from it. Such a rejection carries the mark of sectarianism. Women's movements originate among neither workers nor the bourgeoisie. Evidently reformist, their demands transform neither the everyday, nor the mode of production; they are, for example, content to improve the division of labour at the level of daily life.

The fact that the most comfortably off middle class seeks to reoccupy the centre of large towns does not militate against centrality and the renovation of the centres. It simply demonstrates that those concerned, being sensible folk, appreciate that everyday life is more pleasant in towns, for all their drawbacks, than in isolated outskirts. For a long time, who did not desire a country house or residence? The model and mode once again came from a section of the middle classes, the measures taken by the political authorities favouring their expansion. Disillusionment followed. Urban reconstruction – centres and monuments – can stimulate a new fashion. It is only a pity that workers abandoned positions they once occupied in certain major towns and cities without much resistance. In this respect, the case of Paris is exemplary. Who was responsible for the withdrawal? This is not the place to answer that question.

Thus, in the twentieth century, the middle classes provided the site where the everyday and its models took shape, but also protest and contestation, as well as rather naive attempts to transform and transfigure things that were becoming established: modes of fiction, of the supernatural, the surreal, the imaginary, modernism, and so on. Here too arose the mystification of a cultural revolution by the middle classes and their ways of life, destined in this novelistic fiction to abolish classes by absorbing the various categories of workers. This fiction is becoming ideology in the United States, and could spread to Europe. The Marxist current of thought has not challenged it successfully, for it continues to bank on the working class as if its existence as a class and a political subject were self-evident.

To talk about models and modes is also to talk about imitation. Mimesis rules, but a model is accepted only when people feel that it reflects what is most profound about them, and hence when it is 'freely' accepted.

The critique of daily life exposes this situation. It demonstrates that with the predominance of the middle classes everything becomes illusory certainty and problematic. The word 'problem' features in an incalculable number of expressions. And what a lot of researchers there are! And research! People search and search without finding anything very much. Rather than *oeuvres*, we have essays, attempts, cross-references, overtures. The word 'problem' is becoming intolerable, yet how is it to be avoided? How, getting through to the end of the night, can we cross the problem zone that is nothing but a symptom of total crisis?

Are the innovations in and through the middle classes being consolidated? This is a difficult question to answer. The modes and models of consumption? They quickly become obsolescent; a kind of febrile pseudo-dynamic, visible in advertising campaigns, carries them off: there are always new things, and better things, for doing the same thing.

The middle strata and classes lack substance. They are threatened with dislocation and disintegration. Their political parties cannot guarantee or restore their cohesion. The elitism to which they give rise contrasts with the profound stupidity of short-sighted people who believe they have sound judgement and good taste and are full of good sense, when in fact they possess only a meagre know-how, and the corollary of their distinction is vulgarity.

2 The Abstract–Concrete and the Fictitious–Real

A mode of social existence has gradually emerged, confirming other studies: the fictitious–real and the abstract–concrete. The mode of production involves and entails a mode of existence. The real? It exists; yet it no longer corresponds to the classical notion: something solid, being, independent of all subjectivity, all mental or social activity. This object is there. Its place depends on a choice, a decision. Its reality likewise, since it is the result of a production whose function, form, structure, and even material have been predetermined. Its social objectivity has nothing in common with the objectivity of the *things* of nature, which served as a model for philosophers. The reality of the product should be distinguished from the reality attributed to 'things', but it is difficult to differentiate it. Assigned a signification connected with a use, the produced object enters into multiple networks: it passes through the market, an intermediate but important stage. It is then that it is on the verge of being absorbed into language and signs, without this derealizing absorption being accomplished and 'realized'. The produced object thus crosses through abstraction, never vanishes into it, and yet never quits it. The abstract is not the duplicate of something concrete, but the abstract and the concrete are inseparable, and their unity makes up the everyday. Critical analysis of daily life is thus situated in a region that is difficult to grasp and express. The concrete existence of objects through the abstract assimilates them to abstract idealities that lead to practical, concrete actions: law, right, the accord between wills promoted to the title of contract, and so on. Thus, the abstract–concrete and the fictitious–real, in their ambiguity and duality, extend from simple products to major incarnations of positive knowledge, possessions and power; from humble babbling to higher brain activity, to the empire of signs and the information with which this empire ends. In the course of this enormous deployment, there is no rupture or discontinuity. From daily life to the state, the mode of existence does not alter fundamentally. Yet the various degrees of this deployment do not tally. They conceal one another. Daily life masks the state level while referring the reflective consciousness to it. Likewise, security measures, which are simultaneously fictitious and real, refer to menaces that are no less fictitious and no less real. Daily life conceals and contains the state, but the two taken together mask the tragic element they contain. In this way, daily life enters into the system of equivalents guaranteed by the state. But the identical, the repetitive and the redundant appear differently in daily life and in the state. The state promulgates identity – that of all 'subjects' in the general order – although it may mean subsequently contradicting this promulgation, and circumventing its own law. As for daily life, it endures identity, redundancy and repetition without understanding them.

Compared with the types and models derived either from philosophy or from science, this is a unique mode of existence. It is not a substantial or essential mode of existence. Hence the impression of escape, (bad) dream, even unreality conveyed by daily life, but also by the state-political, when thought attempts to define them. This is no longer the mode of existence of a relation between two terms, a relation that can be grasped – so that, according to positivism, there is no need to define the terms in themselves. Relations in daily life, as in the political and the economic, disclose the terms they connect; they declare them. Positivism and empiricism, which claim to make do with relations, overlook what is most important in the social. For its part, critical knowledge can only indicate an ambiguity, a contradiction that is masked and crystallized in a pseudo-knowledge, which is nevertheless 'realized' on the ground.

Over and above what philosophers thought to define as truth and falsity, there thus develops the real–unreal. The state itself sums up these paradoxes: fictitious but terribly real; abstract but ever so concrete. It is thus that it is the keystone and yet '*rests*' on this foundation, daily life.

This situation, which is intolerable and yet tolerated, doubtless accounts for another paradox: the return in strength of (and to) the Sacred. The Sacred seemingly escapes ambiguity. It gives the impression of strength, of true and authentically concrete *being*, whether we are dealing with the signs of the zodiac, the preaching of a foreign religion, or the traditions of the established church. The most venerable words acquire the appeal of genuine novelty; they emerge either through pathos or through ethos, above this gleaming or benighted unreality that we call the 'social' in contemporary society.

The preceding account is thus situated on the borders of philosophy and the social sciences. Philosophical categories – real and unreal, appearance and essence – are embodied in daily life, but extending beyond themselves to be integrated into elements derived from the various fragmented sciences. Daily life is not inscribed in one of the partial domains or fields. In order to deepen itself, its concept seizes what it needs, and what is its by right, anywhere and everywhere. The concept of daily life is, in its fashion, comprehensive; in the course of its deployment, it concerns and interrogates the totality. To seek to grasp and define daily life at its apparent level, the *micro* – micro-decisions, micro-effects – is to let it slip; to seek to grasp the macro without it is likewise to let the totality slip.

The conclusion of this work will be deliberately metaphilosophical, this term encompassing philosophy while carrying it beyond itself. In accordance with the philosophical approach, it turns towards what underlies daily life in time and space, towards the origin and history, towards the surpassed and superseded. But it also looks to what exceeds the actual, to the possible and the impossible. Philosophy has never gone so far as to demand or proclaim a project for society or a project for civilization. At the highpoint of research, the summit of philosophy, Hegel simply suggested a political model: the state founded on absolute knowledge. Philosophical utopia, like technocratic utopia, must be surmounted in the name of daily life.

(a) If revolution – in other words, the radical transformation of society – cannot have as its goal and end either faster growth or a mere change of political personnel, it can only have as its goal and end the transformation of daily life.

(b) As has already been established on many occasions, this implies not zero growth or reduced growth, but different growth – that is to say, *qualitative development*, and hence a greater complexity, not a simplification, of social relations.

(c) This equally implies a different way of living, extending to the creation of a new social space, a different social time; the creation of a different mode of existence of social relations and different situations, liberated from models that reproduce the existing order.

(d) This also assumes a different form of thought, to be defined later. Let me say straight away: to be defined while taking account of the negative. The project is thus not to know or recognize daily life, in order to accept or affirm it as such in the name of positive knowledge, but, on the contrary, to create it by controlling its ambiguity. Thus the project no longer consists in unfolding daily life to disclose what is concealed in it (first version of the *Critique*); or in an effort to transcend it (second version), but in a metamorphosis through action and works – hence through thought, poetry, love. Once we have obtained knowledge of it and defined it, we must leave it without hesitating before the risk we face: the risk of involvement. Daily life is simultaneously the arena and the total stake.

Contemporary society is sinking into hidden contradictions which form such a tight knot that people do not know which end to approach it from in order to unravel it. It is better to sever it.

Here is a contradiction indicated *en route*, which seems minor but has some serious implications. Modern society disposes of death. People no longer die; they disappear (Kostas Axelos). This society thus also disposes of tragedy, returning it to the spectacle or to aestheticism. Yet it is not enough for it to set the mortal power of the state over it; it runs on death. This other power creates the vacuums that techniques, production and satisfaction arrive to fill. It is enough in this context to recall the importance of arms in today's economy. It should also be remembered that the countries most devastated by the war – the defeated countries of Japan and Germany – are today at the forefront of progress, are comparatively rich and prosperous countries, with a strong currency, and so on. As is well known but rarely stated, wars and crises do their job; they perform the function of the negative, unnoticed as such; they purge the mode of production of its temporary surpluses, and prime a resumption of accumulation on a new technological basis. Destructive capacity creates the premises of prosperity. Thus moulded into a mockery of a full life, daily life itself enables the mode of production to function. It is true that the everyday offers much satisfaction and many amenities to those who live above the level of infra-daily life. That is precisely the trap. This tragic age repudiates the tragic. Moreover, there is no more reason to experience the feeling of tragedy than there is to ratify its elimination. In and through a knowledge of this age, a different form of thought is instituted. How? In the first instance, through knowledge of the negative powers driving this society, which aims and claims to be so positive – and is, moreover, in that it presupposes the positivity of what is operational and profitable. Thinking is born out of contradic-

tions and consideration of the negative, but above all from the relations between the triads we have encountered *en route*, where daily life
always figures in a larger whole – the mode of production. The
thinking that clarifies daily life also discovers that it carries within it
what it negates and what negates it. The negation daily life carries
within it, and which it tries in vain to dispose of, is the tragic. In philosophical terminology and from a metaphilosophical viewpoint, it is
the negative. A fundamental triad is thus disclosed: daily life–the
ludic–the tragic.

Labour and non-labour, verbal language and non-verbal sign-
systems (music, architecture, painting, etc.), are integrated into daily
life. Daily life seeks to integrate the ludic and the tragic; it does not
succeed. The most it can do is to detach some fragments, some scraps,
of the ludic and the tragic.

Marx's thought now appears in a different light, casting him as a
thinker of the negative (and not of the economic, the historical, or techniques), who has been widely misunderstood as a realist – a
theoretician of positive reality and political realism. Workers, let us
remember, have as their historical mission the negation of work. As
has been indicated in the course of this text, when computer science
makes it possible to alter work and, ultimately, to abolish it as manual
labour, this problematic becomes topical once more. This is the
negative mission, historical or trans-historical, of information technology; for the time being, no-one is proposing to see it through. The
transformation of daily life can serve as a guiding thread. In daily life,
work and non-work already confront one another according to conflictual relations whose analysis has been begun in outline in this and
previous works. The end of work? Not yet. Its indication? No doubt,
but with what conflicts and problems! Non-work includes not only
leisure, but unemployment, absenteeism, the search for interesting or
temporary work, festivals, various games. Daily life thus seems to be
entirely taken up by and engaged in the positive; and yet we can see
the negative at work in it. What are we to conclude from this? Is daily
life, which seemed so solid at first, merely a kind of island floating in
a swamp and ferment of technological and social forces?

This daily life trails along with it no more than fragments of the
subject and subjectivity, which is endlessly fragmented within rational
homogeneity. This dissolution was proclaimed by philosophy and

critical thinking. The subject and self-consciousness generated historically, during the era of bourgeois ascendancy, have long been in crisis.
Is this sufficient reason to abandon them? Just because philosophers
have manipulated the subject/object relation in every imaginable way
(from the tautology 'no subject without an object, and vice versa' to the
widest horizons of past or future subject–object identity), is that a
reason to shelve the problematic? No. The crisis, itself total, demands
a total response. Like everything else, the subject is to be reconstructed.
How? In the first instance, through action in the everyday pursuing a
course opposed to the operational schema of the existing order: that is
to say, by opposing difference to homogeneity, unity to fragmentation,
concrete equality to pitiless hierarchization, in a real struggle. This as
regards practice. In theoretical thought, the subject must be reconstructed in accordance with a new approach that foregrounds not the
positive, but the negative and all that it involves. Without shying away
or giving up, but looking it straight in the eye, the subject braves death,
conflict and struggle, including the struggle against time. To use a word
that remains philosophical, the subject regards the *other* in all senses of
the term. Philosophy used not to envisage all these senses: the remote
and the close, horizon and surroundings, ascendancy and decline, difference and indifference, but also debt, dues, contract – and generosity,
gifts, grace.

Physical energy and biological life are already defined solely by possibilities and potentialities. The organism is torn from its habitat to
perform its vital functions. The living self, which is not yet a subject,
exists only for and by the other – not transcendental, metaphysical or
ontological, but concrete and practical: the prey, the sexual object
from reproduction by mating, progeny, above all from fertilization.
Just as it is difficult completely to separate so-called inert matter and
its forms from living matter, so it is difficult to demarcate between
living species and the human species. Continuity? To a certain extent,
yes. But there are also discontinuities. While it is true that human
action impacts back upon the *physis* it issues from, it is in order to
unfurl it in a second, infinitely rich and complex, nature – products
and works – but at the risk of destroying the first nature and severing
the increasingly frail nutritive bond that links the two (we might say,
with Spinoza: *natura naturans* and *natura naturandum*). Social practice
unfolds the life of the living being, but in another space and in

analogical fashion: sooner or later, it wrecks the attempts of groups to isolate themselves and of individuals to shut themselves off. Whence, probably, the incest taboo, exogamy, ritual and symbolic exchanges, and so on. Other-orientated people (Robert Jaulin) always prevail, though not without great suffering. Systemic, functional or structural reality cannot be established in a sustained equilibrium. Even a self-regulated system, closed off to evolution and emergent phenomena, disappears in the face of unforeseen aggression or through internal decline. In the more or less long term, self-sufficiency kills. In this way, the relational character of human beings becomes more pronounced via language, communication and exchange, and the displacement of Eros towards creation through prohibitions and conflicts. Is this how we make the transition from one logic to another, from the logic of life to that of social exchange? Should we not say instead that every logic is inscribed in a dialectical movement that envelops it and carries it beyond itself? Biological life and social life prefigure thought in the sense that they are constantly resumed, recover themselves for a new effort, so that the singularity of individuals and the impact of constraints prevent neither permanent creation and the irruption of possibilities, nor decline. The other is also novelty, emergence, history. The triads 'alterity–alteration–alienation' and 'procreation–production–creation' are dissociated only in the course of evolution – dramatically, in a way that is unforeseen by the actors and yet retrospectively foreseeable. Biological life, like social practice and individual thinking, always present a totality, but one that is constantly evolving, always going beyond (meta) itself, despite the simultaneously formal, functional and structural coherence required by practical existence. This is how coherent organicism and systemic logic sooner or later shatter, thereby opening up to directionality (direction and orientation). Thus is posed the problem of life, from organic spontaneity to social daily life. From this standpoint, there is an analogy between problematics at the different levels. Daily life, the organic body of modern society, summons up its *beyond* in time and space. The work that is now concluding has consistently adopted this (relatively) optimistic perspective, despite the introduction of tragic knowledge – or rather, precisely because of it!

Even so, various anxieties remain. The notion of an ascending life, of an evolution that passes through revolutions in order to progress towards more successful forms, prompts more than one objection and several questions that remain unanswered. How far does entropy extend? Do possibilities suddenly emerge, bursts of possibilities and spurts of energy that counter degradation in biological and social life? We can find arguments to support this hypothesis of a constant dissipation counteracted by irruptions all over the place. But for now, it is unproven. In the biological and historical spheres alike, does not time always bring decline and degeneration? Some regard ageing, and the terrible certainty that it will occur, as proof of the existence of an infinitely cruel, as well as ingenious and powerful god, of an infinity that is simultaneously diabolical and divine, but forever inventive in the ways of spitefulness. Death and even pain are one thing, but growing old? Life recedes slowly, implacably, while we are fully conscious. For consciousness ages only in becoming more refined, improving – unless, that is, it hits upon a way of concealing, through representation or stupidity, what is occurring within and without: the body's treachery, the source that runs dry, the light and heat that fade. Is not ageing the dereliction that some philosophers have described, but without referring to it as such, avoiding it by offering a metaphysical picture? But we do not know how far this ordeal extends. Do societies grow old too – and peoples, and nations, and civilizations or cultures? Are the symptoms interpreted as those of a 'crisis', which a skilful initiative would lead us out of, in fact symptoms of an irreversible decline? Of whom, and what? These questions will remain unanswered here.

But wait a moment. Thought has some privileges. Like all ordeals, those just described have their compensations, at least at an individual level. So why not when it comes to groups and peoples? Consciousness of time and thinking about time struggle *for life*, so to speak, against time. Dominating the process that starts from the outset, dominating ageing and anguish at the same time: this is the force of life to the second degree – thinking, not to be confused with reflection, which knows only how to attend to the first level. At the first level, spontaneity and youth, vitality, spring forth. They are free gifts. From whom? From that same cruel infinity we call *nature*. At the second level, which is not that of a rhetoric, a reflexive decoding or a discourse on the first, but a quite different force, the capacity to master the ordeal, to counter time and prevail, is created. This strength used to be called 'spiritual'; it is thought, which cannot be defined by discourse but as an act.

Today, no one is unaware of the fact that the elementary forms of life are steeped in immortality. The greater the differentiation that culminates in the human species, where everyone is unique, as is each situation, each thought and each love, ageing and death make themselves ever more cruelly felt. We are thus begining to think that the human species and, consequently, its social history spring from a decline in cosmic life, which possibly comes to a halt with humanity, a frontier in the void. A catastrophic, even nihilistic thesis, which is widely endorsed, whether consciously or not.

Objections: the bursts and spurts, the moments when a bundle of possibilities suddenly arises. There are bursts that inject energy into the *reality* of decline. And then, above all, there is the new arrival – the thinking that does not shy away from the horror of the world, the darkness, but looks it straight in the face, and thus passes over into a different kingdom, which is not the kingdom of darkness. This thinking asserts itself while wandering among illusions and lies, beyond truth as well as error. If a consciousness of ineluctability wins out, then we have nihilism and the confirmation of decline. Tragic knowledge does not betoken melancholy science. Quite the reverse. If there is a reconciliation, or at least a compromise, between first and second natures, it will occur not in the name of an anthropological or historical positive knowledge, but in and through daily life transformed from within by tragic knowledge. Sensed by Nietzsche, who drifted towards the 'over-human', this knowledge conceives the negative in all its strength, in order to turn it against itself and try to overcome it. Daily life has served as a refuge from the tragic, and still does: above all else, people seek, and find, security there. To traverse daily life under the lightning flash of tragic knowledge is already to transform it – through thought.

Epilogue

To finish this conclusion, which is in no sense definitive or conclusive, two remarks:

(a) By virtue of its situation in contemporary social practice, daily life functions as the non-tragic *par excellence*, as the anti-tragic. The seeming reversibility of everyday time, demonstrated in the course of this work, establishes a sort of bulwark against anguish. Like a fortress that has been painstakingly built over the centuries, but above all in 'modern' times, objects are piled up against death and consciousness of the end. The same goes for utensils as kitsch objects, for the interior of dwellings as the spatial and architectural organization of contemporary towns. What is described as a 'beautiful' *oeuvre* has a quite different significance and a quite different effect. The tragic is the non-everyday, the anti-everyday. So that the irruption of the tragic in daily life turns it upside down. It is thus possible to make out a dialectical dynamic between tragedy and daily life. The everyday tends to abolish what tragic words and actions brutally restore: acts of violence, crimes, wars, aggression. Whence an extremely serious interaction in the permanent separation and mutual penetration of tragedy and daily life. Tragedy as an *oeuvre* reconnects these aspects: it seeks both to transform daily life through poetry and to conquer death through the resurrection of the tragic character.

(b) The end of work promises to be a long and difficult process which is already permeating the everyday, and which will have very varied forms, improvements and regressions. This is distantly foreshadowed by the end of work as *value*: the *end* of work as a meaning and *end* 'in and for itself'.

Paris, November 1980–May 1981

172

Index

A NOTE ON THE TYPE

The original punches of the types cut by John Baskervillle of Birmingham were sold by Baskerville's widow to Beaumarchais and descended through various French foundaries to Beberny and Peignot. Some of the material survives and is now at the Cambridge University Press. Baskerville has been called the first of the transitional romans in England. Compared with Caslon there is more differentiation of thick and thin strokes, the serifs on the lower-case letters are more nearly horizontal and the stress nearer the vertical.

Critique of Everyday Life Volume 1
HENRI LEFEBVRE

Translated by John Moore

Paperback 0 86091 587 5
$22/£15/$33CAN
320 pages • 6 x 9 inches

'A savage critique of consumerist society.' *Publishers Weekly*

Critique of Everyday Life Volume II
Foundations for a Sociology of the Everyday
HENRI LEFEBVRE

Translated by John Moore

Hardback 1 85984 650 5
$35/£22/$51CAN
416 pages • 6 x 9 inches

'A brilliant example of how theory can be joined with experience to critique and better understand contemporary society.' *Frontlist*

Ethics
An Essay on the Understanding of Evil
ALAIN BADIOU

Translated by Peter Hallward

Paperback I 85984 435 9
$16/£12/$24CAN
224 pages • 5.5 x 7.5 inches

PRAISE FOR *ETHICS*

'A book that aims at the very heart of politically correct "radical" intellectuals,
undermining the foundations of their very mode of life!' *Slavoj Žižek*

Metapolitics
ALAIN BADIOU

Translated by Jason Barker

Hardback I 84467 035 X
$27/£18/$38CAN
208 pages • 5.5 x 7.5 inches

In this follow-up to his highly acclaimed volume *Ethics*, a searing critique of liberalism,
Alain Badiou discusses the limits of political philosophy.

'Scarcely any other moral thinker of our day is as politically clear-sighted and
courageously polemical, so prepared to put notions of truth and universality back on
our agenda.' *Terry Eagleton*

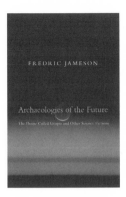

Archaeologies of the Future
The Desire Called Utopia and Other Science Fictions
FREDRIC JAMESON

Hardback 1 84467 033 3
$35/£20/$49CAN
480 pages • 6 x 9 inches

'There is no better example of a "Marxist scholastic" than Fredric Jameson.'
The Economist

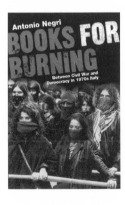

Books for Burning
Between Civil War and Democracy in 1970s Italy
ANTONIO NEGRI

Edited by Timothy S Murphy
Translated by Arianna Bove, Ed Emery,
Timothy S Murphy and Francesco Novello

Paperback Original 1 84467 034 1
$25/£16/$35CAN
336 pages • 6 x 9 inches

PRAISE FOR *MULTITUDE*
'Far left thinking with clarity, measured reasoning and humour, major accomplishments in
and of themselves.' *Publishers Weekly*

Afflicted Powers
Capital and Spectacle in a New Age of War
RETORT

Paperback Original 1 84467 031 7
$16/£9.99/$24CAN
224 pages • 5.5 x 7.5 inches

'A comprehensive analysis of America's relationship with the world. No stone is left unturned. The maggots exposed are grotesque.' *Harold Pinter*

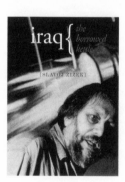

Iraq
The Borrowed Kettle
SLAVOJ ŽIŽEK

Paperback 1 84467 540 8
$16/£8.99/$23CAN
192 pages • 5.5 x 7.5 inches

'Žižek leaves no social or natural phenomenon untheorized, and is master of the counter-intuitive observation.' *New Yorker*

'Žižek has the knack of conjuring the most audacious conclusions between politics, popular culture and high theory.' *Time Out*

Firing Back
Against the Tyranny of the Market 2
PIERRE BOURDIEU

Paperback 1 85984 658 0
£9 UK only
96 pages • 5.5 x 8 inches

'The most convincing embodiment of the politically active intellectual since Jean-Paul Sartre or Michel Foucault.' *The Times*

'Bourdieu once again selects the right targets and, as always, has much to say that is incisive and enlightening.' *Noam Chomsky*

What Should the Left Propose?
ROBERTO MANGABEIRA UNGER

Hardback 1 84467 048 1
$23/£15/$32CAN
112 pages • 5.5 x 7.5 inches

PRAISE FOR *POLITICS*
'Unger does not make moves in any game we know how to play ... His book may someday make possible a new national romance ... It will help the literate ... citizens of some country to see vistas where before they saw only dangers ... see a hitherto undreamt-of national future.' *Richard Rorty*

MORE TITLES AVAILABLE FROM VERSO

Theodor Adorno	In Search of Wagner
1 84467 500 9	$18/£12/$25CAN
Louis Althusser	Machiavelli and Us
1 85984 282 8	$19/£13/$27CAN
Etienne Balibar	Politics and the Other Scene
1 85984 267 4	$20/£15/$29CAN
Jean Baudrillard	Cool Memories IV, 1995–2000
1 85984 462 6	$20/£13/$30CAN
Jean Baudrillard	Passwords
1 85984 463 4	$20/£13/$30CAN
Butler, Laclau, Žižek	Contingency, Hegemony, Universality
1 85984 278 X	$20/£15/$28CAN
Regis Debray	God: An Itinerary
1 85984 589 4	$35/£25/$52CAN
Ernesto Laclau	On Populist Reason
1 85984 651 3	$26/£15/$38CAN
Francisco Panizza, ed.	Populism and the Mirror of Democracy
1 85984 489 8	$25/£15/$36CAN
Jean-Paul Sartre	Critique of Dialectical Reason
1 85984 485 5	$23/£18/$34CAN
Susan Willis	Portents of the Real: A Primer for Post-9/11 America
1 84467 023 6	$23/£15.99/$36CAN
Ellen Meiksins Wood	Empire of Capital
1 84467 518 1	$15/£10/$22CAN

ALL VERSO TITLES ARE AVAILABLE FROM:

(USA) WW Norton **Tel:** 800-233-4830. Alternatively, please visit www.versobooks.com

(UK AND REST OF WORLD) Marston Book Services, Unit 160,
Milton Park, Abingdon, Oxon, OX14 4SD
Tel: +44 (0)1235 465500 / **Fax:** +44 (0)1235 465556 / **Email:** direct.order@marston.co.uk

(AUSTRALIA AND NEW ZEALAND) Palgrave Macmillan, Levels 4 & 5,
627 Chapel Street, South Yarra, Victoria 3141
Tel: 1300 135 113 / **Fax:** 1300 135 103 / **Email:** palgrave@macmillan.com.au

Macmillan New Zealand, 6 Ride Way, Albany, Auckland
Tel: (09) 414 0350 / **Fax:** (09) 414 0351

Credit cards accepted